Women, Power

and Consciousness

Attic Press
Dublin

Women, Power

and Consciousness

in 19th-Century Ireland

Eight Biographical Studies

Edited by

Mary Cullen and Maria Luddy

Attic Press
Dublin

First published in Ireland in 1995 by
Attic Press
29 Upper Mount Street
Dublin 2

ISBN 1 85594 0 787

A catalogue record for this book is available from the British Library.

The moral right of individual authors to be identified as authors of this work is asserted.

Cover design: Mick O'Dwyer
Cover photograph: Anne Jellicoe
Origination: Attic Press
Printing: Guernsey Press Co. Ltd

Attic Press receives assistance from the Arts Council/An Comhairle Ealaíon.

Erratum
Page 17. Lines 7 to 12 from the top should read:

Parnell was a Protestant who worked constructively and harmoniously with Catholic colleagues in Nationalist politics and the Ladies' Land League. O'Brien was a Protestant who became a Catholic, and whose work in emigration freely crossed religious boundaries.

Contents

Notes on Contributors

Jane Côté is a Canadian and an independent scholar and writer. She is the author of *Fanny and Anna Parnell: Ireland's Patriot Sisters*.

Mary Cullen is a research associate at St Patrick's College, Maynooth, and at Trinity College, Dublin

Dolores Dooley lectures at University College, Cork, in philosophy, women's studies and medical ethics.

Dana Hearne teachers feminist theory, gender studies and literature at John Abbott College and Concordia University, Quebec.

Marie Luddy teaches history at the Institute of Education, University of Warwick, England.

Anne O'Connell completed her MA at the University of Limerick and is now researching her PhD dissertation on women and emigration in the nineteenth century.

Jacinta Prunty is a lecturer in geography at University College, Dublin, and a member of the Congregation of the Holy Faith.

Deirdre Raftery is a lecturer at Trinity College, Dublin, and is joint author of *Emily Davis: Portrait of a Pioneer* (forthcoming).

List of illustrations

Permission to reproduce all photographs, which are held in private collections, was obtained by the individual authors and editors.

The publishers would like to thank the following:

Alexandra College, Dublin, for the cover photograph of Anne Jellico which is taken from a portrait in the college library.

Board of Trinity College, Dublin, for the photograph of Frances Power Cobbe on page 89.

Jane McL Côté for the photograph of Anna Parnell on page 263 which is reproduced from her book *Fanny & Anna Parnell: Ireland's Patriot Sisters* (1991).

Introduction

Individuals make history, women as well as men. This collection of biographical studies retrieves the 'lost' histories of eight Irish women of the nineteenth century. These women were well known in their day, many of them achieving international as well as national importance. Of the eight, two perhaps will have already entered the public consciousness as being significant historical figures. Anna Parnell, because of her connections with the Land League and Anna Haslam, due to her long connection with the suffrage campaign, a subject which has received some attention from historians. The other women in this book have been largely forgotten. They have for the most part disappeared from popular memory, and historians have either ignored or been unaware of their significant roles in the shaping of Irish society.

Anna Wheeler was a philosopher of the early socialist movement and played an important role in disseminating socialist and cooperative principles. Frances Power Cobbe became a prominent propagandist for women's rights in England. Anne Jellicoe was committed to improving the quality of education for women and girls and spent her life successfully pursuing that aim. Isabella Tod and Anna Haslam were leading figures in a range of campaigns, that included fighting for changes in the married women's property laws, education, opposition to sexual double standards and suffrage. Charlotte Grace O'Brien's social and political activism was directed towards improving conditions for Irish emigrants, particularly women. Anna Parnell is well known for her work with the Ladies' Land League. Her attitude to the Land War was much more radical than that of her brother, Charles Stewart Parnell. Margaret Aylward stands out from the other women in this book as a major philanthropic figure whose work was channelled through a religious community.

Our original intention was to study a number of Irish women who were consciously feminist and played key roles in campaigns to improve the status of women in the nineteenth century. This plan was modified by the research which was actually in progress and on which we could draw. As a result we were forced to rethink and broaden our original criterion for inclusion which was direct support and work for women's rights. Not all the women here explicitly espoused 'women's rights'. Not all may have even implicitly supported such claims. But each, by her life and work, challenged and contributed to change in accepted nineteenth-century gender roles. Though their work was varied, and contacts between them were few, this theme links them all.

The consequences of being born male or female makes as profound an impact on an individual's life and on the structure of society as do class, wealth and religion. In the nineteenth century, as in earlier centuries, the central issue for women was that of autonomy, the power to direct one's life to ends of one's own choosing. Conventional thinking, backed up by law, regulation and custom, laid down axioms for the behaviour deemed appropriate for women. Society was then always ready to define women's 'nature' to fit the required behaviour. The result was that a wide range of human activity was said to be either beyond the capacity of women, or, when women demonstrated that this was not the case, was castigated as unfeminine, unsuitable, scandalous or flying in the face of God. The underlying paradigm saw women as essentially subordinate to men and subject to male authority in decisions about their lives.

The eight women studied in this book were all aware of the consequences of their sex. Some challenged the rules and the paradigm explicitly and devoted their lives to changing both. Others did not protest but simply ignored or by-passed them by their actions and behaviour. Many combined both responses. Wheeler, Cobbe, Jellicoe, Haslam and Tod all explicitly set out to contest and overturn existing gender roles, as well as becoming important contributors to a wide range of social and political campaigns which concerned the interests of both men and women.

Aylward was at the same time part of the Catholic Church's engagement with the rapidly changing society of nineteenth-century Ireland, and also part of the movement by religious women to assert their place in that engagement. In her campaign to improve the conditions of passenger transport, O'Brien rejected very publicly the non-leadership role assigned to women. Parnell similarly ignored the axiom that public politics were a male preserve.

All of these women achieved a degree of public standing in their own lifetimes. Isabella Tod, for example, was perhaps the best known Irish women's activist of the last half of the nineteenth century, and was the motivating force behind numerous societies which lobbied for change in a range of areas. Margaret Aylward received both public acclaim and notoriety for her engagement with proselytism. Few of these women worked together, or it appears even knew each other. They were in many cases divided by religion and politics. Isabella Tod and Anna Haslam were certainly aware of each other's work and communicated with each other about the campaigns and issues which held their interest. Both were strong unionists and Tod in particular would have had little in common, or indeed little sympathy with the political beliefs of someone like Anna Parnell or Charlotte Grace O'Brien. While it seems likely that many of the women in this book would have been familiar with, or at least aware of, the theoretical formulations of Frances Power Cobbe, few personal contacts were recorded. Indeed, Cobbe appears to have retained few, if any, links with Ireland after her move to England in the 1860s.

These women came from a variety of religious backgrounds: Catholic, Quaker, Presbyterian and Church of Ireland. Only one had a Catholic upbringing and she became a nun. The interaction of different religions with women's claims to determine their own life choices is an aspect of history that is coming under increasing scrutiny and that will undoubtedly repay further examination.

As adults some of these women lost their religion, while a greater number retained and were motivated to action by their religious beliefs. The early philanthropic work of Jellicoe, Aylward, Haslam and Tod was a direct response to the call of Christian duty and led to a belief in the need for political action in order to bring about social change. While political and social alliances were formed between Quakers and Presbyterians, and members of the Church of Ireland, such alliances rarely breached the walls of Catholicism. Indeed, the sectarian divide became more entrenched as the result of the activities of people like Aylward and Tod. Aylward's identification of Protestantism as a threatening force led her into a bitter struggle over schools and orphanages with Church of Ireland activists who saw Catholicism in a similar light. Tod's opposition to Home Rule was rooted in her conviction that the social, economic and political benefits won for Ireland by people like herself, would not survive in a Catholic state.

On the other hand, the commitment of Haslam, a Quaker, to the 'advancement of women' led her to continually encourage women to cross barriers of religion and politics to work together in their common cause. Parnell was a Protestant who became a Catholic and who worked constructively and harmoniously with Catholic colleagues in nationalist politics and the Ladies' Land League. O'Brien, too, was a Protestant whose work in emigration freely crossed religious boundaries.

The personal circumstances of all eight women allowed them a freedom of action not shared by most Irish women. Anna Wheeler left a brutal husband, taking her children with her. Tod, Aylward, Cobbe, O'Brien and Parnell remained unmarried. Jellicoe was widowed. Haslam is the only woman among the group who combined marriage with social and political activism throughout her adult life. Her husband was unusual among Irish men for the interest and support he gave to campaigns around women's interests, and was a significant feminist in his own right. For most of their activist lives none of these women was encumbered by family responsibilities. While Jellicoe and Haslam married, neither had children. All, except Anna Parnell, became financially independent, either through inherited means or, in contradiction to popular understanding of the lives of women in Victorian society, by earning their own living. All of these women were intellectually independent. Few had acquired formal education but all had the ability to argue for their beliefs on public platforms and in print.

These women were from the middle and upper classes, the classes which generally involved themselves in women's issues in the last century. Their work was mostly class based, often with the explicit understanding that a social superior had a duty to help a social inferior. Many of them sought access to political decision-making only for women of their own class, believing that such access would be advantageous both to women of lower social classes and to society as a whole. Wheeler is a notable exception with her commitment to socialism and a society based on mutual cooperation. These women generally saw themselves as responsible not only to and for women, but also to their country. For some, like Tod and Haslam, that country was Ireland as part of the United Kingdom, while for others, like Parnell and O'Brien, it was an independent Irish state.

It took many of these women their adult lives to bring their causes and campaigns to a successful conclusion. Indeed, some of the campaigns failed and others achieved success only after the death of the campaigner. Progress resulted from persistence and also an acute political sense of when to lobby, debate or make public issues relating to their campaigns. Women like O'Brien, Haslam and Tod were public figures who realised that the more visible and persistent they were the more likely it was that they would succeed in gaining progress for their causes. By their activism and visibility they were instrumental in inserting women into the nation's consciousness. In their different ways many of them associated women with mainstream political movements and campaigns. Wheeler was a figure of standing in early nineteenth-century European socialist circles. Cobbe was a high-profile participant in the anti-vivisection campaign. Parnell associated women publicly with the Land War and the campaign for Irish independence, while Tod associated women publicly with the anti-Home Rule campaign. The fact that socialism, the Land War and opposition to Home Rule are generally seen as the preserves of male politicians illustrates the extent to which women's political activism has been ignored by historians.

In presenting these particular lives we wish to show that relationships between the sexes, and between different groups of women, form an integral part of the history of any society. The complexities of women's individual lives, and women's responses to society's expectations of them, interacted with relationships such as class, wealth, education, religion and politics to create the fabric of Irish society.

Mary Cullen and Maria Luddy
October 1995

Anna Doyle Wheeler

(1785-_c_1850)

Dolores Dooley

Anna Doyle Wheeler's story begins in 1785 in Clonbeg Parish, County Tipperary, where she was the youngest of three children born to Anna Dunbar and Nicholas Doyle. Little is known about her father except that he was a Dean in the Church of Ireland for the diocese of Fenner and Leighlen.[1] He died when Anna was very young leaving the job of surrogate father to her bachelor uncle and army general, Sir John Doyle. The Doyle name in Tipperary was synonymous with a tradition of military achievements where women were mentioned only as wives or mothers of men who achieved public recognition.[2]

19

Anna was raised in a bourgeois, liberal Protestant home where a tutored education exposed her to the French *philosophes*, gave her fluency in the French language and abundant opportunities to learn social skills and courtesies. In 1800, aged fifteen, she married Francis Massey Wheeler, a wealthy local man with a family estate at Ballywire in County Limerick. Her mother opposed the marriage, judging that her prospective son-in-law was as irresponsible as he was rich. The marriage survived twelve precarious years, during which the young Anna had multiple pregnancies and miscarriages. By all accounts she also lived with on-going marital abuse and neglect from her husband. Two daughters, Henrietta and Rosina, born in 1800 and 1801 respectively, survived into adulthood. Rosina recalled how

> ... my mother would be stretched on one sofa, deep in perusal of some French or German philosophical work that had reached her translated via London (and who was unfortunately deeply imbued with the pernicious fallacies of the French Revolution, which had then more or less seared their traces through Europe, and who was besides strongly tainted by the corresponding poison of Mrs Wollstonecraft's book) ...[3]

Anna Wheeler indeed acknowledged Wollstonecraft as an inspiration, especially her defence of democratic rights for women in *A Vindication of the Rights of Woman*, published in 1792. Wheeler read widely the works of eighteenth-century philosophers who supported the eventual French Revolution of 1789. A favourite, read more than once, was *System of Nature*, jointly authored by Denis Diderot (1713-84), and the German Baron Paul von Holbach (1723-89). As Wheeler noted,

> ... if everyone would read it, they would soon discover by reasoning the most correct and conclusive that man has hitherto been taught nothing but the most pernicious errors - the consequence of which is his present moral degradation and deplorable wretchedness, alas![4]

In 1812 Wheeler left her husband and, with the help of her brother, John Milley Doyle, travelled to the island of Guernsey where her uncle, General John Doyle was governor. Here with her young daughters, Henrietta and Rosina, and her sister Bessie, she spent several years in a social milieu of visiting diplomats and became immersed in the political debates of the day.[5] Around 1816 she left Guernsey and moved to Caen in France, becoming part of an active group of social philosophers and reformers, 'to the support of whose doctrines she devoted both her purse and her pen'.[6]

I have not found published material from Wheeler during her Caen years. From what we know about her later life in Paris and London, it is plausible to assume that she set up a salon. The reference to 'purse and pen' suggests that she became a patron to young intellectuals. From the seventeenth century onwards the roles of patron and *salonnière* were respectable and acceptable for middle- and upper-class women in the dominantly male literary parlours of the time.[7]

For Wheeler this was a formative period of philosophical development among the 'freethinkers' in Caen, as noted by her daughter. These were mainly Saint-Simonians, followers of the French political philosopher and founder of French socialism, Count Claude-Henri Saint-Simon.[8] Wheeler became known as the 'Goddess of Reason' and was perceived by the 'local intelligentsia' in Caen as 'the most gifted woman of the age'.[9] Saint-Simon himself wrote little about women and did not consider sexual equality a subject for special consideration. However, in his view of a new social world, he claimed women would fill 'useful and productive' roles. He believed that a cooperative philosophy could achieve integration and cooperation among the European states. Wheeler learned the language of cooperation from the Saint-Simonians, and developed a conviction that human society could achieve substantial progress if it accepted this challenge of change.

Saint-Simon died in 1825, but his followers, women and men, bourgeois and labouring classes, perpetuated his ideas well into the 1830s. Women's emancipation gradually became a central component of the Saint-Simonian vision of a reconstructed society.

Wheeler's stay in Caen ended when her husband died in Ireland in 1820. Since Wheeler left him in 1812 he had rarely communicated with her except indirectly, through their daughters. She returned to Ireland for the funeral and then moved between London and Dublin for several years, meeting a community of like-minded philosophers and workers among London Utilitarians and members of British Cooperative Societies.

During the years 1820-23 Wheeler became known in the London centres of the Cooperative Movement, where followers of Robert Owen[10] socialised, heard lectures on the ideas of Owenites and attended classes in a variety of useful subjects. These were pivotal years for Wheeler as she began to appreciate the close links between Owenite and Saint-Simonian ideas for the reform of society. Both aimed to exploit the widespread alienation caused by rapid industrialisation and the mechanisation of labour. Wheeler learned about this alienation at first hand at meetings with workers in the Cooperative centres, Trade Associations and Mechanics Institutes. From her first meeting with Robert Owen, the manufacturer-philanthropist leader of the Cooperative Movement, she became a close ally and co-worker.[11] She regularly introduced him to French and Irish political reformers, and circulated his writings to enthusiasts in both countries. Wheeler excelled at facilitating meetings with potential disciples, expanding networks and smoothing differences between Owen and some of his antagonists.[12]

In this context Wheeler met Jeremy Bentham[13], the English Utilitarian and leader of the Philosophical Radicals, vocal proponents of social and legal change in early nineteenth-century England. Wheeler endorsed the basic Utilitarian premise that the criterion for decisions should be whether they were likely to 'promote the greatest happiness of the greatest number of people'. Her analysis of sexual inequality, its causes and consequences, is always in the context of diminished happiness. This concentration on the social factors which affect the amount and quality of human happiness she shared with a friend, educationalist and Cooperative worker, Frances (Fanny) Wright (1795-1852).

Wright was also a familiar visitor at the house of Bentham, whose ward she had become when orphaned at an early age. Wheeler admired Wright's lectures on education and her experiments in developing black communities in the United States in Nashoba, Tennessee.[14] Wright dedicated her years in America to the goal of gradual emancipation, helping slaves to buy their freedom, as well as to education, development of self-subsistence and organisation of labour.[15] The Nashoba communities confirmed for many Owenites that such projects, while facing serious difficulties, were realisable.

Finally, during the early 1820s, Wheeler met an Irishman, William Thompson from West Cork, a collaborator with both Jeremy Bentham and Robert Owen. Thompson is recognised as the outstanding economist and theorist[16] in the Owenite movement and as eminently more practical than Owen about the details of Cooperative communities.[17] Wheeler's meeting with Thompson was a turning point in her professional and personal life, especially when, in 1825, they collaborated in writing a treatise on sexual equality. In this process they became close friends and colleagues in Cooperative efforts.

By 1823 Wheeler was in Paris where she met the social critic and utopian socialist, François Marie Charles Fourier (1772-1837). Fourier's biographer recorded that:

> Sometime in 1823 Fourier made the acquaintance of an Irishwoman who was able to tell him more about Owen and his work. Mrs Anna Doyle Wheeler was a much-travelled Irish feminist of high birth and radical opinions ... within a short time after their first meeting he [Fourier] seems to have become a regular visitor to her salon.[18]

Fourier produced elaborate plans for the reconstruction of society into small harmonious communities called *Phalanxes*. His followers, including Wheeler, saw such communities as realisable projects. To spread Fourier's often obscure and complex ideas, Wheeler rephrased many of them in accessible language, and delivered them in lectures or incorporated them into journal articles. One fundamental belief in Fourier's system which sustained Wheeler in the propagation of his views in France, England and Ireland was that the true test of social progress in a society is measured by the liberty that women enjoy.[19]

Life in Paris ended in tragedy for Wheeler in 1825 when her daughter Henrietta died at twenty-five from a 'wasting disease' which had afflicted her for several months. Henrietta had lived with her mother in Paris and both had become known among Fourier supporters as well as in a group of Liberal advocates of the cause of Greek national independence, a cause which spanned the years 1821-1830. A close collaborator with Wheeler and Henrietta in this association of philhellenists, or 'lovers of Greece', was Marc Antoine Jullien who composed an elegy in memory of Henrietta. The elegy, read at a public gathering of the Société Philotechnique de Paris in May 1827, commemorated Anna Wheeler as much as Henrietta in the eyes of the many French women - mothers and daughters - who brought flowers to the tomb.[20] The elegy was a public testimony to Wheeler's maternal role and to her support of liberty for Greeks.

Henrietta's death temporarily depleted Wheeler's energies for work, and she seems, for several years, to have withdrawn from writing and social functions. She left Paris and moved back to London, subsequently expressing regret at not being financially able to travel back to France. She found French society more broadly liberated than English, and I suspect her own work was more enthusiastically received in France.

In 1827 Wheeler's remaining daughter, Rosina, married Edward Bulwer Lytton, a well-known literary figure of the time. By 1831 Wheeler had two grandchildren, Emily Elizabeth and Edward Robert. In 1848 Emily died of typhoid fever, but Wheeler's grandson, Edward Robert, lived to write a memoir of his father which denigrated Anna Wheeler as little more than a ranting lunatic on the issue of women's emancipation.[21] Ironically, Edward Robert's third child, Constance Georgina Lytton (1869-1923), became a prominent feminist who, in 1908, began collaboration with Emmeline Pankhurst's 'militant' suffrage organisation, the Women's Social and Political Union, which was prepared to break the law if necessary to win the vote for women. One can only imagine Anna Wheeler's pride if she could have known that her great-granddaughter would be imprisoned for suffrage activism in 1909.[22]

By 1832 Wheeler, depleted in energy, wondered if she could continue her social project. Her health 'is so invariably suffering that I am forced to withdraw myself very much from all society.'[23] Fortunately her indispositions were not long-lasting. Like the phoenix rising from its ashes to new life, Wheeler regularly followed bouts of depression and neuralgia with bursts of involvement and writing. In 1833 she was again applying her energy to realising a community of socialist-inspired equals, and debating current topics in

Cooperative journals.

Wheeler was in London when her daughter, Rosina, went through an acrimonious and public divorce from Bulwer Lytton in 1836.[24] She did not live until 1858 to see Rosina kidnapped and incarcerated in a mental asylum by her husband, who aimed to silence Rosina's publications which gave her side of the divorce, including charges of philandering and abusive behaviour by Bulwer Lytton.[25] Such incarcerations revealed the culturally backed powers of husbands to banish 'problem' wives, and Wheeler herself believed that mental institutions often colluded with men in allowing a facile disposal of difficult domestic problems.

I have not found reliable data about when Anna Doyle Wheeler died. Certainly she was alive to celebrate the revolution of 1848 in France. Hugh Doherty, a friend and prominent British disciple of Fourier, sent her a knot of tricolour worn at the barricades, and urged her to come to Paris. This was a deeply symbolic gesture since women had, for years, been forbidden to wear the tricolour in order to keep the patriotic symbol respectable. Doherty wrote:

> The clubs and the press are discussing social questions, and the rights of women are constantly put forth in all the clubs though not as yet in the public press. It would do you good to be over here now. The moral atmosphere would give you life. Could you not come over?[26]

There is some circumstantial evidence, in the memoirs of James Elishama Smith, a Saint-Simonian theologian, to suggest that Wheeler was dead by 1851. Incidentally, Smith claimed that his introduction to Wheeler was 'a most important providential epoch' in his life.[27]

This sketch of Anna Doyle Wheeler's life indicates the multiple dimensions shaping her intellectual and personal identity. During the many hours of searching for clues and signposts to illuminate Wheeler's life, I came to feel I was in the company of a friend on a journey during which I learned her ideas for social and political reform.

There now follows a selective survey of some of these ideas thematically and in order of their appearance. They are drawn from her book, jointly written with William

Thompson, her correspondence and journal articles.

In early nineteenth-century England a man rarely publicly acknowledged the collaboration of a woman in the writing of a major political work.[28] To do so was considered indiscreet and offensive to the modesty of women. In 1825 Anna Wheeler was acknowledged by William Thompson in a study which is the first complete statement of a socialist defence of sexual equality. The full title is a synopsis of the content: *Appeal of one Half of the Human Race, Women, Against the Pretensions of the Other Half Men, To Retain Them in Political, and Thence in Civil and Domestic Slavery.*[29] The book cites William Thompson as the sole author, but an 'Introductory letter to Mrs Wheeler' clarifies her role:

> ... I have endeavoured to arrange the expression of those feelings, sentiments and reasoning, which have emanated from your mind ... . Though I do not *feel* like you - thanks to the chance of having been born a man ... to you am I indebted for those bolder and more comprehensive views which perhaps can only be elicited by concentration of the mind on one darling though terrific theme. To separate your thoughts from mine were now to me impossible, so amalgamated are they with my own; I address you then simply to perform towards you a debt of justice; to show myself possessed of that sincerity which I profess to admire.[30]

Thompson regrets that Wheeler did not write the book herself:

> Anxious that you should take up the cause of your proscribed sex, and state to the world in writing, in your own name, what you have so often and so well stated in conversation and under feigned names in such of the periodical publications of the day as would tolerate such a theme, I long hesitated to arrange our common ideas ... . Anxious that the hand of a woman should have the honor ... I hesitated to write. But the leisure and resolution to undertake the drudgery of the task were wanting. A few only therefore of the following pages are the exclusive produce of your mind and pen and written with your own

hand. The remainder are our joint property, I being your interpreter and the scribe of your sentiments.[31]

Thompson praises Mary Wollstonecraft's *A Vindication of the Rights of Woman* (1792) and 'the gentle eloquence' of Mary Hays, (1759-1843), a novelist, English women's rights advocate and close friend of Wollstonecraft. However, Thompson sees Wheeler's thinking as more comprehensive than the 'narrow views which too often marred' Wollstonecraft's writings, in particular her reinforcement of traditional roles for men and women and unwillingness to analyse critically the existing oppressive economy of capitalist individualism. Wollstonecraft's arguments for equality did not go far enough, and he believed that Wheeler could have provided a more thorough critique of society as well as concrete plans for the establishment of cooperative communities as an alternative to the 'tooth and claw' existence of competitive society.[32]

The *Appeal* was written primarily to refute the argument of the Utilitarian philosopher, historian and economist, James Mill (1773-1836). In his treatise *On Government*, published in 1820,[33] Mill claimed that

... all those individuals whose interests are indisputably included in those of other individuals, may be struck off [from political rights] without inconvenience. In this light may be viewed all children up to a certain age, whose interests are involved in those of their parents. In this light, also, women may be regarded, the interest of almost all of whom is involved either in that of their fathers or in that of their husbands.[34]

Thompson and Wheeler expected Bentham or other prominent Utilitarians to repudiate publicly James Mill's anti-woman position, but their patience ran out and in 1825 the *Appeal* was published.

Weary of waiting, the protest of at least one man and one woman is here put forward against doctrines which disgrace the principle of Utility ... . Advocates as we are of the principle of Utility as the only test of morals, conduct so disgraceful to its admirers we will not follow.[35]

The *Appeal* set out to show that Mill's claim that women share an identity of interest with men was incoherent and untenable, a 'fiction' constructed to shore up an unwillingness to give women the vote, and developed into a comprehensive study of the social and economic causes of sexual inequality.

Essentially the *Appeal* is a sustained critique of the principle of Utility which aims 'to promote in all things that which is likely to bring about the greatest happiness of the greatest number of people'. Wheeler and Thompson believed that the principle had become corrupt and it was time to provide a 'true development of this principle of human happiness'. How, they asked, could one be committed to the 'greatest happiness of the greatest number' and deprive half the human race of the rights which would ensure access to happiness?

The inheritance of the Enlightenment defenders of women's rights was especially familiar to Wheeler. In the *Appeal* the argument for equal rights, civil, domestic and political, is based mainly on the desirable benefits of self-respect. Wheeler always linked self-respect to the power of self-government, the power to exercise all of one's human capacities. Those who, by whatever means, exclude women from the free exercise of their intellect and will are engaged only in mockery:

> How is it possible that this equality of enjoyments, proportioned to natural or acquired powers, should ever be attained by women, if they are by laws, regulations, or the diseased arbitrary will of men called public opinion, debarred from the equal culture of their natural powers or faculties with men?[36]

Wheeler and Thompson do not claim that women will automatically achieve emancipation from oppression when laws are changed. Culture, public opinion and the attitudes of men and women have to be transformed as well. Wheeler reinforces this case in later writings. Women's equal chance for happiness is only feasible if changes occur: a) in laws affecting intestate property, particularly of land which now prefer male heirs; b) in laws excluding women, directly or indirectly, from almost all lucrative, professional or intellectual occupations and practices excluding women from places of education in all higher branches of knowledge; c) through new laws to protect married women from personal assaults and restraints; d) by the removal of exclusions now in place whereby a woman cannot 'get rid of a worthless and vicious husband', though men 'had such liberties'.[37] Without equality, not only can women not show respect for themselves but men will not respect them either.

> Without them [equal rights] they can never be regarded by men as really their equals, they can never attain that respectability and dignity in the social scale ... they could not respect themselves.[38]

This is a recurring feature of arguments among Utilitarians, and it is central in Wheeler's writings. When a case is being made for changes in the condition of women, the benefits are always predicted for both women and men. If men's interests and happiness were reduced as a result of women's equality, then the 'greatest happiness of the greatest number' would not result. This focus on the goal of achieving self-respect through equality undermined the idea that the objective of achieving equality was somehow to make women the same as men. As I try to show, arguments for equality in Wheeler never imply that women should be like men. Quite the contrary. In a marvellous passage from the 'Letter to Mrs Wheeler' in the *Appeal*, Thompson states bluntly:

> I hear you indignantly reject the boon of equality with such creatures as men now are. With you I would equally elevate both sexes. Really enlightened women ... would find it difficult to meet with associates worthy of them in men as now formed, full of ignorance and vanity, priding themselves on a *sexual* superiority, entirely independent of any merit ... . Unworthy of such women, are the great majority of the existing race of men.[39]

Equality of rights is not enough. A new economics of redistribution of wealth is necessary. Without economic changes, women and many male labourers are without minimal assets to allow them to exercise the freedoms given in equal rights. In explaining this goal for change, the *Appeal* takes issue with the 'competitive political economists':

> In truth, the system of the most enlightened of the school of those reformers called political economists, is still founded on exclusions. Its basis is too narrow for human happiness.[40]

Many early nineteenth-century political economists were advocating a form of individual competition within a capitalist form of economy as the only viable way forward to economic growth. Wheeler and Thompson, and their cooperative worker colleagues, looked for a very different kind of society

> ... where the principle of benevolence shall supersede that of fear; where restless and anxious individual competition shall give place to mutual cooperation and joint possession; where individuals in large numbers, male and female, forming voluntary associations, shall become a mutual guarantee to each other for the supply of all useful wants; where perfect freedom of opinion and perfect equality will reign amongst the cooperators; and where the children of all will be equally educated and provided for by the whole.[41]

The period in which the early socialists were developing their positions was one of extensive social and economic upheaval. In most western societies, the development of industrial capitalism was causing radical adjustments to the situation of different social groups. Most significantly, it was a period in which a new working class was being created, a class seen by socialists as a receptive audience and willing participant for newly proposed forms of cooperative associations.

This developing working class was neither an integrated nor homogeneous group. There were differences between the agricultural and manufacturing sectors, and between artisans and handicraft workers. In its own way each viewed mechanised production as potentially threatening to its livelihood, and needed persuading that it could be otherwise. As a result, social and economic dislocation and new demands on individual competition were facts of life that proved disruptive and alienating for many workers. The essential values of communitarian socialism may be seen as a response to this problem. They represent various attempts to formulate new normative systems in a period of upheaval.[42]

One such plan was given in the *Appeal*, although it was eclipsed for over a century. It offered perhaps the most comprehensive treatise on sexual equality and on social and economic reform provided in the nineteenth century, and can be read as a detailed script which Karl Marx knew and utilised to his advantage.[43] Only a few of the critical issues in this text can be looked at in this essay, and so a reading of the *Appeal* itself is strongly recommended.

It is not always easy to determine precisely what Wheeler wrote in the pages of the *Appeal*, but many long passages have a style of writing and a set of expressions very characteristic of her, diffuse and dense at the same time, exclamatory and graphic in description. This is much less typical of Thompson, to judge by the stylistic evidence from his other writings.[44] Wheeler may well have penned these words which are searing in their condemnation of legalised marriage, depicting it as little more than potential prostitution and slavery, and contrasting it with the benefits of a life of equal rights between the sexes in communities of voluntary association:

> Here no dread of being deserted by a husband with a helpless pining family, could compel a woman to submit to the barbarities of an exclusive master ... the vile trade of prostitution, consigning to untimely graves the youth and beauty of every civilised land, and gloated on by men pursuing individual wealth and upholding the sexual and partial system of morals, could not here exist. Man has, here, no individual wealth more than woman, with which to buy her person for the animal use of a few years. Man, like woman, if he wish to be beloved, must learn the art of pleasing, of benevolence, of deserving love.[45]

But are such changes possible? Who will motivate men to change? Who will convince women and men that these changes will make them happier? This is a difficulty which meets Wheeler at every point in her writing. How is one to persuade women and men that it is truly in their best interests and happiness to undergo the difficult adjustments required by cooperative communities? Radical changes in the institutions and decision-making procedures of society were required.

One can only speculate about the level of disappointment that Wheeler experienced when Daniel O'Connell, the leader of the Catholic Emancipation Campaign in Ireland, issued his political creed. Describing himself as a 'radical reformer', he explains that his constitutional reform will give the

> ... right of voting to every male inhabitant of the British Islands who attains the legal age - for example, the age of 21 - and who is sane in point of intellect, and unconvicted of crime: in other words, I insist upon universal suffrage.[46]

Many Owenite women and men were impatient with this kind of overt exclusion of women in suffrage reform measures. However, they were by philosophy non-violent and non-revolutionary in their politics. Most believed that social changes would be very gradual; in the meantime, micro-communities of just societies could be established and could prove to the larger society that cooperative living among equals was a real option. Such mini-societies were the Voluntary Communities defended by Thompson and Wheeler, self-sustaining communities consisting of about 2,000 people, carefully recruited and then more rigorously selected from applicants to ensure a like-mindedness of objectives, cooperation in means and determination to make these schemes work.

> This scheme of social arrangements is the only one which will complete and for ever insure the perfect equality and entire reciprocity of happiness between women and men. Those evils, which neither an equality of civil and criminal laws, nor of political laws, nor any equal system of morals upheld by an enlightened public opinion, can entirely

obviate, *this scheme of human exertion will remove or abundantly compensate.*[47]

This picture of what male-female relationships could be like under cooperation is effectively giving incentives to men and women to take up the challenge of such living experiments. Wheeler was showing that society would gain through communities by diminishing social evils, and individuals would gain from opportunities for 'genuine happiness'.

Finally, the *Appeal* asks men and women to look at the condition of the world under male legislators, and poses the question: could women do a better job if given a chance? If we look at the qualities women have developed in their subordinate social positions, is it a worthwhile gamble to bet that women would do a better job as legislators and government leaders?

> Is it possible to conceive that legislative power lodged exclusively in the hands of women, without force, the weaker half of the race, could have produced atrocities and wretchedness equal to those with which exclusive male legislation has desolated the globe? Is there no hope that under the exclusive legislation of women, some at least of these palpable and avowed evils would have been obviated or lessened? [48]

The answer is given: it is almost certain that exclusive legislation by women would have been more beneficent. Why? Because women have greater or deeper sympathies for the whole race, and certainly for the weaker members of society, by virtue of their own inferior physical strength and positions of dependency. On these grounds women would be more inclined to promote impartially the happiness of all. 'The important truth is ... that sympathy for the happiness of those for whom laws are made is the most indispensable quality in the makers of laws.'[49]

This discussion about the qualities of character in women relative to men focuses on three such qualities and comes to these conclusions: a) moral aptitude - women as exclusive legislators would be more apt to possess this quality than men; b) intellectual aptitude - in the ability to comprehend the needs of the people, the inclination to meet these needs and the appropriate knowledge of how best to meet these needs, women would be on a par with men; c) activity or active talent - 'women have the habit and the capacity for that species of activity which is *most appropriate* to the end in view'.

Whereas male politicians might use force to compel obedience, women would use their skills of persuasion to achieve compliance with the law. The downside is that women's need to take time out for child-bearing and rearing reduces their active availability. Weighing the pros and cons against each other, on balance women came out only marginally inferior to men in regard to active availability for public offices.[50]

At this point the critic of Wheeler might ask why change things, if conditions of inequality can in fact yield good results in the long run? Wheeler was well aware that subordination damaged women's characters in many ways. It is perhaps a more accurate interpretation of what she and Thompson mean here to see them as arguing, not that it is because of oppressive subordination that women have these qualities, but that in spite of negative conditions, women have developed resilience, strength of character, sympathy and other positive human qualities.

In the end, for feminist utilitarians in the nineteenth century, the difficult challenge was to show clearly how one choice of social policies was likely to deliver greater human satisfaction and human happiness for the greatest number of people.

A final passage will conclude this brief glance at the *Appeal*. Almost certainly from Wheeler's pen, it depicts in graphic language the quiet desperation of many women's lives in the nineteenth century.

O woman, from your auspicious hands may the new destiny of your species proceed! The collective voices of your sex raised against oppression will ultimately make men themselves your advocates and debtors. Reflect then seriously on your miserable and degraded position - your youth, your beauty, your feelings, your opinions, your actions, your time, your few years' fever of meretricious life - all made tributary to the appetites and passions of men. Nothing is your own; protection of person and of property are alike withheld from you. Nothing is yours, but secret pangs, the bitter burning tears of regret, the stifled sobs of outraged nature thrown back upon your own hearts, ... until body and mind become the frequent prey to overwhelming disease; now finding vent in sudden frenzy, now plunged in pining melancholy, or bursting the weak tenement of reason, seeking relief in self-destruction. How many thousand of your sex *daily* perish thus unpitied and unknown; often victims of pressing want, always of privation and the arbitrary laws of heartless custom.[51]

The urgency of Wheeler's appeal for a 'collective voice' among women recurs in all of her work: it is at once an expression of the necessity for political strategy and change and a challenge to determine if women know what their 'collective voice' is.

In 1830 Wheeler published a lecture, delivered a year earlier, in *The British Co-operator*, a short-lived journal sympathetic to 'radical causes'.[52] At the time she was continuing her collaborations with Saint-Simonians and Fourier supporters in England and France. The lecture reflects some of the developments in the debate about the 'true natures' of women and men.[53] Wheeler is aware she may find hostility in her audience:

> I am ... but too well aware, that the remarks I am about to make, will draw upon me the hate of most men, together with that of the greater portion of the *very sex* whose *rights* I attempt to advocate, with a distinterestedness which finds no rallying point in the self.[54]

This anxiety is outweighed by her desire to fulfil her debt to society by making this public appeal for women.

> To die and make no sign expressive of my horror, indignation and bitter contempt for that state of society called civilized, which in fact is nothing more than barbarism masked ... would, I feel, complete the measure of my regret for having lived only to serve and suffer, in my capacity of slave and woman; but the opportunity afforded me now, to leave *one* parting admonition to society, will

35

greatly mitigate those *regrets* which I feel, in common with
every good mind, when denied the power of being more
actively useful.[55]

Wheeler's indication that this is her 'parting admonition to
society' can be interpreted in the light of her increasingly
painful neuralgia and vacillating energies for public work.
This lecture was given at a low point in her health and in her
optimism about changing 'rotten institutions', and as a result
Wheeler greatly underestimates her own power in argument.

A dominant theme in this lecture is the manner and
extent to which the 'true natures' of women and men are
distorted by social institutions and social policies. A theory
of environmental conditioning is central to these early
communitarian ideas, a conditioning which can frustrate
human nature's positive development. The thesis is that we
have an original nature which is benevolent, cooperative,
and given to harmony. The mistakes of human beings and
the misguided appropriations of power in organising social
institutions have corrupted the original good in human
nature. Wheeler explains that she will expose this distortion
by holding the mirror up

> ... not indeed to nature (for man's cruel social code has
> stultified, if not stifled nature in him), but to some mockery
> of himself, some distorted image of a goodly nature, warped
> in all its fair proportions by the evil genius vanity, who
> condemns him to be his own tormentor, in being the enemy
> and oppressor of WOMAN![56]

This rational argument may not meet with agreement from
men, but Wheeler's point is that men's universal tendency to
keep women subordinate, disenfranchised and ill educated
affects them negatively also, making them victims of their
own unjust behaviour towards women. Wheeler never sees
women as engaged in adversarial combat against
unregenerate men:

> I have ... no leaning to the interests of one sex above the
> other; my object is to deprecate that narrow, stupid policy

which divides their interests, and in so doing, makes a pandemonium of our earth, by forcing its inhabitants to be in constant opposition to each other! ... I beg to be understood, as speaking, more in sorrow than in anger; more with *regret* for the loss of happiness to both sexes than to either in particular. It is not in the nature of woman (when she has strength of character sufficient to preserve original feelings, and reject those which are forced upon her adoption) to wish to mete out undue proportions of good, for one sex above the other ... [57]

If men could understand, they would see that behaviour which consistently deprives women of equality and just treatment results in discord, suffering and even crime between men and women and also crimes among women themselves. Men's behaviour also seriously diminishes their own happiness. Women's nature can be equally distorted and, when acting wrongly (destructively and thus out of keeping with their true nature), they contribute equally to social evils:

The *vices* of women, always those of the slave, no more belong to their *nature*, than the anguish they endure in becoming mothers belongs to their organization; but those vices are the more mischievous because they undermine *public virtue*, and painful as it is to me, I must observe, that the enmity women entertain towards each other, their active malice or secret jealousy, their delight in the punishment, privations and disgrace of their sex, individually and collectively; their apathy and indifference to *general good*, their sole engrossment of their minds, to keep and secure their masters' favour, and through that their own personal comforts, are not only the causes of their degradation as a body, but the fruitful source also of the crimes and shocking matrimonial murders which disgrace our land.[58]

Wheeler here addresses the problem of discord, enmity and disunity among women. If the cause of women's equality and emancipation is to succeed, women's own divisions must be addressed. Divisions may arise because of class, or discord may come from jealousy, or even from angry indifference to the cause of women's equality.

Concern about disunity was a focus of action among Saint-Simonian women in France and England during the 1830s. Wheeler is explicit that one cause of women's on-going degradation is precisely divisions among themselves, on which they seem to thrive rather than try to remove. 'Thus divided, women have no friends amongst themselves, and benevolence, stinted of its growth, dwindles to the size of a dwarf, while its natural stature is that of a giant!'[59]

The 'natural stature' of benevolence is much greater than women allow it to be in practice. The point is made again that both social institutions and women themselves can prevent the positive potential in women's natures from developing. Wheeler again stresses that she is pleading the cause of both women and men in arguing for equal rights. Women are urged to recognise their power to contribute to the totality of social happiness, including the happiness of men. Woman's moral role is to develop their own true, benevolent nature and to shoulder their responsibility to society.

> I am also pleading the cause of men by showing the mighty influence women hold over the happiness or misery of men themselves, according as they are instructed or ignorant, as they are fettered or free, as they *act on principles* ... acquired through the full development of their *own faculties* ... So true it is that, though men make the law, it is women who mould the manners and morals of society; and according as they are enlightened or ignorant, do they spin the web of human destiny ... [women's] destiny is to be the *mother* of both [sexes], and nature, whose laws are general and not partial, makes no distinctions in a mother's love.[60]

A new idealisation of woman was developing during these years, and it is consistent with the views of the French socialist women that Wheeler knew well. Women were encouraged as part of their 'moral duties' to be helpers in man's regeneration, to facilitate his improved happiness as well as their own. Men were chastised for not facilitating women's happiness, especially the happiness of their wives, but nowhere do we see men being exhorted to help in the 'regeneration' of women.

This view, which put women - but not men - on a

pedestal of moral responsibility, ran parallel with vigorous campaigning for equal rights. The pursuit of equality in this historical context neither encouraged nor wanted to imply an adversarial relationship between men and women, though later moves towards sexual equality might often suggest competitive or adversarial attitudes between the sexes.

Wheeler argued that a radical renewal of society cannot be accomplished while women are ignorant, without rights and thus without self-respect. The task given to women of helping social regeneration is in their power only if they have equality of rights and education. There was public concern that equality might compromise women's special qualities and diminish their motivation to fulfil their role of moral reconstruction. Wheeler answers that if society is to benefit from women's aptitude in promoting manners and morals, it must remove ignorance and inequalities from their lives. Far from women's equality being at odds with their special moral mission, it is in fact essential to its success.

For centuries various arguments have tried to prove that women (but not men) have disabilities, inherent weaknesses, making them unsuitable for full political rights. Wheeler is not persuaded.

> Let us examine the grounds of disabilities set up by men, to disfranchise half the human race, Women; the effects of this treatment on us and on themselves; and whether indeed there is any essential difference between the sexes, which can authorise the superiority men claim over women? ... What are the causes of, and who are accountable, for the seeming difference ...? [61]

Two grounds are most commonly given: first, women's deficiency of muscular strength; second, the assumed moral incapacity which, in this context, means intellectual incapacity, of women. A true Utilitarian, Wheeler produces empirical evidence from anthropology to refute an innate muscular weakness in women:

> Monsieur de Chateaubriand, in his book of martyrs (an appropriate place to find a chapter on Women), brings a host of evidence, from travellers and naturalists, to prove

that this deficiency of strength in Women, is nothing but a *civilized disease*, imposed no doubt, on women, to shorten the duration of life, and to provide men with a rapid succession of youthful slaves ... so this supposed organic weakness, which condemns women to be slaves, is by no means borne out by fact.[62]

The most obvious causes of these presumed physical 'disabilities' can be removed by social changes. The presumed 'intellectual inferiority of women' is rejected in the same way. The causes of the disabilities, physical or intellectual and moral, come from cultural practices and customs of 'female fragility' which are both encouraged and rewarded in women. If nature were given a chance, women would be seen to be equal in abilities. The absence of universal and equal education (not a special 'female' education) is one of the most serious factors causing women's debased condition. Women's given nature is not to blame; rather, such allegations of 'nature being such' are camouflaging the social causes of exclusion - all of which men have established and women have often colluded in maintaining. Men are

... jealous of their power, [and] will ever be inclined to exercise it on those whom oppression holds captive, and will wish to render those already weak, *still weaker*, by destroying the moral energy which would resist oppression.[63]

In a final plea for 'rational education' to develop all women's faculties, Wheeler praises Fanny Wright's work for universal education.

Wheeler believed that women were partly reponsible for their own continuing degradation. Depending on her strength and buoyancy at the time of writing, Wheeler assigns more or less blame to women for not resisting their own oppression. Sometimes she is discouraged at how little women show will or energy for changes in their condition. She never questions whether, or to what extent, women agree with the diagnosis that their condition is a degraded one. However, even if women believed they were not degraded, she would argue they were deluded, and that the delusion was itself a result of their oppression. She writes:

> The emancipation of women till they win it by their own resolute efforts to obtain it would, even were it likely to be granted by men, prove a useless boon. The love of rational liberty forms no part of the nature of this willingly degraded sex, and their very propensity for slavery is indeed a justification of the dogma that they originated the fall of man. Women are capable of great personal courage and certainly they possess in a more eminant [sic] degree than men the courage of endurance, but their personal courage is never exerted but to fight for a master and their mental courage is chiefly exhibited in the indurance [sic] of oppression.[64]

Women's courage is recognised but this is often misguided.

> Women are not so ignorant but they are passive and indifferent to the suffering of their species. Whether from superstition or its stupefying effects on the characters of women, their hearts seem incapable of loving anything but man as he is tyrannical, cruel, selfish, oppressive. There is something very depressing in contemplating this true, but dark side of the human picture.[65]

The causes of women's indifference are rooted in institutions and public opinion. Blindness to their degraded condition is encouraged in society. This is a refrain which is heard in the French and English socialists of this period. Transformation of society is necessary if minds are to be freed to even recognise their oppression.

The attempt to analyse the causes of sexual oppression is pursued again during the year 1833, when Wheeler was especially prolific in her writing. William Thompson had died in West Cork in March of that year. Under her pseudonym, Vlasta, Wheeler wrote to Lord Hampden, a supporter of the Cooperative movement and a long-time friend of Thompson. The use of 'Vlasta' suggests that she expected the letter would be read to Owenite groups gathering at Lord Hampden's. The letter is a eulogy to Thompson, showing deep love and respect, and is the final response to his famous 'Letter' to her in the *Appeal*. [66]

In her letter Wheeler voices the sociopolitical views she shared with Thompson. As a political essay it echoes sentiments of the Saint-Simonians in its faith in humanity and belief in the progessive improvement of human beings, though Wheeler constantly reminds us that it is a long road, through a labyrinth of errors. 'It is the very nature of error ... to restrict progress, and keep man stationary, against all the laws of universal nature'. [67]

A combination of utopian hope and depression at disunity makes this letter a realistic statement of the mixed feelings among community socialists in the 1830s.

> But the night of ignorance is passing away, and the dawn of a brighter day than humanity has ever yet witnessed is fast breaking upon us! ... Yet there is something depressing in the reflection ... that this unity of purpose, this simultaneous march of public opinion, must meet with many formidable obstacles ... the human mind has never been trained to think ... never permitted in two large divisions of the community - the labouring poor, and women: every device has been resorted to, to keep down the intelligence of these two portions of the human race ... this has ever been the mind-extinguishing destiny of woman. [68]

Wheeler's memorial to Thompson was a resumé of her political views, and a record of her deep personal loss at the death of an intimate friend. Her relationship with Thompson was not unlike that which later developed between John Stuart Mill and Harriet Taylor. [69] But, as Wheeler explains in this letter, neither Thompson nor she could endorse the legal slavery that they both believed marriage to be at the time.

During 1833 numerous debates on the nature and social role of women were published in the *Crisis*, the journal of the Cooperative Trade Associations. In August 1833 the *Crisis* published a series of views about Robert Owen's intention of publishing a code of laws for the human race, women as well as men. In France, Fourier was also putting finishing touches to his *Phalanx* plans. Legislation for this was also anticipated, and Saint-Simonians were spelling out terms for 'a new religious sect'. A central issue in the debate was whether men were competent to legislate in women's interests. One correspondent, Concordia, was a regular voice and debated with Wheeler on this question of men legislating for women - a question that quickly moves onto women's nature and their knowledge of themselves.

> When you attempt to make regulations for women ... you will not succeed in regulating properly for beings whose feelings and habits are so little known to any but themselves ... never can there be a code of laws framed in harmony with the laws of nature and truth, until woman shall be permitted to have a voice in all enactments that concern her ... until ... she shall be permitted to *legislate for herself*.[70]

Yes, she argues, there are universal principles of feeling and action which both women and men share, but there are also 'individual feelings and principles peculiar to each party'. The respective natures of men and women share these similarities but also show irreducible differences.

> The nature of men induces a set of habits and emotions differing materially from those induced by the nature of women; neither can, therefore, entirely and fully understand the other.[71]

Exchanges of sympathy and affection are possible but it is impossible for one to wisely legislate for the other. In today's categories, Concordia is the voice of the essentialist feminist, who argues that there are innate differences between the sexes and women only have knowledge of their own nature - a nature which especially excels in the capacity to love.

> Nature cannot be reversed; and *she*, in her infinite wisdom, has stamped upon men and women a moral and intellectual difference, which no social arrangement can ever amalgamate. Woman, to be the loved and loving being for which she is so beautifully qualified, must preserve her own distinct moral peculiarities, and these, men can never

understand ... . Who, but herself, can tell of feelings which are the holiest and purest of her nature? ... There is not a man ... who can tell of the enduring love that beats in her bosom.[72]

Concordia believes that the 'false arrangements of society' have led women down a path not true to their nature. She asks each woman 'to become acquainted with herself ... learn and teach the habit of analyzing her wishes'.[73]

Vlasta (Wheeler) in reply explains that the good legislator asserts the

> ... *equal* rights of both sexes - involving equal education; mankind having a common nature, the wants of one human being are the wants of *every* other; therefore, the whole business of legislation ... should confine itself to discovering the best means of supplying these *common* wants of *all*, taking especial care that the interests of any one individual of *either sex* should not clash with the interests of any other.[74]

Wheeler is radical in arguing that equal rights must be aimed at giving both sexes the knowledge, liberty and self-respect required to fulfil individual needs and wants. Legislation provides for wants common to all human beings. Women, however, cannot claim a 'collective voice'. In 'her ignorance of the infinite *shades* of difference in female ... character', any one woman can only accurately know her own peculiar feelings.[75] Women then cannot presume understanding of other women simply by virtue of a shared biology. The differences among women are seen to be significant. Wheeler urges women of all classes and religions to try to appreciate these differences.

As a first step to alleviate a sense of strangeness and even hostility towards each other, women are encouraged to come together more often and learn to appreciate, if not comprehend, differences of feelings and aspirations. Wheeler translates an article from a Paris woman's journal chosen as a combination of arguments central to her own writings.

We are born as free as men - their infancy is as helpless as ours, and ours as theirs. Without our tenderness, our sympathy and care, they could never grow up to be our oppressors ... . Let us understand our rights - let us also understand our powers - and let us learn how to employ *usefully* the intelligence and the attractions that nature has bestowed upon us ... Let us no longer form two camps - that of women of the people, and that of women of the privileged class ... Women of the privileged class - those amongst you who are young, beautiful and rich, and who think yourselves happy, when in your splendid salons you breathe the incense of flattery ... when you return home you are slaves, you find there a master who makes you feel his power ... it is for us to tell them [men] that this ... system must terminate, that the social edifice must be re-built ... .[76]

Men are being given a new role and this is made clear. If man is to be a worthy associate for woman and legislate justly for her, he must of necessity become intimately acquainted with her 'more refined sentiments and capabilities'.[77]

Finally, Wheeler is concerned about the adverse implications of romanticising women's capacity for passionate loving, a capacity proclaimed, in almost messianic terms, by Prosper Enfantin, a Saint-Simonian well known to Wheeler. Women's love is like religion, says Wheeler. It has been made a superstitition. She is cautious in dealing with these sensitive subjects of love and religion, but claims that the power to love in woman is 'a fearful gift' and 'hurtful to society because it has been made an antisocial passion; she must love to excess one, and hate or be indifferent to all the world besides'.[78]

This view of monogamous marital loving as 'anti-social' is clearly that of Charles Fourier, and Wheeler criticises the dubious new exaltation of women's power of loving, which could all too easily become another social tyranny.

Anna Wheeler's legacy is that of a critic of social structures that promoted competition, discord and individual pursuit of progress without concern for those who are disabled by being disenfranchised from having a public voice. She excelled at emotional negotiation which allowed people with differences to search for the unity in their aspiration. In her translations for the early socialists she did more than change languages for them; she interpreted for them the cultural means and understandings that could facilitate cooperation.

Her legacy also includes her challenge to the authorised canon of Utilitarian ideas. The founding 'fathers' such as James Mill and Jeremy Bentham needed revision to include women in their calculation of happiness. Wheeler and Thompson gave a critique of Utilitarian assumptions about general happiness, and showed that their ideas of generality excluded women's prospects for happiness.

Wheeler believed it was necessary to argue for equal rights for both sexes and yet not compromise on the assumption that women could make unique contributions towards a more humane, just and non-competitive society. Women and men would both be the beneficiaries of Wheeler's politics, which she shared with her contemporaries in France. Women and men equally valued freedom to govern themselves. This freedom would have to be facilitated by the legal provision of equal rights.

Wheeler's vision included the broader community of cooperation and sympathy that society could become. Social regeneration was more than rhetoric for this epoch in women's history. The discord and 'tooth and claw' of competitive society made painful demands on Wheeler's health and mental peace. She often withdrew to renew her energies and bolster her beliefs that progress in institutional change was possible.

In their political project, Wheeler and her contemporary women supporters showed a first serious effort to combine what was later seen as the 'liberal' goal of procuring equal rights with the more explicitly 'socialist' claim that radical social and economic changes were required for human emancipation. In this endeavour, Wheeler's work was a bridging voice, showing the necessary transitions from Enlightenment claims for equality and individual freedoms to a preoccupation with socialism under Karl Marx and his successors.

Wheeler's utopian imaginings of what could become reality can be appreciated by those feminists today who believe that when women stop envisaging alternatives to the patriarchal order - 'the weight of the father' as the French call it - this dearth of dreaming will signal the end of worthwhile human civilisation. In her vision women and men are not opponents in the race to improvement or happiness. She called for the mobilisation of both sexes to respect the 'differences of their unique natures', but made clear the need for cooperation and mutual understanding.

Braving the hazards of historical anachronism, one might see a prophetic character in nineteenth-century discussions about the social constructions of 'meanings' which women inherit, meanings which are often oppressive and not freely chosen. The questioning about differences among women and the limits of legal equality provides a humbling read, reminding us that our contemporary theorising cannot claim radical originality. Wheeler is among the earliest of women in social science, and her 'science for happiness' offers a human project which assumes cooperation among equals who in their equality can affirm their profound differences. She never minimises the difficulty of that collective journey.

I have taken you over a rugged road, that of error, leading, however, to truth; so we must not mind the sharp thorns and briars that lay hold of us on the way. We shall compare scratches when we get to the end of our journey, which is a long day's march yet ... who cares for brambles, or briars, or flints, or stocks, or stones? We shall make new roads in a short time, when we all go to work together.[79]

NOTES

1 Doyle, Colonel Arthur. 1911. *A Hundred Years of Conflict: some Records of the Services of Six Generals of the Doyle Family 1756-1856.* London, p.187.

2 The sources available for Wheeler's life are mainly the following. Lytton, Edward. 1883. *The Life, Letters and Literary Remains of E Bulwer, Lord Lytton, by his son,* 2 volumes. London; Devey, Louisa. 1884. *Letters of the Late Edward Bulwer, Lord Lytton, to his Wife with Extracts from her Ms. 'Autobiography' and other Documents Published in Vindication of her Memory,* London; idem. 1887. *Life of Rosina, Lady Lytton.* London; Ellis, S M (ed.) 1914. *Unpublished Letters of Lady Bulwer Lytton to A W Chalon, RA.* London; Sadleir, Michael. 1931. *Bulwer and His Wife: A Panorama 1803-1836.* London.

3 Devey, *Letters of the late Edward Bulwer,* pp7-8. Mary Wollstonecraft (1759-1797) critiqued Rousseau's views on women with the same vigour that Wheeler used in denouncing James Mill's exclusion of women from the political franchise.

4 Wheeler to Robert Owen, 19 July 1831, Owen Correspondence, no. 426, available at Cooperative Union Library, Manchester, England (hereafter C.U.L., Manchester).

5 Devey, *Life of Lady Lytton,* pp16-7

6 Lytton, *Life, Letters and Literary Remains,* p.34.

7 There is an extensive literature on salons as 'institutions' facilitating a semi-public role for women. Especially relevant to my study of Wheeler were the following: Landes, Joan B 1988. *Women and the Public Sphere in the Age of the French Revolution.* New York; Goodman, Dena. 1991. 'Governing the republic of letters: the politics of culture in the French Enlightenment'. In *History of European Ideas* 13, 3, pp183-199.

8 Henri, Comte de Saint Simon (1760-1825) barely escaped the guillotine during the French Revolution and spent years attempting to construct a new social structure to replace the ineffective regime which brought about the 1789 Revolution.

9 Sadleir, *Bulwer and His Wife,* pp76-81. This biography provides a number of deprecating judgments of Anna Wheeler, such as that when she became known as the 'Goddess of Reason' it was 'to a small group of embittered cranks in Caen. Her unhappy children played acolyte on either side of her altar', p.76. Sources on Wheeler are difficult to interpret when trying to achieve an accurate picture of her as a person. They were often written in contexts of family acrimony where sides were mainly interested in either publicly eulogising and defending someone or alternatively excoriating their character. There seems to be a consensus, however, that she was single-minded in her political objectives and did not suffer fools gladly.

10 Robert Owen (1771-1858), born at Newtown in Wales, established his international reputation by 1812 with his blueprint for a

reformed society, *A New View of Society*, a foundation text in British social history. In the extensive literature on Owen the following proved especially helpful in my work on Wheeler. Goodwin, Barbara. 1978. *Social Science and Utopia*. Sussex; Taylor, Barbara. 1983. *Eve and the New Jerusalem*. London.

11 Correspondence from Wheeler to Owen can be found in the Owen Correspondence C U L, Manchester.

12 Owen's followers organised a series of meetings in Dublin, Ireland during 1823. It is probable that Wheeler would have attended these meetings if she were in Dublin. Owen was laying out his plans for Ireland and trying to prove their practicality. It is likely that Daniel O'Connell became familiar with Owen's ideas at this time. The records of these Dublin meetings are available in the Royal Irish Academy in Dawson St, Dublin.

13 Jeremy Bentham (1748-1832) became a close friend and confidant of Wheeler, who regularly visited him and borrowed his writings in order to keep up with the development of Utilitarian ideas.

14 *The Cooperative News and Journal of Associated Industry*, (1904), C U L , Manchester. During the period 2 April-6 August 1904, G J Holyoake wrote detailed summaries of correspondence from the Robert Owen family, including detailed reporting on the work and life of Frances (Fanny) Wright.

15 The ideas of Fanny Wright and her influence on the ideas among nineteenth-century Utilitarians and the Owenites are discussed in Taylor, *Eve and the New Jerusalem*.

16 See Pankhurst, Richard. 1954. *William Thompson (1775-1833) Pioneer Socialist*. London.

17 Robert Owen is known as the father of cooperation, though this is inaccurate since many organised cooperative endeavours preceded him in other countries. He was instrumental in establishing a number of cooperative communities in New Lanark, Scotland, New Harmony, Indiana, North America, and one in Ralahine, County Clare, Ireland which lasted only a short time, 1831-1833, under the local organisers, John Vandeleur and E T Craig. See: Garnett, R G 1972. *Co-operation and the Owenite Socialist Communities in Britain, 1825-1845*. Manchester, and Pollard, Sidney and Salt John (eds.)1971. *Robert Owen, Prophet of the Poor*. London. An excellent study of the ideology of gender in the American Owenite communities is Kolmerten, Carol A 1990. *Women in Utopia* Bloomington.

18 Beecher, Jonathan. 1986. *Charles Fourier, the Visionary and his World*. Berkeley, pp366-367.

19 Fourier, François Marie Charles. 1808. *Théorie des Quatre Mouvements et des Destinées Générales: Prospectus et Annonce de la Découverte*. In *Oeuvres Complètes*, vol 1 Paris 1841-45. Wheeler regularly gave journal materials about Fourier's philosophy to interested persons in England, a point she makes clear in her correspondence.

20 Jullien de Paris, Marc Antoine. 1827. 'Le tombeau d'une jeune philhellène'. In *Revue Encyclopedique*, 3, pp334-9. The elegy is

dedicated to Anna Wheeler: *'Adressée à Madame Anna Wheeler, Irlandaise, amie dévouée de la cause des Grecs, sur la mort de sa fille Henriette.'*

21 Lytton, *Life of E Bulwer* I, pp33-4; For details about Rosina in the decades 1830-1860, see Ellis, *Unpublished Letters of Lady Bulwer Lytton*.

22 Banks, Olive. 1985. *The Biographical Dictionary of British Feminists, Volume 1: 1800-1930*. Brighton, pp112-4.

23 A.D. Wheeler, writing from London to Marc Antoine Jullien, 15 November 1832, in Stephen Burke, 'Letter from a pioneer feminist' in Noyce, John L. (ed.) 1976. *Studies in Labour History* 1. p.22. Anna is always candid with her friends about her energies lost through illness or grief. In this letter to Marc Antoine Jullien, she refers to her 'constant state of mental and bodily suffering' and apologises for her penmanship: 'I hope you may be able to read this, the cruel nervous malady I labour under, deprives me the free use of both arms.' Wheeler's neuralgia increasingly diminished her mobility.

24 A D Wheeler to M Charles Fourier, 29 October 1836. 'My present existance [sic] is much afflicted with many causes of domestic pain.' The reference is to Rosina's divorce which had occurred just a few months previously.

25 Devey, *Letters of the Late Edward Bulwer*, p.303. Lady Bulwer Lytton (Rosina) published her own defence in the *Appeal to the Justice and Charity of the English Public* (London, 1857). Rosina's forced incarceration followed soon after.

26 Hugh Doherty to Mrs Wheeler, 7 May 1848, in Owen Correspondence, no. 1, 613. C U L , Manchester.

27 Smith, W. Anderson. 1892. *Shepherd Smith the Universalist*. London, p.336. A letter to Rosina referring to 'the memory of your mother' is dated 29 April 1851, p.333.

28 For detailed discussion of men's use of women's talents without acknowledgement see: Spender, Dale. 1989. *The Writing or the Sex*. New York.

29 Hereafter referred to as *Appeal*. The edition of the *Appeal* which I use for the references given here was published by Virago Press in 1983 with a new introduction by Richard Pankhurst. Pankhurst's *William Thompson*, first published in 1954 and republished in 1991, is a general introduction to Thompson's ideas. There is a closer look at Wheeler's life in Pankhurst's article, 'Anna Wheeler: a pioneer socialist and feminist', *The Political Quarterly* 25, 2 (1954), pp132-43. See my *Equality in Community* which includes biographies of Thompson and Wheeler and details their philosophy of sexual equality. Forthcoming Autumn 1995, Cork University Press.

30 *Appeal*, ppxxi-xxii.

31 *Ibid.*, ppxxii-xxiii.

32 See: Wanklyn, Wendy. 1988. 'The Feminisms of Mary Wollstonecraft and William Thompson'. Unpublished DPhil, Oxford.

33 For an excellent study of this period in Utilitarian politics see: Lively, Jack and Rees, John (eds.). 1978. *Utilitarian Logic and Politics*. Oxford.

34 Mill, James. *On Government*, as quoted by Thompson in *Appeal*, p.9.

35 *Appeal*, p.xxv.

36 *Ibid.*, pp149 and 159.

37 *Ibid.*, p.164.

38 *Ibid.*, p.182.

39 *Ibid.*, p.xxviii.

40 *Ibid.*, p.xxx.

41 *Ibid.*, p.xxvi. In the concluding sections of the *Appeal*, pp195-213, there is an expanded explanation of the profound differences between economies based on individual competition and voluntary associations of mutual cooperation.

42 Taylor, Keith. 1982. *The Political Ideas of the Utopian Socialists*. London, p.3. See also: Manuel, Frank and Fritzie. 1979. *Utopian Thought in the Western World*. Oxford.

43 It is not clear from Wheeler's later writing precisely where she stood on this issue of equality of distribution of wealth or equality of governing within Fourier's plans for a *Phalanx* community. Inequality of distribution is certainly a central feature of Charles Fourier's system of cooperation, as are features of his proposed mode of government. There were rather strong inconsistencies for Wheeler to deal with on this issue if she compared Thompson's plans for a Cooperative community with Fourier's.

44 See forthcoming annotated student edition of the *Appeal*; D Dooley (ed.) Cork University Press, Autumn 1995. In addition to the *Appeal* (1825), William Thompson published three other major works: *An Inquiry into the Principles of the Distribution of Wealth most Conducive to Human Happiness* (London, 1824); *Labour Rewarded: The Claims of Labour and Capital Conciliated* (London, 1827); and *Practical Directions for the Speedy and Economical Establishment of Communities on the Principles of Mutual Co-operation, United Possessions and Equality*, (London, 1830). He also published numerous articles in Cooperative journals and London labour newspapers of the day. The *Cork Southern Reporter* contains a series of articles from Thompson, written as early as 1818.

45 *Appeal*, pp200-1. Following the publication of the *Appeal*, Wheeler's critiques of marriage and religion became a source of concern for some of her Owenite friends. P O Skene, a close confidante and worker with Wheeler in the British Association for Promoting Cooperative Knowledge, wrote to Robert Owen on 9 October 1828: 'I had the pleasure of seeing Mrs Wheeler lately in London and of finding her mind in a good measure tranquillized and her opinion altered as to the propriety of violent attacks on marriage and religion.' Owen Correspondence, no. 83. C U L , Manchester.

46 'Mr O'Connell's Political Creed'. 1828. In *The Weekly Free Press of Trade, Manufacturers and Commerce*, IV, 167, (20 September).

47 *Appeal*, p.199.

48 *Ibid.*, p.131.

49 *Ibid.*, p.129.

50 *Ibid.*, p.141. Compare these points with those given by John Stuart Mill in *The Subjection of Women* (London, 1869).

51 *Appeal*, pp212-3. Recent studies document the extent to which women in centuries past suffered anxiety, neuroses and chronic physical complaints caused or greatly influenced in complex ways by women's alienation, and social deprivation. See: Gilbert, Sandra and Gubar, Susan. 1979. *The Madwoman in the Attic*, New Haven; and Showalter, Elaine. 1987. *The Female Malady*, London.

52 Wheeler. 1830. 'Rights of women'. In *The British Co-operator* 1, April, pp12-5, and 2, May, pp33-6.

53 For the ideas of French socialists and Owenites see: Goodwin, Barbara. 1978. *Social Science and Utopia, Nineteenth-Century Models of Social Harmony*. Sussex; Grogan, Susan. 1992. *French Socialism and Sexual Difference: Women and the New Society 1803-44*. London.

54 Wheeler, 'Rights of women', p.12.

55 *Ibid.*, pp12-3. Emphasis on words is Wheeler's own unless otherwise specified. Language characterising women as 'slaves' was commonly used as political rhetoric at this period in British history. Pamphlets protesting against the slave trade had been published in abundance for at least fifty years prior to this lecture. Listeners would have caught the emotive connotations of the term and associated 'slaves' with the opposition to British toleration of black slavery in West India and the southern United States. For a history of racism, and slave trade practices in Britain see: Shyllon, Folarin. 1977. *Black People in Britain 1555-1833*. London.

56 Wheeler, 'Rights of women', p.13. Wheeler has many stylistic emphases in her writing, using upper case and underlining or highlighting words frequently.

57 *Ibid.*, p.13.

58 *Ibid.*, p.35. For crimes committed by 'respectable' English and French women see Hartman, Mary S 1985. *Victorian Murderesses*. London. For research materials on crimes against and by women see the London Cooperative labour papers, especially the trades newspapers and *Weekly Free Press* during the period of 1820-1835.

59 Wheeler, 'Rights of Women', p.35.

60 *Ibid.*, p.13.

61 *Ibid.*, p.15.

62 *Ibid.*, p.15.

63 *Ibid.*, p.36.

64 Wheeler to Jullien, 15 November, 1832. See footnote 23 above.

65 *Ibid*

66 Minter Morgan, John. 1834. *Hampden in the Nineteenth Century, Volume II*. London, p.326. The letter from Vlasta in its entirety is in Chapter X, pp301-25. Vlasta was the name of a sixteenth-century Swedish woman who allegedly headed a female army fighting for the protection of women against various kinds of attack.

67 *Ibid.*, p.305.

68 *Ibid.*, pp 305-12. Another friend and co-worker of Wheeler's was Flora Tristan (1803-44), who argued that women and labourers should join forces in fighting for unions to support political unity.

Around 1839, Wheeler gave Tristan a tour and a detailed account of the mental hospitals in England, showing her concern with afflictions of the mind. The event is recorded in *The London Journal of Flora Tristan* (1842), translated by Jean Hawkes, (London, 1982), p.208.

69 See: Rossi, Alice S. (ed.). 1970. *Essays on Sex Equality*. Chicago. Rossi gives a chapter to the story of John Stuart Mill and Harriet Taylor, both of whom were considerably younger than Thompson and Wheeler, but knew of them and would have known the *Appeal*.

70 Concordia. 1833. 'To Robert Owen, Esq.' In *Crisis*, II, 31-32, 10 August, pp254-5.

71 *Ibid.*

72 *Ibid.*

73 *Ibid.*, p.255.

74 Vlasta. 1833. 'To the editor of the *Crisis*'. In *Crisis*, II, 35-36, 31 August, p.279.

75 *Ibid.*, p.280. See further: 'Plan of a practical moral union of the women of Great Britain and Ireland, for the purpose of enabling them to attain a superior physical, moral, and intellectual character'. In *Crisis*, II, 33, 17 August, p.v.263. No author is given. Also see: 'Woman' by Suzanne. 1834. *Crisis*, III, 28, 8 March.

76 Victoire, Jeanne. 1833. 'The women of the future', translated by A.D. Wheeler. In *Crisis*, II, 23, 15 June, p.182.

77 *Ibid.*

78 Vlasta, *Crisis*, 31 August 1833, p.280.

79 *Ibid.*, pp280-1.

I dedicate this chapter to the memory of my mother, Marie Talbot Dooley (1908-1995). Her active listening was her great power. I am grateful for a grant received from the Development Fund of UCC which enabled me to do the research required for this project. The assistance of the editors, Mary Cullen and Maria Luddy, was invaluable and greatly appreciated.

Margaret Louisa Aylward

(1810-1889)

Jacinta Prunty

Margaret Aylward declined to have a portrait painted or a photograph taken during her lifetime. Therefore no image of her exists.

Margaret Louisa Aylward, wealthy, well-educated and unmarried, was passionately committed to the poor of her adopted city of Dublin. Her very varied activities during a long life of charitable endeavour have tended to be overshadowed by her most public achievement, the founding of a religious congregation, the Sisters of the Holy Faith, canonically approved in 1867. Most certainly a reluctant foundress, her story extends far outside the confines of any conventual enclosure, and is intertwined with the stories of many Irish women. She was a confirmed believer in the ability of women to organise themselves and spearhead change, and in the special contribution women make in tackling society's ills. Her life story also provides fascinating insights into the power structures of the Roman Catholic Church in Ireland in the second half of the nineteenth century, and the particular skills and ecclesiastical contacts required of women to secure church sanction and support for their charitable enterprises.

Aylward's family background was one of privilege and civic responsibility. It was into one of the most prominent of Waterford merchant families that Aylward was born on 23 November 1810, the fifth child of William Aylward and Ellen, née Murphy. There were ten children in all, and a half-brother, Maurice, from her mother's first marriage. One daughter, Anne, died in childhood, while two brothers, Francis and Richard, died in their teens. Mary, John, William and Catherine were older than Margaret; Ellen and Jane followed.[1]

The Aylward wealth was based on the lucrative eighteenth-century provisions trade, with the family occupying a prominent position in the civic and merchant life of the city, and both parents patronised various local charities. Politically the family sympathies were with the Young Ireland movement, while both Thomas Francis Meagher, a native of Waterford, and Daniel O'Connell were frequent visitors to the family home at 11 Thomas Street.

Much of the family's considerable wealth originated on the mother's side, with two unmarried sisters, Mary and Margaret Murphy, selling to their brother-in-law William Aylward 'all the property he possessed in King Street, Waterford and in Thomas Street and other places'.[2] These two ladies still possessed and managed considerable property portfolios until their deaths in 1858, when their wealth came to their sister Ellen, Margaret's mother.[3] Margaret Aylward was therefore familiar with women as substantial property holders and administrators in their own right. Through familiarity with her parents' and aunts' financial affairs Aylward developed sound business skills, including a grasp of the complexities of investment options, legal terms, and property rights. These abilities, combined with meticulous book-keeping, and a driving zeal to bring her projects to fruition, made her a formidable businesswoman and entrepreneur.

William Aylward passed on extensive business concerns to the two older sons, John and William Jr, in 1834, six years before his death. It was a time of declining fortunes in Waterford commerce, as trade contracted following the Act of Union and the end of the Napoleonic wars. The failure to adapt to shifts in market patterns and changing technologies all combined to leave traditional Waterford enterprises well behind their competitors.[4] The collapse of the Aylward family business, under the mismanagement of the two sons, was just one of many such business failures. However, the poor health and lengthy absences of John from Waterford, and the protracted and very bitter divorce proceedings of his brother William, hastened the collapse.[5]

As befitted their status as citizens of substance, William and Ellen Aylward sent their children to the best Catholic schools available: Margaret to the Ursulines in Thurles, Jane to the Benedictines in Princethorpe in England, and the sons to Stoneyhurst, also in England, and to Clongowes Wood.[6] Until she reached ten years of age, Margaret Aylward received her early education in a small Quaker school, after which she moved to the Ursulines in Thurles. Here she became fluent in French, the daily language of the school, and developed her talents as an artist, as her surviving watercolours show. Following on her second-level schooling she continued for an extra three years studying Sacred Scripture, Latin, classics, art and embroidery.[7]

Aylward spent about four years after school living at home and applying herself, with her sisters, to various charities in Waterford. She worked in the Mont de Piété, a charitable pawnshop designed to protect the poor from the exorbitant rates of interest charged by regular pawnshops.[8] Family connections with both the Presentation Sisters and the Christian Brothers provided Aylward with an introduction to the operation of poor schools in the city, where she taught for some time.[9] When she later moved to Dublin the circle of people who had supported her Waterford endeavours undertook some fundraising for her Dublin projects, under the able organisation of her sister Ellen. Surviving references to her philanthropic work in Waterford point to her first-hand experience of the appalling city slums and her familiarity with the harsh regime of the local house of industry.[10] It is clear that she belonged to a well-developed network of charitable middle-class Catholic women, who had more than ample scope for their efforts in a port city ravaged by economic depression.

Records of Aylward's activities are more complete from

1834, when she followed her sister Catherine into the Irish Sisters of Charity in Dublin. She had, as had Catherine, the full backing of her father, who writes affectionately 'You know not the feelings of a fond parent on an occasion of this kind. But if you feel it is for your happiness most cheerfully will I bear it'.[11] Aylward taught in King's Inn Street national school as a novice, but according to one source she suffered from 'weakness of the spine which obliged her to keep in a lying posture', and reputedly left under the advice of her confessor.[12]

There was, however, another angle to her time with the Sisters of Charity, recorded in their annals as 'Troubles from Within'. The novice mistress, Sr Ignatius (Ellen Augustine Bodenham) was dismissed from the congregation by its foundress and first superior, Mary Aikenhead, for allegedly creating 'mischief'. It was claimed that Bodenham had stirred up the young recruits to believe that they were 'squandering intellectual gifts' by devoting their lives to the poor.[13] Her forcible removal caused havoc in the community, with some believing Aikenhead's handling of the situation unjust and sympathising with the undoubtedly accomplished and attractive mistress of novices. On her dismissal thirteen of the twenty-two novices, and two young professed sisters, left.

This exodus included Aylward, with whom Miss Bodenham continued to correspond from 1839 to 1842.[14] The letters which Aylward received from Bodenham have survived, making it clear that the former novice mistress put Aylward under considerable pressure to join with her in founding a new congregation in Hastings, England. Aylward's own reflections on this turbulent period have not survived, but it can be deduced from Bodenham's letters that while Aylward had not abandoned all thoughts of religious life, she was more interested in assisting the establishment of religious orders in Waterford than in Bodenham's complex schemes.

Religious life was a major family consideration, and while Catherine was the only one to persevere in this vocation, each of the Aylward sisters and several of their friends gave it serious thought. Mary and Ellen each gave the convent a short trial, while Jane's first unsuccessful attempt was followed by an unhappy marriage and desertion, after which she joined Margaret's embryonic community. Aylward twice entered religious congregations, and eventually began her own. The serious consideration which the Aylward sisters and their circle of young women friends gave to the possibility of religious life was not atypical in mid nineteenth-century Waterford. Geographically the city was at the core of the 'Catholic heartland', a compact area of Catholic large farms, with an overwhelmingly Catholic urban population, a continental-educated clergy, and the wealth and political confidence required for the endowment of Catholic convents and schools.[15] The post-penal re-establishment and modernisation of the church in Ireland was spearheaded by stable Catholic communities with surplus wealth such as that into which Aylward was born. In such a social and religious climate the consideration of religious life by so many of Margaret's circle is understandable. On a personal level the attractiveness of religious life for many middle-class women in nineteenth-century Ireland has been strongly argued:

Many had no real marriage prospects, no prospect of ever moving out of the family home, and faced a future of single idleness or perpetual dependence upon the whims of older relatives. Becoming a nun offered the comfort of the familiar and the challenge of a new way of life, and in an evangelical age, it apparently ensured salvation.[16]

The attraction could vary according to class; for many women with money the choice lay between marriage and convent life, and the latter provided opportunities 'to give expression to their intellectual and vocational aspirations'.[17] In Aylward's case the choice between lay or religious life was an agonising struggle; at the mature age of 35, she made one further attempt by entering the Ursuline convent in Waterford.[18] However, almost immediately she found it unbearable, apparently finding the loss of liberty and innumerable 'annoyances' too great a strain.[19] In January 1846, after no more than two months, Aylward left, to the disapproval of some family members and friends. She moved to Dublin, both to avoid the local gossip which inevitably followed on this second failure in religious life, and to consult with doctors.

Materials relating to Aylward's family life in Waterford reveal her closeness to her father, some strain in relations with her mother, and intense and affectionate involvement throughout her life with her brothers and sisters. Although the fifth child, she was to prove the mainstay of her family, as numerous letters directed to her, on matters of great and small import, testify. It was Aylward who had the worry of finding accommodation for Ellen, unmarried, and Jane, deserted, in Dublin in 1854. She had also the anxiety of dealing with her brother William and his wife Maria, throughout traumatic divorce proceedings. Aylward's role as counsellor, mediator and financial manager in her family circle was maintained, and indeed intensified, despite what were to be exceptionally demanding activities in Dublin.[20]

On moving to Dublin in 1848 Aylward came into contact with the Ladies' Association of Charity of St Vincent de Paul for the Spiritual and Temporal Relief of the Sick Poor. This lay charity opened its first Irish branch in Kingstown (Dún Laoghaire) in 1843. Aylward worked there with a Miss Margaret Kelly, director of the branch, before founding the Metropolitan Branch in the Catholic parish of St Mary's in Dublin, in May 1851. This was Aylward's first major Dublin project and the enterprise which was to lead her, unwittingly, to more complex and ambitious ventures.

Geographically this new branch of the Ladies' Association covered the two Catholic parishes of St Mary's, Marlborough Street, and St Michan's, Anne Street, including most of the city north of the Liffey. The general valuation of 1854 reveals several highly desirable residential streets in this area. However, behind the fine thoroughfares and Georgian squares was a warren of back lanes, enclosed courts and alleyways, with some of Europe's worst slum housing. The sector bounded by Gloucester Street Lower and Montgomery Street was also in poor physical condition, but was more notorious as the heart of the 'Monto', the red-light district famed in Joyce's *Ulysses* as 'Nighttown', and by mid-century already an area of ill repute.[21]

Famine had swelled the numbers of destitute thronging the city, while its function as a port acted as a magnet to the dispossessed *en route* to what they hoped would be a better future in Britain and, via Liverpool, in America and Australia. Chronic under- and unemployment, the general unavailability of outdoor relief under the statutory Poor Law system, and a widespread abhorrence among many of the poor for the relief provided in the workhouses, made the provision of assistance to the 'sick poor' a very apparent and urgent area of need. Existing voluntary provision was grossly inadequate.

Distressed by the inhuman poverty she witnessed on a massive scale in the Dublin slums, and frustrated with the lethargy which seemed to paralyse much of the Catholic middle class, Aylward saw the Ladies' Association as a means by which she could harness the energies of like-minded women and attempt to ameliorate at least some of the poverty she witnessed. From her standpoint, religious and humanitarian values were inextricably bound together, and the women visitors were to adopt an all-inclusive pro-active strategy. They were directed not alone to distribute the 'relief orders' but to catechise, advise in the matter of parenting, and 'to insist, as far as they can, upon cleanliness, order, [and] industry ... in their homes'.[22]

Active membership of the Association was open to all women, who were requested to have 'the consent of those to whom they are subject in their families'.[23] The necessity of stifling potential opposition to women's involvement outside the home was necessary in mid nineteenth-century Dublin, and potential for hostility was further reduced by Aylward's public emphasis on the traditional role of women as home-makers, coming from happy homes to bring relief to the poor and bringing the blessings of the poor back to their own families.[24]

Acutely aware that large numbers of Dublin women were the sole support of themselves and their families, her initial concerns were essentially practical. Her support of working women was based on this belief, and included plans to establish a pre-school to allow mothers to avail of work, releasing clothes from pawn to allow a servant girl 'make an appearance', setting women up 'in business', and apprenticing a 'poor lame girl to the boot-closing trade'.[25] While her vision was firmly grounded in the Christian call to consider the most exploited and vulnerable as brother and sister, it was constructed in class terms; her formal appeals for members depict the lady visitors as graciously reaching out of their social circle to silently relieve the poor, who accepted the ministrations of 'persons above them in life' with a mixture of gratitude and awe.[26]

Aylward, with her 'very imposing appearance and attractive and engaging manner'[27] personally took the platform at the yearly public meetings which she convened to launch the annual reports, an unusual role for any woman

61

in Dublin at the time. To engender support, an on-going requirement was to publicise the position of the poor and the success of the Association. Aylward graphically described, in her published annual reports, the pitiful scenes witnessed daily by her visitors. Aylward's passionate and eloquent appeals on behalf of the poor of the parish were based on extensive personal visitation, and powered by a certitude that at least something could be done to improve the lives of the poor. She was driven by a conviction that at least part of the problem was the unwillingness of the Catholic middle classes to cross the social and spatial divide that allowed the better-off to inhabit the high-status streets and gracious squares without ever really needing to face the squalor of the city's slums. If 'the Ladies of the Parish and of the city' could be induced to visit, she was confident that untold improvement could be effected.[28]

Almost all the women who joined as active members were drawn from the north city parishes in which they served, and included three social groups: the wives and daughters of solicitors, barristers, and doctors; the wives and daughters of wine merchants; women from manufacturing and business families, particularly from families engaged in the provisions trade, but also in drapery, baking, candlemaking, and pawnbroking.

The visitation of the poor in their own homes and the publication of graphic accounts of the scenes witnessed was adopted as a means of securing support by a variety of charitable and missionary societies throughout the nineteenth century. The Dublin Bible Woman Mission and the Dublin Visiting Branch of the Irish Church Missions, both operating in connection with the Church of Ireland, for example, were very active in the north city parishes covered by the Ladies' Association of Charity, and were similarly eloquent in advertising the plight of the poor, although from their perspective the people laboured under the double calamity of poverty and adherence to 'popish superstition'.[29]

While the Ladies' Association was not founded as a direct foil to such evangelical organisations it had much in common with the evangelical societies in terms of organisation, methods of fundraising, advertising, class involvement, and relief provided. What was certainly original was Aylward's ability to mobilise the Catholic womenfolk of some standing in the community to involve themselves first-hand in ministering to the poorest, to consider themselves bound by 'family' ties to improve the lot of their poorer co-religionists, and to emulate the wealthy Protestant women who were, proportionately, more visible on the streets of Dublin.[30] Within five years her branch had a network of 148 lady visitors, but its effect extended beyond its parish boundaries as it assisted the establishment of several other city and suburban branches.[31]

Aylward's entrepreneurial skills are very evident in the vital business of fundraising, and she succeeded in supplementing the annual subscriptions and private collections with money raised from raffles, charity sermons and an annual bazaar. Equally, if not more important, was the clerical support she secured from the foundation of her branch of the Ladies' Association. On the 'auspicious advent' of Dr Paul Cullen to the Dublin diocese in 1852, the first year of operations of the Dublin branch, Aylward and her Kingstown friend, Margaret Kelly, immediately and publicly sought his 'episcopal benediction upon their works' and secured a powerful and generous ally.[32] While the alliance between Aylward and Cullen was to prove immensely useful to both, politically and strategically, Aylward maintained a startling independence of thought and action. However, such close association with Cullen led to his being credited with some of her most notable achievements, a practice which she seems to have done nothing to correct. The most obvious of such inaccurate credits is the absence of any reference to Aylward concerning the arrival in Dublin of the Daughters of Charity of St Vincent de Paul.[33] That congregation had been formed in France in 1633 with the specific purpose of attending to the poor.

The negotiations which Aylward conducted with the Dublin diocesan authorities, the Vincentian leadership and her own women workers to establish the first Dublin foundation of the Daughters of Charity extended over eight years from 1851. Aylward hoped that the lay charity she was directing would, in time, come under the supervision of that sisterhood. The protracted and well-documented negotiations, combined with other evidence, reveal much about Aylward's style of leadership, especially under pressure. In the core group, a committee of five women, she made every effort to be collegial. While the Ladies had 'willingly consented' to Aylward's proposal that this religious community should take over the direction of their 'sick poor' visitation and the outdoor orphanage which was to develop from it, they were actively involved in every step of the complex negotiations which followed. The Dublin women teased out each section in successive drafts of the contract between the two organisations, refusing to sign when items about which they had not been consulted were introduced by the French party, 'nor would they agree to being charged with the support of a servant'.[34] Aylward acted as mediator and messenger, but found the endless delays stressful, complaining that 'tis such a misery to be eternally humouring every one'.[35] The negotiations were not concluded until 1859.

Meanwhile the Ladies' Association of Charity launched St Mary's Industrial Institute in 1853, an ambitious effort to tackle the root cause of much local distress, namely the great dearth of work for poor women, and the impossibility of securing an adequate wage in an oversupplied market. It was begun in response to repeated requests from the women themselves, and under the direction of a qualified seamstress from Northern Ireland 'who understands the sewed muslin work or embroidery in all its branches', and aimed 'to teach the same gratuitously to all who may wish to learn'.[36] Home needlework, whereby piecework was undertaken, was a traditional area of employment. The initial advertising for the Institute optimistically claimed that demand for ornamental needlework, such as sewed muslin, was unlimited. To ensure success St Mary's aimed to admit only 'such persons as will be free to devote to it their whole time, and to follow it up as a regular pursuit of industry'. It was also proposed that a pre-school be established so that, 'mothers would be free to avail themselves of the work available in the Institute'.[37] It was intended for the very poorest, but as the training would require regular attendance and perseverance before a decent income could be generated in practice, Aylward realised it was 'expecting too much to think, that they will sit down patiently to learn, or to improve themselves, with scarcely any remuneration whilst so doing, and no other means of support'.[38]

The initial optimism was almost extinguished in the first year. The reasons St Mary's Industrial Institute failed are a good indicator of the insurmountable difficulties facing Dublin women who attempted to secure an adequate livelihood by needlework alone. The women who applied to the Institute were not experienced, and thus earned too little to be induced to persevere. The biggest difficulty, however, was structural, as the only work available was poorly paid 'shopwork', the demand for which fluctuated greatly. The training, or retraining, of women, apparently a wise response to the unskilled female labour surplus in Dublin in the 1850s, was here unworkable. The large gap between the Institute's income and expenditure could not continue to be bridged by fundraising, and by 1856 the Institute had folded up.[39]

It was the family visitation undertaken by the Ladies of Charity which alerted Aylward to the extent of Protestant missionary activity in the Dublin slums, to which she responded by a systematic campaign of publicising the operations of the mission agents.[40] Denominational considerations dominated public discussion of state involvement in education and health, and the operation of the Poor Law in the nineteenth century. It was in the context of evangelicalism that Church-sponsored charities drew up their manifestos. The role of women, both as major providers and recipients of social services, and as committed agents and counter-agents of Church missions, reveals the essential impact that the evangelical movement had on shaping Irish women's involvement in charitable organisations in the nineteenth century.

Aylward was particularly critical of the Irish Church Missions (ICM) and its associated network of schools. Founded by Alexander Dallas in direct response to the ravages of the famine holocaust of 1847, the relationship of the society with 'souperism' in the poorest parts of the West made it particularly vulnerable to attack.[41] Dallas considered the establishment of poor schools and residential homes legitimate 'missionary' activity, and arranged, in the case of Dublin, that the Irish Church Missions should take charge of education, with the support of school committees.[42] While the ICM aspired to cover all Ireland, the large population in Dublin provided an irresistible challenge, and was seen as the ideal location for the society's training and model schools.[43] Here, with the support of several influential individuals, most notably Ellen Smyly and her family, a number of poor day-schools, followed by residential homes, were founded. As the care and education of children were viewed as essentially religious and moral tasks, to be conducted along strict denominational lines, bitter inter-church rivalry was inevitable, especially with the involvement of very able and fearless women campaigners such as Ellen Smyly and Margaret Aylward.

The ICM revelled in open controversy, calling on supporters: 'Let us remember that Rome knows no neutrality. If we are not aggressive towards her, she is aggressive towards us.'[44] Their very publicly-reported successes alarmed Catholic clergy and charities, who felt they were facing unfair competition, anxieties which were fuelled by the data collected by Aylward and her fieldworkers, and forwarded to Cullen. Aylward herself contributed substantially to the very bitter public debate, berating especially those Catholics who ignored the problem, or who claimed that it did not exist, and focusing repeatedly on proselytism as the exploitation of the poorest and most vulnerable.[45] To those who accused her of doing exactly the same for Catholicism, by providing schoolchildren with food and clothing, she replied that it was fundamentally different, in that the children were already baptised Catholics, and that her organisation was so hard pressed to 'rescue even a fraction of our own', that it could have no possible interest in, or indeed resources, to devote to making converts.[46]

Aylward's first-hand encounters with mission agents dated from her apprenticeship as a Lady of Charity in Kingstown, one of the first mission areas of the ICM. In the first year of operations of Aylward's metropolitan branch, several of the branch members, styled the 'anti-proselytising department', organised a fact-finding mission throughout the city and through interviews and the compilation of a register of schools they suspected of proselytising, claimed to uncover 'a fearfully extended and active organisation' committed to 'the perversion of the children of the Catholic poor'.[47] The fact-finding excursions very rapidly became 'open warfare', with the zealous Ladies of Charity actively involved in physically removing Catholic children from Protestant institutions, and equally zealous Protestant missionaries determined to persevere in their evangelising activity. Aylward and her friends picketed the Sunday schools where, it was claimed, 'crowds of unhappy Catholics, men, and women, were to be found, lured by the offer of a small cut of bread, and then obliged in return to listen to blasphemous language, and a sermon from a minister'.[48]

There are reports of children being dragged away by the schoolmistresses to prevent them being interviewed by the Ladies of Charity; of the Catholic ladies distributing crucifixes among the children, and the Protestant missionaries removing these 'idols' from them; of crowds of Dublin men, women, and children assembling to join in the excitement, urging on the disputing parties with cries of 'more power to you!'[49]

Accounts of the 'battles' fought by the Ladies of Charity for the souls of the Catholic poor were included in the annual reports of the Association for the purposes of generating moral support and attracting recruits and finances to the branch. Aylward's writings were not solely or even principally for propaganda purposes. Just as the Protestant evangelicals reeled in horror at the 'mass of souls' in Dublin, crushed by the darkness of popery, 'rushing on to destruction, and no cry raised to warn them of their danger',[50] Aylward held an unshakeable conviction in the value of the Catholic faith, a priceless treasure 'compared with which, this whole world, nay a thousand worlds, would not weigh as a grain of sand'.[51] Following from that conviction, talk without action infuriated her. To put down proselytising, effective organisation was necessary. She challenged her fellow Catholics to emulate the commitment and organisation of the 'auxiliaries and agents and correspondents' of the ICM, whose zeal outshone that of their Catholic adversaries.[52]

Based on her first-hand experience of the destitution which left women with children most vulnerable, and her increasing familiarity with the Protestant missionary movement, Aylward decided on a large Catholic outdoor orphanage as the most urgent requirement, and a special committee drawn from the Ladies of Charity was established. The proposal met with some opposition. Archbishop Cullen, despite his regard for the Ladies of Charity and public concern with child proselytism, refused permission, for he saw what appeared a rash undertaking, an immense orphanage to be founded, depending almost entirely on an invalid who might at any moment be struck down by sickness, and in that case the whole responsibility falling upon him.[53]

Aylward's stubborn attachment to the 'boarding out' system, whereby children were reared in families rather than in an institution, and which could not be as closely monitored as the traditional orphanage, also caused real concern. Aylward was acutely aware that the backing of the diocesan priests was vital for the assessment of suitable cases, the collection of funds and the creation of a climate of support. Through continued pressure Aylward received the necessary approbation, and on 1 January 1857, the first child was received.

The boarding-out system of rearing young, deserted children in families had been greatly discredited when it operated as the policy of the Dublin Foundling Hospital from 1703 to 1838,[54] and although there were some charity children 'at nurse', there was a general wariness about the system's suitability for large numbers of children. To convince the public of how well-regulated and necessary St Brigid's system was, and to generate the necessary funds for its support, public meetings were held at which Aylward launched the annual reports. These included details on the institution's philosophy and practice, current statistics, financial position, and subscription lists; charity sermons, letters to the newspapers, and the personal recommendation of friends of the institution, especially clergy, were also used to full effect.

Applications to the orphanage were made 'from clergymen, communities, societies and from the poor themselves, who come to the door without any recommendation',[55] but the managers insisted on being free to make their own investigations and decide whom to admit.[56] Pressure from individual clergy to receive particular cases could be immense, and refusals often led to bitter, and generally unfounded, criticism of the institution by some priests. St Brigid's would receive only those who could not be cared for among their relatives, insisting that 'the separation of parent and child is one of the greatest social evils, and that in all cases where it is possible, the parent ought to support and bring up his own child'.[57]

Analysis of the register case histories for a sample period, 1868-1875, reveals that the vast bulk, just over 75 per cent, of the children admitted were in the charge of single women, who had been widowed, deserted, or simply left behind as their husbands sought work outside the city. These women were now too ill or destitute to provide for their children, at least for a given period. This also explains the large percentage of children each year 'restored to mother' or other relative; few of the children were orphans in the sense of having neither parent. Many of the truly 'orphaned' children were adopted by their foster families, a happy outcome, which was given extensive publicity on every possible occasion.[58]

The primary requirement of the system was good 'nurses' or foster mothers, recommended in writing by the local clergy, or by another nurse, and willing to 'act towards St Brigid's children as if they were her own and be a true mother to them'.[59] The foster families 'are all small farmers, except one, all in possession of more or less land, with a greater or less stock of cows',[60] with the children grouped in twos and threes, which allowed for rearing boys and girls together.

The care taken in engaging nurses is evident. Families with a foster child generally recommended others, but they had to meet Aylward's standards first. John Lacken of Blessington, for example, was asked to send up a nurse for an infant, but warned 'not to send any person with whom a child died or from whom a child was removed or any one that I find fault with', and in particular not to dare send his daughter, 'as the child she had minded returned with fleas & I will remove every child who is not *perfectly* clean'.[61] Close supervision of the families tried to ensure the children were well cared for, with 'unannounced visits that the lady visitor might see everything in their real, everyday state', for 'then there can be no making up'.[62] The principal control, however, was through twice-yearly general inspections, the award of premiums, the fining or withholding of the nurse's money in cases of neglect, and the removal of children to other nurses.[63] Threats of removal were carried out. The nurses' payment books for 1868-1874 detail occasions when part of monies due were held back for a month to allow the nurse one chance to remedy some minor neglect, and several instances of a child's removal due to 'incapacity', or 'not thriving'.[64]

The orphanage met with widespread initial Catholic support, and was hailed as the 'chief bulwark in Dublin against the multiplied machinations' of the proselytisers, and, along with the Ladies' Association, received special mention in Cullen's pastorals, their services being 'above all praise'.[65] Such success demanded exceptional administrative and diplomatic skills, for it was entirely reliant on public fundraising and goodwill in a city that was already stretched to support a myriad of competing charities. Although the length of time spent by individual children in the care of the institution varied from a few weeks or months to the full span of childhood, the overall numbers were large, with

2,717 admissions recorded from its foundation in 1857 up to Aylward's death in 1889.

The active support of the clergy was always crucial, as a favourable word from the altar, or better still a charity sermon, could provide substantial funds, while it was very often through the clergy that suitable 'cases' were directed. Rose Gaughren, who worked with Aylward from 1861, reported that Aylward 'visited almost all the Archbishops and Bishops of Ireland who afterwards became subscribers to the Orphanage and good friends as long as they lived'.[66]

Aylward's orphanage project was run on an exclusively volunteer basis, which was certainly of value in nurturing moral and financial support, as the public was repeatedly alerted to the boast that 'there is not one paid officer or collector in the whole organisation' and 'every shilling goes to the orphan'.[67] The rapid expansion of the institution meant that large sums were committed well into the future, as each child accepted had to be supported until aged fifteen or sixteen years, and some disabled or 'sickly' children even beyond that.

Behind the impassioned public appeals for funds and volunteers, characteristic of the published reports of all such charities, there are real indications of the pressures Aylward endured in keeping the orphanage in operation. From the outset she was determined to secure its long-term viability, by establishing some framework for the direction of the volunteer helpers, and making the supply of funds more reliable. The means to achieve both was eminently simple: attach it to an established religious community and, as she herself noted, 'once it becomes known that it is in the hands of the Sisters every kind of aid will be given to it'.[68] The targeted group, the Daughters of Charity of St Vincent de Paul, appeared, at least from initial communications with their superior general in Paris, Père Etienne, willing to undertake the task.

There were, however, complications on the diocesan side. Cullen was resolutely opposed to the matter at first, and Fr Philip Dowley, superior of the Irish province of the Vincentian congregation, warned Aylward against further lobbying as Cullen might take it 'as rather a troublesome intrusion, having so latterly decided against it so strongly'.[69] However, several months later, her enthusiasm undimmed, Aylward was again in direct communication with the Vincentian superior general, who promised sisters as soon as the house which she intended for them should be ready.[70]

Aylward kept up the pressure on Cullen through the medium of the annual reports which expressed the hope 'that ere long it may be given to us to welcome them to this land, as children of a common parent, and claim from them their counsel and their aid'.[71] After lengthy negotiations the French sisters were eventually granted the premises of the Carmelite Community in William Street.[72] Experienced in running orphanages very successfully along traditional lines, they were unwilling to experiment with 'boarding out', a point on which Aylward and her co-workers would not compromise. The proprietorial attitude of the women's group towards the new arrivals also made for considerable animosity. A very cool parting of ways was the end result, with the sisters developing their Dublin mission independently of Aylward.[73]

Aylward's correspondence, in this and other organisational matters, provides very useful insights into the ecclesiastical and lay power structures within which all philanthropic women had to steer a course. Aylward proposed that the French sisters include a school for the blind in William Street, not only a great necessity but an enterprise which was likely to attract generous financial support. The takeover of Catholic lay charities by religious congregations was a prevalent practice in nineteenth-century Dublin, so that Aylward's plans for the Daughters of Charity, and the subsequent refashioning of her own core group of women running St Brigid's Orphanage and poor schools into a religious congregation, are variations on the same theme.[74]

Alongside Aylward's day-to-day concerns with the orphans and the 'sick poor', and her many associated enterprises, she continued her energetic campaign of exposing the activities of the various state and voluntary institutions which she accused of engaging in child proselytism. Quoting extensively from the published reports of such societies, and publicly naming particular persons, were provocative practices which inevitably made her, and St Brigid's, targets for retaliatory action.

Additional fuel was added by Aylward's interest in protecting the orphaned and destitute Catholic children of interdenominational marriages, a minefield into which charities from both sides of the religious divide were repeatedly drawn. It was such a circumstance that almost caused the collapse of the orphanage, just four years after its foundation. The controversial case, which centred around the abduction of an infant, Mary Mathews, provided the media with high drama and debate. It epitomised the denominational, legal and political struggles which surrounded the care of charity children in Ireland throughout the nineteenth century.

Mary Mathews was entrusted to the care of St Brigid's orphanage in April 1858. Her father was Catholic, and a native of Dublin; the mother was English and converted to Catholicism before her marriage. The couple had moved to England and the marriage was in crisis by 1857. In October of that year Maria Mathews took their youngest child and left England to take up a position as nursemaid with a family in the Bahamas, despite her husband's strenuous objections. Left to care for two children alone, Mathews tried every avenue to have the children reared as Catholics in London, but failed. He returned to Dublin where he committed his two children to the care of a woman in Sir Patrick Dun's hospital, instructing that they were to be reared as Catholics. The father died in January 1858. The girl, Mary, was admitted to St Brigid's and sent to a nurse in Saggart. At the same time the mother, Maria, was expelled from the Bahamas on the instructions of Governor Bayley, who stated that during 'the whole of her stay here she had exhibited continued bad temper' and had 'shamelessly neglected' the child she was employed to mind.[75] She was deported to England, and after an interval of four months began to enquire after her children, encouraged, it was claimed, by the Smyly family of the Irish Church Missions.[76] Tracing them to Dublin she removed the boy from Brown Street Orphanage, and demanded the girl from St Brigid's, determined to rear them as Protestants. The infant could not be traced, and, as it emerged years later, had been spirited away to France by a gentleman from North Great Georges Street, and later moved to Belgium.[77] The first Aylward knew of the abduction was eleven days later, when the nurse visited Dublin to express her regret at the loss of the child. Lengthy legal proceedings were instituted by the mother, and under a writ of *habeas corpus* Aylward was ordered to produce the child in court.

The fact that she had not reported the matter to the police immediately on hearing of the child's removal was held against her, and opposing counsel also rejected her protestations that she had no means of tracing the self-appointed guardian of the child, and berated her for her passivity.[78] That the child was known as 'Mary Farrell' in her foster home laid Aylward wide open to the accusation of purposely thwarting the efforts of any Protestant relatives who might seek to trace her. The father's verbal instructions, although witnessed by a woman visitor and by a nurse, were not acceptable as evidence.

The mother's four-month delay in making any inquiries after her children after her return from the West Indies, and her previous neglect of them, according to counsel for Aylward, made it 'plain, therefore, that the mother was not the moving party here. The question was between a Roman Catholic Institution and a Protestant Institution'.[79] Judge Lefroy, who, although now aged eighty-four years, was still stubbornly holding office, had a family interest in the case; his sisters' involvement as collectors for a branch of the Irish Church Missions had received special mention in St Brigid's report of 1859.[80] Aylward had previously taken charge of several Catholic children of mixed marriages, each of whom, on the application of Protestant relatives, had been returned to them, so that general accusations of 'child stealing' cannot fairly be levelled against St Brigid's. In the case of Mary Mathews it appears certain that the child would have been returned by Aylward, albeit with expressions of regret and fears for her eternal salvation, had it not been for the intervention of a third party. Once the abduction had taken place there was no turning the clock back.

Sentence was finally delivered on 7 November 1860. The court found Aylward innocent of kidnapping and complicity, but sentenced her to six months' imprisonment on the lesser charge of contempt of court, for not producing the child.

Impassioned speeches were made in Aylward's defence, and many letters of support arrived in Eccles Street and at Grangegorman Prison.[81] During her imprisonment she directed arrangements for the fourth annual meeting of St Brigid's Orphanage, which was rescheduled for 16 January 1861.[82] It was a provocative display of clerical support, with Archbishop Cullen in the chair, flanked by the bishops of Kerry and Dromore, and an impressive array of high-ranking clergymen. Ostensibly to launch the fourth report and encourage the members in their charitable endeavours, it was an occasion to show support publicly for the imprisoned 'lady manager' and a platform for speeches defending St Brigid's against counter-charges of proselytism. The proceedings were widely reported in the press. The response from the opposing camp was outrage, led by the London *Times*, which accused Cullen, 'the athletic Catholic whitewasher', of 'rank cowardice' in urging 'poor, weak, fanatical women to go a child-stealing for the glory of the Church'.[83]

Further public controversy and private anguish was caused by the refusal of the judges to rule on the conditions under which Aylward was to be held. This was left to the discretion of the Board of Superintendence of the Prisons, which led to numerous divisions in the prison administration, some members objecting to the harsh conditions under which Aylward was held, and threatening to resign their places on the Board.[84] The hardships of the period in prison, confined to a cubicle off the hospital ward, the first three months without even a single break for exercise, in the company of maternity cases, the idiotic, epileptic and lunatic, were publicised by her supporters. For Aylward personally the most distressing aspect was the enforced inaction as calumnies continued to be circulated about her and her institute, and she continued to be denied the minimum conditions granted her by the Board and of which the Board believed her to be possessed. Aylward forwarded futile appeals to the Lord Lieutenant and the Chief Justice,[85] and a month before her release signed and had distributed a printed circular addressed from Grangegorman Prison in defence of her case.[86]

While Aylward considered herself greatly constrained by the prison regime she had practically unlimited time for correspondence, reflection and planning, and there were no restrictions on access to writing materials. She continued to complete an immense amount of daily business, directing the outdoor relief efforts of the Ladies' Association and the multifarious concerns of St Brigid's.[87]

The appointment of Fr John Gowan CM, as spiritual director to St Brigid's in April 1861, was of immense personal importance to Aylward. To him she disclosed her deepest worries and anxieties, and her future plans as they evolved. The surviving correspondence (which regrettably consists almost solely of Gowan's replies to Aylward) is one of the principal sources for learning of Aylward's vulnerability and feelings of inadequacy. She had repeated anxieties about receiving Holy Communion, overpowered by feelings of unworthiness which prevented her from approaching the altar even when urged by her confessors.[88] She agonised about the Lenten fast and abstinence, and indulged morbid anxieties about death, a self-criticism that left her mind 'clouded and bewildered'.[89] She worried about family affairs, and distrusted her own ability to provide leadership among the women volunteers.[90]

The long-term consequences of the prison episode were serious. With a characteristic lack of self-pity Aylward admitted 'my health has got a little shake here, but when my day comes for being emancipated I hope to be quite well again'.[91] She was, however, never to know good health again. In the Ladies' Association of Charity 'some want of vigour and a little chilliness' was recorded, and the untimely death of Mrs Frances Murray, one of the first and most generous of the volunteers, further compounded the morale problems resulting from the scandal of Aylward's imprisonment.[92]

The managing group of St Brigid's Orphanage (initially drawn from the Ladies of Charity), consisted of six women, unmarried and widowed, who had barely started living together under the title of 'Daughters of St Brigid' when Aylward was imprisoned. This core group, excepting Ada Allingham, aged twenty-two, and the elderly Eliza Monahan, dispersed while the Ladies' Association of Charity continued their operations on a reduced scale, with Aylward's involvement reduced to that of a supportive role, through fundraising and advertising.

Far from cooling her zeal for the protection of Catholic children from the attentions of equally zealous evangelicals, Aylward's incarceration in prison and the advice of John Gowan determined her on the course she should follow on her discharge: small poor schools spread throughout the Dublin slums, taking in 'the more abandoned and more destitute'.[93] Within five months of her release the first such school was opened, in 10 Crow Street, in the Temple Bar area, the premises granted rent-free by the Oblate Fathers. Aylward's interest in schools was long standing, from her first experience as a volunteer lay teacher in the Presentation Poor Schools in her native Waterford, to the adult catechism classes in Gardiner Street and first communion classes in the parish schools of St Michan's under the care of the Ladies of Charity. In the Christian Brothers' model of school management she found both inspiration and practical support, adopting a similarly independent stance from the National Board, and receiving the assistance of their superior general in the preparation of school texts.[94]

The anti-proselytising stance which characterised the foundation of the orphanage was also to determine the spirit and progress of the schools network. Aylward's approach was typically aggressive, choosing to locate her schools in the poorest areas where the Protestant mission schools, particularly those of the Irish Church Missions, had been operating most successfully. The parish of Francis Street, 'a stronghold of papal darkness and intolerance' according to the ICM, was to be one of the more notable battlefields.[95] Here an ICM school had been in operation from 1853, while the Catholic Ragged School, founded in 1851, was taken over by Aylward in 1865. To supply the undoubted needs of these pupils, Aylward endeavoured to provide them with food, clothing, and bread to take home, advantages already enjoyed by those attending the ICM schools, but an approach which opened her to charges of proselytism; in the annual reports of the schools she passionately defended this practice.[96] Aylward's efforts 'to carry the schooling into the poor localities, to the doors of the room-keepers and the inhabitants of cellars' progressed steadily in Dublin, with six foundations from 1861 to 1870.[97]

Despite pressure from clergy to open many more such schools both in the city and outside it, Aylward proceeded slowly. A major restriction on development was her commitment to remain independent of the National Board of Education. Her schools were to be Catholic 'Schools of Faith' and free: free to the poor, free from government control, and under the authority of the Church alone; and she warned that 'English statesmen present a subsidy education with the one hand and a manacle with the other'.[98] Four foundations were made between 1873 and 1879: in Kilcullen and Celbridge, County Kildare, Skerries, County Dublin, and Mullinavat in County Kilkenny. Aylward promoted such 'village schools' not alone for the advantages they would confer on the local children, including in some instances St Brigid's 'nurse children' at care in the district, but also with a view to recruiting young teachers. The schools could be maintained and extended only with large numbers of committed persons, unlike the orphanage which even at its most populous required only a small management team. Rural schools would, it was hoped, also 'foster and develop religious vocations among the daughters of the Irish farmers', who were regarded as the most promising material for teaching in the city schools as they have 'enthusiasm and buoyancy and mental power and strength of constitution, and withal a simplicity of character'.[99]

Aylward's decision to allow her group to be formed into a religious congregation was intimately bound up with her hopes for a Catholic poor-school network, and her determination to maintain the unpaid character of all her charitable work. To ensure stability, the voluntary services of like-minded women who would bind themselves permanently to this mission was required, and a religious congregation could make this possible. However, earlier attempts to attach a ready-made lay branch, complete with well-established ministry, to an existing religious congregation had proved unworkable, so that there appeared no alternative to founding a new religious congregation. Aylward did not see herself as at all equipped for the role of foundress, and indeed in her late forties, in very poor health, with two unsuccessful novitiate attempts behind her and with her media notoriety, she was an unlikely candidate to direct the formation of a new congregation. The idea progressed gradually, from the hope expressed in 1858 that 'a few Ladies will come and live with me and devote their time to our charities', without being under any tie whatsoever, but open to whatever 'form and permanence', might evolve from the experiment.[100]

It was the prison experience which proved the catalyst for action. Aylward was faced, on the one hand, with the likely collapse of the orphanage venture, but on the other had the loyalty of Ada Allingham and Eliza Monahan, while there were several hopeful applicants. She was under pressure from Cullen, who had allied himself publicly with the prisoner and her charities, but she was also fired by her personal ambition to see what she had started flourish, and full of new ideas for extending St Brigid's work.[101] The crucial question of 'who would form the congregation' was answered by the appointment of Fr John Gowan as spiritual director of the Institute,[102] while Archbishop Cullen was personally responsible for many aspects of the speedy transformation of the small lay community to a religious congregation, a process which took only seven years. However, Aylward must be credited with some of the most important features of the foundation. While Cullen had requested that it be erected 'for his own Diocese' [*sic*] it was Aylward who questioned if it would not however be better to make it 'general not local'.[103] Aylward's wishes were eventually fulfilled, and the congregation became an institute of pontifical right, under the direct control of Rome (subject only to the ordinary authority of the bishop of the diocese), a matter of much consequence later.

By 1862, one year after the prison episode, Aylward was able to report: 'Eight of us live together now, we have a little Chapel in the house - and we follow a simple rule'.[104] By 1869 the number had risen to twenty-seven. The elderly Eliza Monahan was the only woman not to take vows, but she continued as a full member of the young congregation.[105]

The same cumbersome Church bureaucracy with which Aylward had had so many struggles this time practically smoothed and oiled the way forward, so that one cannot avoid noting the difference in attitude when a lay women's group becomes so much more manageably 'religious'. Religious names were first adopted in 1863, but the adoption of religious dress was even more important, placing an indisputable distance between the 'lay' and 'religious' life and bringing with it a particular code of behaviour. While conversion to a religious congregation was now largely complete, Aylward herself never wore religious dress again. According to Margaret Gaughren, who joined Aylward in 1865, this was because she had 'so much public business to transact, regarding the Orphanage, etc'.[106] Aylward had clearly no intentions of being restrained by public or clerical perceptions regarding what activities or behaviour were 'suitable' for her.

Aylward, foundress and first superior, had her own vision of religious life. The main elements were that dowries would not be required for admission; there was to be no class division such as that between 'lay' and 'choir' sisters; the sisters would be 'walking nuns' untrammelled by cloister, and visiting the 'sick poor' in their own homes, and the kind of extravagances which she had witnessed in some continental convents, such as silver-handled cutlery and watered silk dresses, would have no place among the daughters of St Brigid. She directed, in 1872, that the sisters, 'live in the midst of the poor, looking after their children', residing:

... in an ordinary house attached to the school, and go to Mass like the rest of the faithful ... there will be no need of a chaplain nor of walls of enclosure nor of any ornamentation; and the schools in most localities will be self-supporting.[107]

Analysis of the community Register of Membership reveals the extent to which Aylward's plans were carried out, and modified, as time passed. Of the first 41 entrants between 1859 and 1867, only five brought money.[108] Over time dowries became increasingly common, but even by 1879 still fewer than half of the entrants brought dowries, and a substantial number of these were quite modest, as low as £20. By 1889, the year of Aylward's death, most entrants brought money, and there is a clear target of £100 dower money and £14 to cover clothing. Allowance was always made for persons with no means who wished to join, although some contribution, at least, towards the cost of clothing and noviceship 'pension', was by then expected. Caitriona Clear has noted that the minimum for acceptance as a choir nun to the Presentation Convent, Galway in the early nineteenth century was £500; the lowest dowry accepted in the Galway Mercy from 1840-1857 was £200, while the average was £375.[109] Luddy's analysis of the Presentation convents in County Tipperary 1806-1900 explores how the dowry structure allowed choir nuns maintain their sense of superiority, access to the 'public work' for which the community had been established being limited to those bringing varying but substantial sums with them.[110] Lay sisters, who either brought no dower, or a small one, performed the domestic work of the convent, cooking, scrubbing, serving, gardening, washing and were regarded by many as a necessary substitute for servants.

Aylward's decision to disallow such divisions went against the prevailing wisdom. There could, of course, be persons who might choose to devote themselves to domestic work rather than teach or administer the orphanage, but all who taught were to contribute to the housework, even taking turns at milking cows in Glasnevin before heading off to teach in city schools. Aylward's new community of the Holy Faith, with its relatively modest dower, and accompanying flexibility, brought religious life within the reach of women who wished to enter a community but who were excluded from many of the longer-established convents unless they were prepared to lower their sights and become lay sisters.

Within the day-to-day life of the congregation, Aylward left the spiritual direction of the women to Gowan, while she continued to wear secular dress, travel, solicit funds and audit accounts, directing the development of the school network, and the continuing work of the orphanage, and especially seeing to the ever-increasing burden of correspondence. She played a full part in most of the household matters, from instructing the young sisters in housework and the care of the Chapel, to directing the cutting-out of skirts, the payment of workmen, and the affairs of the dairy.[111] She also had a store of homoeopathic recipes to alleviate every possible affliction, and provided detailed instructions on the treatment of ill sisters.[112]

Aylward suffered severely from erysipelas and rheumatism, and almost died in 1869.[113] The necessary convalescence was combined with business and pleasure, as she travelled throughout Europe and Ireland.[114] She regularly removed herself to friends in Thurstenstown, Beauparc, County Meath, where her hostesses were 'most kind and attentive and never even for a moment intrude on my business or solitude' so that she rejoiced in being able to write in her room for '6 or 7 hours daily'.[115] In her later years she was confined to a wheelchair but remained mentally as sharp as ever, as several stormy incidents testify.

In 1884, aged seventy-four and in very poor health, Aylward became involved in altercations with Dr Donnelly, coadjutor bishop of Dublin, over St Brigid's. The bishop suggested that the orphanage was badly managed and unwilling to take in all the cases offered by the clergy, and urged Aylward to 'regain, if possible, lost popularity amongst the clergy' by trusting to 'general charity' and quietly enlisting 'the good wishes of the clergy without appearing to make them pay for their efforts in rescuing the little souls in danger'.[116] Aylward was outraged, and slated the hypocrisy and ingratitude of those clergy who made a show of 'rescuing' children at risk in their parish, but then expected St Brigid's to admit them instantly while they themselves made no effort to contribute in any way to the cost of their maintenance. In a cutting reference to the spate of church-building then underway she questioned:

Is the seating of a Church or the painting of a Church to be compared with the salvation of the orphan child of the parish? Would it not be lawful to melt and sell the sacred chalice to save him?[117]

The exchanges between Aylward and Donnelly are significant, not alone for the light they throw on Aylward's indomitable personality and her loyalty to her women workers, but for what they reveal about the context within which philanthropic Catholic women, whether religious or lay, operated in late nineteenth-century Dublin. Donnelly undoubtedly expected his paternalistic advice to be accepted submissively and acted upon, perhaps even humbly welcomed. It was the assertiveness of the woman manager of St Brigid's in forcing the parish to support the enterprise that led to the hostility of some of the clergy.[118] Clearly women's contribution to the social mission of the Church was to be welcomed and extolled when it was subservient; efforts to place that mission on a business footing smacked of insolence and were considered troublesome. There was also the question of control, with Archbishop Walsh (1885-1921) expressing a long-standing concern over the pontifical status of the sisterhood, speaking ominously of 'a strong opinion very generally held that the Institute should be under ecclesiastical control and supervision'.[119] However, the esteem and affection in which Aylward was held by influential churchmen in Dublin, Paris, Armagh and Rome had, on the whole, contributed significantly to her success; her congregation and its ministries were, by the 1880s, sufficiently well established to weather some quite serious clerical opposition.

Aylward died on 11 October 1889, aged seventy-nine, and was buried in the convent cemetery, Glasnevin. Fifteen members of her congregation had predeceased her.

Her personal story is one of great courage and colour, a formidable woman taking on the challenge provided by the evangelical missionary movement, and handling it with style and energy. Her impact on the Dublin charity scene from 1851-1889, through the institutions of the Ladies of Charity, St Brigid's Orphanage and Poor Schools, and the Sisters of the Holy Faith, was substantial, particularly the pioneering of the outdoor system of child rearing, and the network of city poor schools. Her youngest sister, Jane Fagan, a member of the congregation, wrote: 'My father looked to his son to perpetuate his name, but now - see - it is not his son, but his daughter who will hand it down in honour to posterity.'[120]

NOTES

1 See Gibson, Romuald. 1982. *Tomorrow Began Yesterday*, Dublin, pp22-3. See also, Prunty, Jacinta 1995. *Margaret Aylward 1810-1889*. Dublin.

2 Account of estate and assets of Mary and Margaret Murphy, 2 December 1858, Holy Faith Archives, Glasnevin (hereafter GA) AP/BR/26 nos. 14, 15; payment to Inland Revenue by Mrs Ellen Aylward, successor, 1858, GA: AP/BR/26 no. 15A.

3 Jane Fagan to Father Gowan, 11 December 1871, GA: AF/PL/15 no. 30; for Aylward family business dealings see files, GA: AF/PL/15; AF/PL/15A; AP/BR/26; AP/LI/27.

4 Cowman, Des. 'Trade and society in Waterford city 1800-1840'. In Nolan, W and Power, T (eds.). 1992. *Waterford: History and Society*, Dublin, pp427-58.

5 John Aylward to Mary Aylward, Dublin 1854, GA, AF/PL/15 no. 14.

6 Gibbons, Margaret. 1928. *The Life of Margaret Aylward*. Dublin, p.20.

7 *Ibid.*, p.28.

8 Ellen Bodenham to Margaret Aylward, 1839-1852, GA: MA/GC/03 no. 69.

9 Her mother Ellen had first married John Mullowney, brother of Teresa Mullowney, the Waterford woman who established the first Presentation community in the city in 1798; Ellen was also a sister of Brother Patrick Joseph Murphy, one of the first recruits to the Christian Brothers and the first superior of Mount Sion, Waterford.

10 Ellen Aylward to Margaret Aylward, 1858, GA: AF/PL/15A no. 51. Margaret Aylward to Dr Kirby, 3 July 1870, MC/K/12 no.30.

11 William Aylward to Margaret Aylward, 30 September 1834, GA: AF/PL/15A no. 48.

12 Gaughren, Sr Rose. n.d. but written prior to 1923. MS, 'A Little Sketch of the History of the Congregation'. GA: HC/S/21 nos. 16, 16A (MS and typed copy); also 2, 2A (earlier MS version); hereafter Gaughren, History.

13 Anon. 1925. *The Life and Work of Mary Aikenhead*. Dublin, p.180.

14 Ellen Bodenham to Margaret Aylward, bundle of letters dated 1839-42, GA: MA/GC/03 no. 69.

15 Whelan, Kevin. 1988. 'The regional impact of Irish Catholicism, 1700-1850'. In Smyth, W J and Whelan, K (eds.). *Common Ground: Essays on the Historical Geography of Ireland*. Dublin, pp253-77.

16 Clear, Caitriona. 1987. *Nuns in Nineteenth-Century Ireland*. Dublin, p.143.

17 Luddy, Maria. 1992. 'Presentation convents in county Tipperary, 1806-1900'. In *Tipperary Historical Journal*, pp84-95.

18 Gibbons, *Life*, pp77-88, also GA: JC/C/13.

19 Clear, *Nuns*, p.143.

20 John Aylward to Mary Aylward, 1854, GA: AL/PF/15 no. 14; John Fagan to Jane Fagan, 11 April 1855, GA: AF/PL/15 no. 43;

Richard Fitzgerald to Margaret Aylward, n.d., GA: AF/PL/15 no. 22; court proceedings and private papers on the separation of Maria Clara née White, petitioner, and William Aylward, respondent, 1848, GA: AP/LI/127 nos. 6, 6a, 7, 8.

21 Finegan, John. 1978. *The Story of Monto: An Account of Dublin's Red Light District.* Dublin. See also, Prunty, Jacinta. 1995. *Dublin Slums 1800-1925, A Study in Urban Geography.* Dublin.

22 Ladies of Charity, Third Report, 1854, pp7-8.

23 As was laid down in 1617, Ladies of Charity, First Report, 1852, p.5.

24 For the application by women of domestic skills to areas outside the home, a feature common to almost all nineteenth-century philanthropy, see Luddy, Maria. 1995. *Women and Philanthropy in Nineteenth-Century Ireland.* Cambridge; Prochaska, F K 1980. *Women and Philanthropy in Nineteenth-Century England.* Oxford.

25 Ladies of Charity, Second Report, 1853, p.15; Fourth Report, 1855, pp11, 20; Fifth Report, 1856, p.6; Eighth Report, 1859, p.6.

26 Ladies of Charity, First Report, 1852, p.9: Third Report, 1854, p.4

27 Gaughren, History.

28 For example, see Ladies of Charity, Tenth Report, 1861, pp6-7.

29 See, for example, an account of social conditions in the vicinity of the Law Courts in the Annual Report of the Dublin Bible Woman Mission in connection with the Church of Ireland, 1877, p.16.

30 For a comparison of the philanthropic work of Margaret Aylward with that of contemporaries of other denominations, see Preston, Margaret H. 1993. 'Lay women and philanthropy in Dublin 1860-1880'. In *Eire-Ireland.* (Winter), pp74-85.

31 Ladies of Charity, Fifth Report, 1856, p.4; Margaret Aylward to Dr Cullen, 10 June 1862, GA: MC/K/12 no. 27a; Margaret Aylward to Dr Kirby, 6 October 1854, GA: MC/K/12 no. 26a.

32 Cullen presided at the annual meetings in 1856 and 1861, from 1854 granted it a Sunday in the Annual Charity Sermon List of the diocese, made generous personal contributions and also directed some of the funds which were entrusted to him for the 'poor of Dublin' to be dispensed by the Ladies; see Ladies of Charity, First Report, 1852, p.31 Appendix; Fifth Report, 1856, p.4; Margaret Aylward to Paul Cullen, 20 December 1856, GA: PC/C/11 no. 1.

33 The archives of the Irish Province of the Daughters of Charity of St Vincent de Paul are very scant for this foundation period, and make reference only to the roles of Dr Cullen and Fr Dowley in establishing the Sisters in Dublin.

34 Margaret Aylward to Fr Dowley, 13 March 1857, GA: MA/CH/02 no. 31B.

35 John Gowan to Margaret Aylward, 12 June 1851, GA: JG/CL/06 no. 6.

36 Ladies of Charity, Second Report, 1853, pp15, 26.

37 *Ibid.*, pp15, 25; Fifth Report, 1856.

38 Ladies of Charity, Third Report, 1854, p.19.

39 *Ibid.*, pp24-5.

40 Ladies of Charity, First Report, 1852, p.20; for the first of several

39 *Ibid.*, pp24-5.
40 Ladies of Charity, First Report, 1852, p.20; for the first of several 'blacklists' of Protestant charities accused of proselytising, see St Brigid's Orphanage, Second Report, 1859, attached to Ladies of Charity, Eighth Report, 1859, pp23-5.
41 See Kerr, Donal. 1995. *A Nation of Beggars: The Whig Government, The Irish Church, The Irish Famine.* Oxford.
42 Smyly, Vivienne. n.d. c1976. *The Early History of Mrs Smyly's Homes and Schools.* Dublin.
43 'Report of Honorary Secretary for Missions, with reference to the reduction of missionary expenditure furnished to the Committee according to minutes 2988, 3028, 3029, 3030, 3085;' Irish Church Missions minutes no. 3087, XVlll, XlX, 9 June 1859. Irish Church Missions, Central Office, London. (Hereafter ICM.)
44 Dublin Visiting Mission in Connexion *[sic]* with the Society for Irish Church Missions, Report for 1894, (Dublin, 1895), p.5.
45 St Brigid's Orphanage for Five Hundred Children, Sixth Annual Report, 1862, p.19. (Hereafter, St Brigid's Orphanage.)
46 St. Brigid's Orphanage, Third Report, 1859, p.14.
47 Ladies of Charity, First Report, 1852, p.21; fragments of one of these lists survives, titled 'Names of women found attending at Weaver's Hall School, the Coombe, on Sunday Feb. 10, 1856', which gives the mothers' names, addresses, and where their children attend school. GA: ML/VP/16 no. 5.
48 Ladies of Charity, Fifth Report, 1856, p.9.
49 Ladies of Charity, First Report, 1852, p.22.
50 Davies, Sarah. 1866. *'Them Also', The Story of the Dublin Mission.* London, p.2.
51 St Brigid's Orphanage, Fourteenth Report, 1870, p.5.
52 St Brigid's Orphanage, Tenth Report, 1866, p.14.
53 St Brigid's Orphanage, Fortieth Report, 1897, p.10.
54 Robins, Joseph. 1980. *The Lost Children: A Study of Charity Children in Ireland 1700-1900.* Dublin, pp10-59.
55 St Brigid's Orphanage, Fifteenth Report, 1872, p.10.
56 St Brigid's Orphanage, Fifth Report, 1861, p.13.
57 St Brigid's Orphanage, Thirteenth Report, 1869, p.6.
58 St Brigid's Orphanage, Eighth Report, 1864, p.10.
59 Instructions to the Nurses (Dublin, 1858) p.4.
60 St Brigid's Orphanage, Second Report, 1858, p.11.
61 Margaret Aylward to Ada Allingham, n.d. but from prison, GA: MA/F/01, no. 15.
62 St Brigid's Orphanage, Twenty-Seventh Report, 1884, p.5. First Report, 1857, p.5.
63 St Brigid's Orphanage, Sixth Report, 1862, p.14.
64 See Orphan Registers, II, entries nos. 183, 189, 264, for examples. These registers are stated in St. Brigid's, The Coombe, Dublin.
65 *The Month*, December 1866, pp568-9; Pastoral Letter on Mary by Dr Cullen, 1864, p.7. *The Workman or Life and Leisure*, 16, 22 April 1865, pp247-8; Taylor, Fanny. 1867. *Irish Homes and Irish Hearts*, London, p.56.

68 Margaret Aylward to Fr Dowley, 17 February 1857; GA: MA/CH/02 no. 33.

69 Philip Dowley CM to Margaret Aylward, 15 January 1851, GA: MA/CH/02 no. 40.

70 Père Etienne to Margaret Aylward, 18 September 1851, original in French. GA: MA/CH/02 no. 50.

71 Ladies of Charity, Third Report, 1854, p.5.

72 The Carmelite community and the orphans in their care moved to Sandymount. Margaret Aylward to Père Etienne, 4 October 1856, GA: MA/CH/02 no. 45a.

73 Sr M. Josephine Virieu to Monsignor, 16 July 1857, GA: MA/GC/03 no.9a

74 For example, the Sisters of Charity took over the Magdalen Asylum, 91 Townsend Street in 1832 and relocated it to Donnybrook in 1837; the Sisters of Our Lady of Charity of Refuge took over a similar asylum in Gloucester Street in 1877; the Sisters of the Holy Faith took over the 'good works' and premises of the men's sodality, Our Lady Queen of Charity, 65 Jervis Street, in 1870.

75 E B A Taylor to Henry Mathews, 12 January (1858), GA: MM/CC/17l no. 8.

76 John Gowan, Thirty-Third Annual Report of St Brigid's Orphanage, and *History of Miss Aylward's Trial and Imprisonment*, Dublin, 1890, p.28.

77 *Ibid*.

78 *Freeman's Journal*, 6 June 1860.

79 *Freeman's Journal*, 18 November 1859.

80 St Brigid's Orphanage, Third Report, 1859, p.19.

81 To Margaret Aylward from Georgina Fullerton, n.d., GA: MA/BL/14 no. 8; John Curtis SJ, no date but clearly November 1860, GA: JC/C/13 no. 1; Dr Kirby, GA: Mc/K/12 nos. 1-4; J. Tully, 27 March 1861, GA: MA/BL/14 no. 17; also letters from Bishops Leahy, Gilhooly, Furlong, Flannery, Kilduff, and various lay and clerical supporters in file GA: MA/BL/14.

82 Margaret Aylward to Dr Kirby, 22 January 1861, GA: Mc/K/12 no. 26c.

83 *Freeman's Journal*, 17 January 1861; *Times*, February 1861.

84 The trial of Miss Margaret Aylward, GA: C/B1, p.77; Margaret Aylward to Ada Allingham, n.d. but apparently February 1861, GA: MA/F/01 no. 22.

85 Margaret Aylward to Lord Lieutenant, draft notes, not dated but must be early February 1861, GA: MM/CC/17L no. 39; Margaret Aylward to Lord Lieutenant, 6 February 1861, GA: MM/CC/17L, no. 35; to Lord Chief Justice, 15 February 1861, GA: MM/CC/17L, no. 37; Lord Chief Justice to Governor, Grangegorman Prison, 19 February 1861, GA: MM/CC/17L, no. 38.

86 3 April 1861, GA: ML/VP/16 no. 9.

87 Margaret Aylward to Ada Allingham, from prison, GA: MA/F/01 nos. 1-38.

88 See, for example, John Gowan to Margaret Aylward, 12 June 1851, GA: JG/CL/06 no. 6.

89 John Gowan to Margaret Aylward, 28 February, GA: JG/CL/06, no. 3; same to same, Fourth Sunday after Easter, undated, GA: JG/CL/06 no. 5.

90 John Gowan to Margaret Aylward, 12 June 1851, GA: JG/CL/06 no.6.

91 Margaret Aylward to Dr Kirby, 24 April 1861, GA: Mc/K/12 no. 26d.

92 Margaret Aylward to Ada Allingham, n.d. but from prison, GA: MA/F/01 nos 13, 16; also Ladies of Charity, Tenth Annual Report, 1861, p.9.

93 Margaret Aylward to Dr Kirby, 29 November 1860, GA: Mc/K/12 no. 26b.

94 Margaret Aylward to Dr Kirby, May 1862, GA: Mc/K/12 no. 27.

95 *Anon*. 1878. *The Story of the Irish Church Missions*. London, p.178.

96 See, for example, St Brigid's Orphanage, Eighteenth Report, 1875, pp7-8.

97 For example, in West Park Street by 1884 over 200 of the children received daily breakfast and a loaf of bread to take home. See *West Park Street School Journal*, 1865-1910, GA: HC/S/21 no. 18; *Crow Street School Journal*; also annual reports of St Brigid's Orphanage and Schools of the Holy Faith, 1861-1906.

98 St Brigid's Orphanage, Twelfth Report, 1868, pp21-2.

99 St Brigid's Orphanage, Fifteenth Report, 1872, pp15-6.

100 Margaret Aylward to Dr Cullen, 29 December 1858, GA: PC/C/11 no. 5.

101 St Brigid's Orphanage, Tenth Report, 1866, p.10.

102 Margaret Aylward to Dr Kirby, 24 April 1861, GA: Mc/K/12 no. 26d.

103 [Cullen] 'kindly told me to write the application' to Rome that 'it may be made a religious congregation or at least that the first steps thereto may be taken that it may receive the sanction and approbation of the Church'. Margaret Aylward to Dr Kirby, 19 June 1866, GA: Mc/K/12 no. 28d.

104 Margaret Aylward to Dr Kirby, May 1862, GA: Mc/K/12 no. 27.

105 Obituary, in Aylward House, Glasnevin, 16 April 1869.

106 Gaughren, History.

107 St Brigid's Orphanage, Fifteenth Report, 1872, pp14-5; See overseas correspondence GA: MA/F/01 nos. 62,69,77 (1864), no. 63 (1867).

108 The term 'dower' is the only term used in Holy Faith records.

109 Clear, *Nuns*, p.87.

110 Luddy, 'Presentation convents', pp84-95.

111 Margaret Aylward to M Frances, 1869, GA: MA/F/01, no. 75; nos. 60, 64, 65, 68, 73, 75.

112 For cures see Margaret Aylward to M Frances, GA: MA/F/01 nos. 47, 60, 64, 68.

113 Margaret Aylward to Dr Kirby, 4 September 1869, GA: Mc/K/12 no. 29.

114 Margaret visited Aix les Bains Saine in 1864, Aix-la-Chapelle in

Mc/K/12 no. 29.

114 Margaret visited Aix les Bains Saine in 1864, Aix-la-Chapelle in 1868, 1872, and Rome in 1864 for the canonisation of St Margaret Mary Alacoque.

115 Margaret Aylward to M. Frances, n.d., GA: MA/F/01 no. 58.

116 Dr Donnelly to Margaret Aylward, 10 January 1884, GA: MA/CH/02 no. 64a.

117 Margaret Aylward to Dr Donnelly, 14 January 1884, GA: MA/CH/02 no. 65a.

118 Ellen Aylward to Margaret Aylward, not dated but contents indicate written early 1888, GA: AF/PL/15A no. 51.

119 Margaret Aylward to Archbishop Walsh, 10 May 1886, MA/CH/02 no. 55; however see also friendly correspondence with John Gowan (after Aylward's death) in GA: JG/ML/07 nos. 11-27, 1 November 1889-19 March 1894.

120 Gibson, *Tomorrow*, p.5.

My thanks to Professor Annagret Simms, Department of Geography, UCD, who directed the PhD research from which this contribution is drawn. For making this study possible, my thanks to Sr Rosemary Duffy, superior general of the Sisters of the Holy Faith, and to Srs Assisi Tattan and Theodore Bugler, archivists, who facilitated the work in every possible way. For access to Irish Church Missions material I am indebted to Mr B E Sloane, (Croydon) and Rev. Bridcott, (Bachelor's Walk) while Sr Margaret Mary DC (Dunardagh, Blackrock) and Mr David Sheehy (Clonliffe) were also most helpful in locating materials.

Frances Power Cobbe

(1822-1904)

Deirdre Raftery

In England, the nineteenth-century women's movement developed from the work of a small group of women who, in the late 1850s, worked from an office in London which housed an employment bureau, a library and a meeting place, and from which was produced the *Englishwoman's Journal*.[1]

During the 1860s the movement grew and diversified. New publications - the *Victoria Magazine* and the *Englishwoman's Review* - began. New concerns were placed on the agenda. To women's education and employment and married women's control of their property were added entry to the medical profession, suffrage, and the repeal of the Contagious Diseases Acts. Separate organisations on different issues were established at various centres. While not formally linked, these societies had overlapping memberships, and many of the best remembered names are found in minute books and membership lists of a number of organisations. The prolific author and journalist Frances Power Cobbe did not lead any of the major campaigns, but was involved in most of them - education, suffrage, and women's position under the law. For her the major strands of the women's movement were inextricably linked: for equality women needed education, remunerative employment and the vote, whereby they could influence changes in the law.

In 1843 the Governesses' Benevolent Institution was established to provide support and employment for 'distressed gentlewomen' who needed to earn a living. By 1851, over 25,000 governesses were registered for work in England. The increase in the number of middle-class women needing gainful employment was partly due to the decline in infant mortality and consequent rise in family size which, with the rising standards of middle-class life, put strains on the incomes of a class already suffering from the economic uncertainties of the time. In addition, increasing numbers of men left for the colonies, or chose to postpone marriage.[2] By 1871, the 'surplus' of females in the age group twenty to thirty-five alone in the population amounted to over a quarter of a million women. With little hope of finding a husband to support them and lacking a formal education, many were ill equipped to fend for themselves.

Between 1861 and 1872, Maria Rye's Society for Promoting the Employment of Women placed 160 women in governessing positions in Australia and New Zealand, although this 'solution' was viewed with cynicism by many feminists, including Frances Power Cobbe. It suggested 'that women were parasitic and unnecessary rather than oppressed'.[3]

Throughout the second half of the nineteenth century, female education remained a pressing question. Bessie

Rayner Parkes, Barbara Bodichon and Emily Davies contributed to the debate, Davies giving it her undivided attention and opening Cambridge University to women when she founded Girton College in 1873.[4] Similarly, Barbara Bodichon concerned herself with the legal status of women. In 1854 she published a pamphlet which was a powerful stimulus to legal reform. It demonstrated that most married and divorced women had virtually no legal rights, and her campaign for a Married Women's Property Bill was supported by Cobbe who, like Bodichon, gathered considerable amounts of empirical information on women and the law. Bodichon summarised the legal position of women in marriage under the English common law:

> A man and wife are one person in law; the wife loses all her rights as a single woman, and her existence is, as it were absorbed in that of her husband ... . A wife's personal property before marriage ... becomes absolutely her husband's, unless when settled in trust for her, and he may assign or dispose of it at his pleasure ... . Money earned by a married woman belongs absolutely to her husband ... . The legal custody of children belongs to the father. During the life time of a sane father, the mother has no rights over her children, except limited power over young infants, and the father may take them from her and dispose of them as he thinks fit.[5]

Bodichon, together with Millicent Garrett Fawcett, was also actively involved in the suffrage campaign of the 1860s. Once again, minute books and journal articles show that Cobbe lent her support.

There are biographies of many of the leaders of the women's movement, including Emily Davies who gained access to university examinations for women, Josephine Butler who led the campaign to repeal the Contagious Diseases Acts, and Millicent Garrett Fawcett, president of the National Union of Women's Suffrage Societies.[6]

Among the unsung heroines of the Victorian women's movement is Frances Power Cobbe, whose greatest contribution to the movement was to improve the domestic position of women, and, in particular, that of married women. Only recently has an exploration of her life appeared, in Barbara Caine's *Victorian Feminists*,[7] which also deals with Davies, Butler and Garrett Fawcett. When Dale Spender and Janet Todd mention Cobbe,[8] they quickly focus on Cobbe's feminist commitment, a commitment which was most evident during her life in England.

Were it not for passing references to her relationship with her father at their home in Donabate, County Dublin, readers might be forgiven for assuming that Frances Power Cobbe was born, or spent all of her life, in England. In fact her feminism had its genesis in the domestic ideology, the philanthropic interests, and the passion for learning to which she was exposed on the family estate north of Dublin, where she lived until she was thirty-six.

The most valuable source for Cobbe's life is her autobiography, published in 1894.[9] She began it in the early 1890s, describing it to Lydia Becker as 'a sketch of my life in which I shall make a point of showing how I came to be concerned with women's rights ... .'[10] The autobiography deals also with her childhood in Ireland, her travels through two continents, her work for homeless children and in the anti-vivisection movement. She prefaced it by stating that she hoped its value would 'partly consist in the evidence it must afford of how pleasant and interesting, and ... not altogether useless a life is open to a woman, though no man has ever desired to share it, nor has she seen the man she would have wished to ask her to do so.'[11]

The two-volume autobiography was an ambitious undertaking in a woman of her years, but while it occasionally betrays both her failing memory and her desire to edit out certain parts of her life, it is one of the few autobiographical sources which embraces almost every facet of the nineteenth-century English women's movement.

In 1904, a posthumous edition of the *Life* was published, containing additions written by Cobbe before her death, and an introduction by a friend, Blanche Atkinson. Although Atkinson indicates that Cobbe sifted through 'old letters and records'[12] while writing the original draft, attempts to evaluate the accuracy of the autobiography are frustrated by the fact that many of Cobbe's personal papers have not survived. This biographical study draws on material from the *Life*, and on all traceable Cobbe papers. Six important sources have been located, and five of these have been examined. Papers relating to Newbridge House have been catalogued by the National Library of Ireland, but remain in the possession of the Cobbe family and are not yet available for consultation. The catalogue indicates that they do not contain personal papers of Frances Power Cobbe. The largest collection of Cobbe's personal papers is at the Huntington Library, California.[13] This collection, consulted in 1992, comprises 854 pieces covering the period 1855-1902, reflecting her interest in women's suffrage, anti-vivisection, and theology. Papers relating to Cobbe have been located and examined at the Bodleian Library, Oxford, among the papers of Mary Somerville, Sir Henry Acland and Sir Henry Taylor, and at the British Library, among the papers of W E Gladstone and Sir Charles Dilke.[14] The papers of Emily Davies and Barbara Bodichon at Girton College, Cambridge, have also been consulted.[15] Finally, three volumes of notes by Cobbe were located and examined at the National Library of Wales.[16] These volumes, dated 1846-1863, are kept with a large collection of Cobbe's published work, and for this reason may have escaped the attention of other scholars who have written on Cobbe. Certainly they are not noted in Spender or Caine. The third volume contains notes for the *Life*, while the first and second volumes contain notes for her theological writings, and some pen-and-ink sketches, probably made in Italy. They do not contain references to her daily life; few of her friends are mentioned, and many entries are undated.

The 'public' Cobbe is accessible through her published writings, while the 'private' Cobbe has either been erased or was not given expression in diaries and letters.

This invisibility of the private Cobbe is possibly linked to her having lived for thirty-five years with Mary Lloyd in what Spender and Caine equally conclude was a lesbian relationship. The exact nature of their relationship is unknown, underlining the argument that history has been impoverished by the self- or other-imposed silence of nineteenth-century lesbians.[17] Lesbian relationships between nineteenth-century women certainly existed, though they were often viewed as 'romantic friendships', a term which gained currency in the eighteenth century. 'Romantic friendships' were often platonic, despite the passion with which women wrote to, and about, each other.[18] However, the contemporary view of all passionate relationships between women as essentially platonic neatly eclipsed the possibility of sexual relations between women.

The best known instance of two women setting up home

was that of two Irish women, Sarah Ponsonby and Eleanor Butler, who, in 1778, eloped together and set up home in Wales, sharing a home and a bed for the rest of their lives. Admired and befriended by Edmund Burke, Sir Walter Scott, the Duke of Wellington and Josiah Wedgewood, their 'romantic friendship' was immortalised in verse by William Wordsworth.[19] That they caused little scandal to contemporary society was due, Lillian Faderman argues, to the fact that their relationship 'was thought to be non-genital ... they were Protestant nuns'.[20] In some circles in nineteenth-century England it was not thought possible that women could engage in active lesbian relationships. In 1811 two school-mistresses won a lawsuit undertaken on foot of an allegation that they engaged in a sexual relationship, when the judge ruled, 'No such case was ever known in Scotland, or in Britain ... I do believe that the crime here alleged has no existence'.[21]

It is not known whether the relationship between Cobbe and Lloyd was sexual, but, like Ponsonby and Butler, they were 'married' in every other sense, sharing a home for thirty-five years, spending vacations together in Europe, and choosing to be buried together near Lloyd's home in North Wales. Lloyd dictated that their relationship would not be recorded in the *Life*. To the second edition, published after Lloyd's death, Cobbe added a note that Lloyd's 'reticence' made her 'always refuse to allow me to lead her into the more public life whereto my work necessarily brought me, and in her last sacred directions she forbids me to commemorate her by any written record'.[22] In the light of this Cobbe may have destroyed personal papers, hence the paucity of source material relating to their shared years.[23] A careful use of the autobiography, selected papers, and Cobbe's published works can, nonetheless, give some idea of the immense contribution that this eminent Victorian made to the rights of women, children and animals.

The Cobbe family originated in Hampshire. In 1717, Charles Cobbe came to Ireland as chaplain to his cousin, the Duke of Bolton, who had been appointed Lord Lieutenant. With this connection, he enjoyed rapid ecclesiastical promotion, becoming 'successively Bishop of Killala, Dromore and Kildare, and Archbishop of Dublin'.[24] In 1736, he purchased land around Donabate in north County Dublin, and built Newbridge House. In 1742, he added a further 510 acres to his estate. Described by Frances Power Cobbe as 'a sensible Whig, and eminently Protestant Archbishop',[25] he was only one of many relatives to hold an important ecclesiastical position. She was also connected to the Beresfords and the Trenches.[26]

Archbishop Cobbe married Dorothea Levinge Rawdon. Their son, Thomas Cobbe MP, represented the Borough of Swords in the Irish Parliament, and Frances Power Cobbe noted with pride that he was one of the few MPs who voted for the Union while refusing 'either a peerage or money compensation for his seat'.[27] Instead, he secured educational endowments for Swords.[28] In 1751 Thomas Cobbe married Lady Eliza Beresford, daughter of the first Earl of Tyrone, and their son, Charles, inherited Newbridge. Charles Cobbe married Anne Power Trench, sister of the first Earl of Clancarty. His premature death resulted in his son, also named Charles, inheriting Newbridge at the age of eighteen.

While his grandfather managed the estate, Charles joined the army and served in India. In 1809, having returned to England for health reasons, he married Frances Conway and brought her to Newbridge. Frances Conway Cobbe and Charles Cobbe had five children, the youngest of which was their only daughter, Frances Power Cobbe, born in 1822.

As a child, Frances was educated at home by her mother, and by governesses. In 1836 she was sent to a school in Brighton, run by a Miss Runciman and a Miss Roberts. There were two English governesses, and teachers of French, German and Italian. 'The din of our large double schoolrooms was something frightful,' Cobbe recalled.

[F]our pianos might be heard going at once in rooms above and around us, while at numerous tables ... there were girls reading aloud to governesses ... everything was taught in the inverse ratio of importance. At the bottom of the scale were morals and religion, at the top were music and dancing.

The pupils were daughters of country gentlemen and members of Parliament, 'full of capabilities for widely extended usefulness and influence [but] ... all this fine material was deplorably wasted. Nobody dreamed that any one of us could in later life be more or less than an ornament of society'.[29] Shortly after Frances was born, her mother had suffered an injury to her ankle and was eventually unable to move without assistance. On returning to Newbridge from boarding school in 1838, Frances assumed the duty of companion and nurse. Her mother was her closest friend during her youth and, while she has left few details about their relationship, at the end of her life she wrote: She was the one being in the world whom I truly loved through all the passionate years of youth and early womanhood; the only one who really loved me.' She describes her as charming, cultivated, and 'an almost omnivorous reader'.[30]

Cobbe herself continued to study, learning a little Greek and geometry with the local parson, and began a programme of rigorous and systematic self-education. She used her allowance to buy books and make visits to Marsh's Library in Dublin, and, in addition to reading English literature and history, she enjoyed astronomy and heraldry.

She had little interest in the social life of the Anglo-Irish gentry. She hated it when her parents forced her to attend Dublin balls, believing that the officers of the Horse Artillery, then under the command of her uncle, danced with her out of duty. Nor had she a wide circle of friends. She liked to read, to nurse her mother, and to visit her close friend and near neighbour, Harriet St Leger, who lived at Ardgillan Castle. In her autobiography, images of genteel life in Ireland are whimsical rather than glamorous: she recalls the excitement at the arrival of the first sponge-bath in Ireland, installed by her cousin, Lady Eliza McClintock, at Drumcar; equally memorable was the first time she ever saw a matchbox, 'a long upright red one containing a bottle of phosphorus and a few matches which were lighted by insertion in the bottle'.[31]

Although the only daughter, Frances did not have a close relationship with her father. Life at Newbridge, dominated by her father's 'fiery temper and despotic will', and 'his ideas concerning the rights of parents, and husbands',[32] must have helped form her views of marriage and the role of women. Cobbe later reflected with irony that her finer 'faculties' were such as her father 'would have regarded as incongruous and unseemly for a daughter'.[33] In her autobiography, her mother emerges as an intelligent but voiceless member of the family, and, despite Cobbe's deep affection for her, she does not seem to have considered imitating her role.

It fell on her, 'as the only active woman of the family, to

play the part of Lady Bountiful on a rather large scale'.[34] She visited the tenants' cottages, taught at the school, and oversaw the distribution of Christmas gifts, which included frieze to make coats and capes, and an ox to be slain and divided among them. She considered her father to be a responsible and generous landlord. He had, she wrote,

> ... as strong a sense as any modern sanitary reformer of the importance of good and healthy cottages; and having found his estate covered with mud and thatched cabins, he ... laboured incessantly, year by year, to replace them by mortared stone and slated cottages, among which were five schoolhouses, all supported by himself ...

It was his daughter's duty 'to draw for him the plans and elevations of these cottages, farmhouses and village shops, with calculations of the cost of each ... .'[35]

On the famine years she makes little comment, beyond recalling the smell of the rotting potato crop around Donabate, and remarking that many gentlewomen who nursed their tenants died of famine fever.

Cobbe never questioned her position as a member of the ruling class. She was shocked by the Young Ireland rebellion in 1848, finding it difficult to believe 'that there were actual pikes imported into well-known cabins, and that there were in the world men stupid and wicked enough to wish to apply them to those who laboured constantly for their benefit'.[36] Her unquestioning acceptance of the *status quo* was influenced by a belief in 'the supremacy of the Anglo-Saxon intellect in every land of its adoption'.[37] She was dismissive of the Catholic clergy, describing the local priests as 'disagreeable-looking men with the coarse mouth and jaw of the Irish peasant ... and often the purple and bloated appearance of their cheeks suggested the too abundant diet of bacon and whiskey-punch'.[38] She resented their sporadic interference in her attempts to teach Catholic children in her tenant schools:

> [The priests] ... worried me dreadfully by clearing out all the Catholic children from my school every now and then on

the pretence of withdrawing them from heretical instruction
.... . What the priests really wanted was to obstruct education
itself and close and friendly intercourse with Protestants ... .
Several times, when the class had been well got together and
began to be interested, the priest announced that he would
give them lessons on the same night ... . A fortnight or so
later, however, I always learnt that the priest's lessons had
dropped and all was to be recommenced.[39]

There are no papers relating to Cobbe's life in Newbridge
against which to measure her account of this period in the
Life, written some fifty years later. But that account is, of
itself, revealing. Cobbe, who considered herself Irish by birth
and Anglo-Saxon by race, writes of her relations with the
Irish tenantry with an unselfconscious superiority. Writing
with the hindsight of fifty years, she offers no analysis of the
socio-political climate of her times, nor does she waver from
her early acceptance of *noblesse oblige*. This sense of duty led
her to teach the children on her father's estate to read and
write, and later drove her to work with destitute incurables
in Bristol. It would lead her to become involved in the
women's movement, believing it was her responsibilty to
alleviate the misery of her more unfortunate sisters. The
thirty-five years which she had spent at Newbridge prepared
Cobbe for such work. They also exposed her to the accepted
lifestyle for a woman of her class, that of charming hostess,
wife and mother; she rejected this lifestyle wholeheartedly.

Her concern for her mother's failing health delayed
Cobbe from revealing her increasing scepticism about the
tenets of Christianity. She had always found religious ideas
'intensely interesting', but knew that her position would
shock and disappoint her mother. 'We had five archbishops
and a bishop among our near kindred, - Cobbe, Beresfords,
and Trenchs ... . I was the first heretic ever known among
us,'[40] she wrote, not without self-irony. At the age of eleven
she was questioning the nature and veracity of Christ's
miracles. By her early twenties, having rejected the basic
tenets of Christianity, she set about working out a set of
beliefs influenced by her reading of American
Transcendentalists. In particular she was influenced by
Theodore Parker's *Discourse of True Religion*, which
supported her belief in a rational God whose moral law was
revealed through human intuition. 'Divine inspiration' was

not, Parker believed, a miraculous thing, but was 'in accordance with the natural relations of the infinite and the finite spirit.'[41] She corresponded with him between 1848 and 1860, and in 1863 she edited his *Collected Works*.[42] Barbara Caine suggests that Cobbe may have been influenced by Parker's critique of the masculine brutality evident in the Christian God. Parker saw God as both father and mother, incorporating both feminine and masculine qualities. This aspect of his thought may have met Cobbe's 'deeply-felt needs ... in a home dominated by an imperious and arrogant man'[43] who had never shown affection for his daughter.

Cobbe kept her theological studies and religious scepticism to herself until after her mother's death, when she declared herself a theist. Her family considered that theism was 'a word in a dictionary, not a religion', and some time around 1853 her father asked her to leave his house. This period of Cobbe's life must have had a great impact on her personal development. It marked her increasing awareness of her 'particular circumstances as the daughter of a man of immense force of will', and signalled her first open challenge to patriarchal power. 'Fathers,' she wrote, 'believed themselves to possess almost boundless rights over their children in the matter of pursuits, professions, marriages and so on ... .'[44] This, she concluded, was a direct result of the 'laws which concerned women ... [which] were so frightfully unjust that the most kindly disposed men inevitably took their cue from them, and looked on their mothers, wives, and sisters as beings ... with no rights, indeed, which should ever stand against theirs'.[45]

For a year she lived with a brother in Donegal. This was a period of 'utter loneliness', in which she first faced the possibility that she might have to earn her own living. Duty dictated that she return to Newbridge to manage her father's household, 'all the time in a sort of moral Coventry', until his death in November 1857. During this time she began to write. As with many women of her time, her writing and study was accomplished secretly, and could not impinge on her domestic duties. She wrote a book, *Essay on the Theory of Intuitive Morals*, in which she articulated her belief in a rational God to whom the individual owed a duty. Human life was not the pursuit of happiness: it was the perfecting of the human soul by fulfilling one's duty. This was the foundation for her feminist thought in the coming decades, when she associated her work for both oppressed and destitute women with her duty to God. The essence of her argument, replicated in her later feminist tracts, is that women's rights are *human* rights; to support them is to act as a philanthropist, motivated by an intuitive sense of what is morally right. Her position echoed that of a number of women, such as Mary Astell (1666-1731), Hannah More (1745-1833) and Mary Wollstonecraft (1759-1797), who argued from the equality of all human souls to the equality of man and woman.[46]

The *Essay* was published in 1855, anonymously, to avoid her father's wrath. It was received with some acclaim, and reviewed as if written by a man. The *Caledonian Mercury*, typical of the early reviews, described it as 'the work of a masculine and lofty mind'. When the sex of the author was revealed, the *Christian Observer* wrote: 'Our dislike is increased when we are told it is a female who has propounded so unfeminine and stoical a theory.'[47] Cobbe's initiation into public life anticipated her career: though she would accomplish much it would be measured against the Victorian yardstick of compromised femininity.

Charles Cobbe had expected that Frances would remain at Newbridge as the guest of her brother and sister-in-law, following his death. Her legacy, comprising a hundred-pound note and an annuity of two hundred pounds a year, just a little more than her usual annual pocket money, indicated that her father had not wished that she would live independently.

Cobbe rejected the role of spinster aunt at Newbridge. With her savings and inheritance she began a year of travelling. This took her to Paris, Rome, Alexandria, Cairo, Beirut, Athens, Trieste, and Antwerp 'in eleven months and at a cost of only £400'.[48] She then settled in Bristol in 1858, where Mary Carpenter, a well-known English philanthropist, needed help with her Ragged School work. Some of Carpenter's letters to Cobbe at this time have survived,[49] although scholars rely on the Cobbe autobiography for details of this period of her life. At Carpenter's suggestion, she came to live at the Red Lodge reformatory. As Cobbe was receiving no wage for her work, it seemed sensible on Carpenter's part to offer lodgings. The situation proved unsatisfactory. While Cobbe enjoyed conversation and good meals, Carpenter's diet was simple, and she rarely discussed anything other than her charitable works. The domestic situation put Cobbe under much strain, and towards the end of 1859 she moved out of Red Lodge and took rooms at Belgrave House.

Jo Manton's biography of Mary Carpenter presents Cobbe as an unwelcome and virtually useless addition to Carpenter's work, and misinterprets passages of the Cobbe autobiography in support of this view. Cobbe is presented as a grotesquely fat woman, attired 'in something resembling a riding habit with a skirt of sensible length'.[50] As Cobbe herself wrote, it was Harriet St Leger who early adopted such a costume, adding that while she admired Harriet's costume, she could not suffer the attention drawn by such an attire.[51] Manton goes beyond the evidence in concluding that Cobbe, 'whose passionate love for her own sex had never found fulfilment, was seeking a soul mate. In this hope she vainly accepted a life unlike anything she had ever known'.[52]

Cobbe elected to work with the children of the streets out of a genuine wish to do something useful with her life. That she had hoped for Carpenter's friendship is not unlikely: they worked closely together and shared a home. While Carpenter's letters indicate that she had neither the time for, nor the interest in, a close friendship with Cobbe, they do not support the suggestion that Cobbe offended Carpenter by proposing a lesbian relationship. If anything, Carpenter's letters indicate a warmth and concern for Cobbe's welfare. However, Carpenter made it clear that she could not alter her ascetic way of life at Red Lodge to accommodate Cobbe's needs. By December 1859, Carpenter advised Cobbe that, as meals and work arrangements did not suit her, she should think of moving elsewhere. Her tone remained friendly as Carpenter tried to bring their work relationship to an amicable end:

I am truly grieved to be the cause of disappointment to you, but, dear friend, I cannot find out that anything is my fault about it. Much as I love and admire you, I have long perceived, and I thought you did so too, that your particular gifts and talents have not their true development in the work of these schools ... . The injury which my mode of living does to your health is a definite reason why you should feel it necessary to remove from my roof ... do not think that there has been any change in my feelings or affections towards you, except of greater anxiety from seeing you suffer and not being able to relieve you.[53]

There was no acrimony between the two women. In 1862 Cobbe praised her former colleague as 'the woman whose philanthropy has been the most perfect ...'[54], and in 1865 Carpenter wrote a lengthy letter to Cobbe indicating her keen understanding of Cobbe's strengths:

> You tried to do something to alleviate the evil but were physically hindered. But your philosopher's mind and literary talents combined with your womanly and loving nature would enable you to do an infinitely greater good to the country by writing.[55]

Upon leaving Red Lodge, Cobbe together with Miss Elliot, daughter of the late Dean of Bristol, published and circulated pamphlets drawing attention to the needs of destitute incurables, and her 'Workhouse Sketches', published in *Macmillan's Magazine*, was the first article for which she earned money - she was paid £14. She was critical of 'the men who ... managed the pauper system', arguing that their attempts to train girls *en masse* 'to be general servants, nurses, cooks or anything else'[56] could not possibly succeed in workhouses which had been designed for quite another purpose. Without proper training, many girls brought up in the workhouses of London found it impossible to keep jobs in service, and eventually ended up on the streets. Cobbe and Miss Elliot began to give Sunday School classes at the Elliot home, to support girls recently gone into service from the workhouse, believing the girls were particularly vulnerable at this stage.

In addition to charity work, Cobbe continued to make occasional journeys abroad. She particularly liked Italy, visiting it six times between 1857 and 1879. On two of these trips she acted as correspondent to the *Daily News*, once from Florence and once from Rome. In Florence she knew the Brownings, Harriet Beecher Stowe and Theodore Parker. In Rome she met a number of distinguished women, including the actress Charlotte Cushman and the sculptors Harriet Hosmer and Emma Stebbins, who shared 'a handsome house in the Via Gregoriana'.[57] In 1858 or 1859, Cushman introduced Cobbe to Mary Lloyd, a friend of Mary

Somerville's, and the acquaintance was renewed two years later at Aix-les-Bains.

In 1860 or 1861, Mary Lloyd bought 26 Hereford Square, in South Kensington, and Cobbe came to live with her. Cobbe felt that she 'had once more a home and a most happy one',[58] and the two women lived at Hereford Square for twenty-five years, before retiring to Lloyd's family home in Wales.

Happily settled in London, Cobbe's career as a writer flourished. With the exception of *Essays on the Pursuits of Women* (1863), her earliest books reflected her theological interests and appeared in quick succession. *Thanksgiving* (1863), *Religious Duty* (1864), *Broken Lights* (1864), *The Cities of the Past* (1864), *Italics* (1864) and *Studies New and Old on Ethical and Social Subjects* (1864) all appeared within the space of two years, during which time her interest in the oppression of women was also evident. In 1862 she entered the contemporary debate about 'surplus women' with two incisive articles for *Fraser's Magazine*: 'Celibacy v. marriage' and 'What shall we do with our old maids?' The latter was written in response to an article suggesting that women without gainful employment were 'in no sense redundant' since they 'discharge a most important and indispensible function in life ... they minister to men'.[59] The article continued that since the 'excess of women over twenty years of age in Great Britain in 1851 was 405,000' these women should be exported to the colonies where there was a shortage of single women of marriageable age.[60] In 'Celibacy v. marriage' Cobbe argued that celibacy should be a viable option for women: specifically, they should be in a position to earn their own bread should they desire to remain single. In 'What shall we do with our old maids?' she challenged the assumption that 'all efforts to make celibacy easy for women are labours in a wrong direction'[61], and launched a scathing attack on the proposal that 'marriage, the only true vocation for women, [should] be promoted at any cost, even by the most enormous schemes for the deportation of 440,000 females'.[62]

Cobbe's articles made her known to the various branches of the women's movement in London, and in the same year she wrote one of her most important essays, 'The education of women, and how it would be affected by university examinations', presented at the National Association for the Promotion of Social Science Congress in London.[63] In this, the first public call for university education for women, Cobbe argued that the fate of upper-class women was 'the wretchedness of an empty brain' and 'the most deplorable depreciation of character',[64] since their education in 'trivial accomplishments' fitted them for no worthwhile employment. She dismissed the well-worn argument that 'there is a natural incompatibility between classical studies and feminine duties'.[65] With brisk logic she concluded:

> Education is, after all, only what its etymology implies - the educing, the drawing out, of the powers of the individual. If we, then, draw out a woman's powers to the very uttermost, we shall only educe her womanliness.[66]

In the 1860s and the 1870s Cobbe particpated in various strands of the women's movement as a member of the Kensington Discussion Society, the Married Women's Property Committee, and, from 1872 to 1879, as a member of the Executive Committee of the London National Society for Women's Suffrage.[67] She read papers to the Kensington Discussion Society, the National Association for the Promotion of Social Science (NAPSS), and the Women's Education Union,[68] and she published at least twenty books and hundreds of articles. Her books continued to explore her theological interests, while her journalism included articles on female celibacy, wife torture, the higher education of women, the duties of daughters, suffrage, and anti-vivisection.[69] She was published in the *Spectator*, *Economist*, *Reader*, *Macmillan's Magazine*, *Fraser's Magazine* and the *Contemporary Review*.

Barbara Caine, noting Cobbe's criticism of the treatment of women by doctors, clerics and social theorists, argues that

> ... in her recognition of the connection between the many different forms of female oppression evident within the family, the Church, and the intellectual and professional worlds, Cobbe came closer to propounding a theory of patriarchy than did any other Victorian feminist. [70]

Cobbe's autobiography does not offer a precise chronology of her interests and publications during the 1860s and 1870s. However, from correspondence with Emily Davies[71] it appears that Cobbe was a well-known member of the feminist circle, while her journalism indicates a sustained commitment to the diverse interests of the women's movement.[72] She contributed a regular 'leader' to the *Echo*, for which she commanded an annual fee of £300,[73] and thus she could carry 'the ideas of the movement to the world at large'.[74] However, as Caine has noted, since many of the journals of the women's movement could not afford to pay for Cobbe's services as a professional journalist, the quantity of material she published in support of the movement is not itself indicative of her considerable personal involvement.

Although Cobbe strove to widen opportunities for her sex, she believed that they had certain duties to which freedom must be sacrificed. In 1865 she read a paper to the Kensington Discussion Society on 'The limits of obedience in daughters'. Cobbe, doubtless influenced by her years at Newbridge, argued that a daughter has an obligation to her parents, above that which she has towards her spouse, to satisfy demands for companionship or nursing. Parents, she believed, were entitled to demand self-sacrifice from their child, but had no right to impinge upon young adults' freedom to choose reading matter, a career, a set of beliefs, or a spouse. In 'Self-development and self-abnegation', she reinforced her position, arguing that a son was as bound by filial duty as a daughter, and that parents were no more entitled to command one than the other.

At this early stage in Cobbe's professional career we see the polarities of her feminist thought. On the one hand, women had duties, and their duties defined the female role. On the other hand, they should have autonomy to negotiate these roles and to reject laws and customs which subordinated them to men.

In 1868 she attacked marriage under the common law in 'Criminals, idiots, women and minors',[75] one of her better-known articles. The prose is lucid, with a witty use of allegory and a veneer of cynicism. The title refers to 'the four categories under which persons are now excluded from many civil, and all political rights in England'.[76] The injustice of this, Cobbe wrote, 'appears most distinctly ... in the regulation of the property of married women under the common law':

By the common law of England a married woman has not legal existence, so far as property is concerned, independently of her husband. The husband and wife are assumed to be one person, and that person is the husband. The wife can make no contract, and can neither sue nor be sued. Whatever she possess of personal property at the time of her marriage, or whatever she may afterwards earn or inherit, belongs to her husband, without control on her part.

This law affected

... only two classes of women, viz. those who marry hurriedly or without proper advisers, and those whose property at the time of marriage is too small to permit of the expense of a settlement; in other words, the whole middle and lower ranks of women, and a certain portion of the upper ranks.[77]

Since parents wealthy enough to afford the legal costs could and did protect their daughters' property against the common law, Cobbe asked why the rule 'is generally considered expedient, yet invariably evaded by all who have means to evade it?'[78] The women most affected were those who had no means of survival should their husbands fail to maintain them. Their vulnerability was a consequence of both their socio-economic position and their sex. Cobbe considered it the duty of the 'women of the upper classes in England' to 'obtain influence in public spheres' and relieve 'the miserable oppression, the bitter griefs, the cruel wrongs [their] sister women are doomed to suffer, and which might be relieved and righted by better legislation'.[79] To Cobbe, herself a single woman of independent means, the category of 'women less fortunate' ultimately included all those who were married, since the legal framework of marriage contributed to women's oppression.[80] She wrote extensively about marriage, criticising the marriage contract for including, in addition to the mutual vows of 'conjugal union' and 'fidelity', a third vow which 'is not mutual ... the vow of conjugal obedience ... . ' She found no grounds for accepting that wives should take this third vow, concluding one lecture with a dismissal of the proffered grounds of 'expediency':

> My dear Friends! Will you please tell me did you ever hear of any sort of despotism ... which was not justified by those who exercised it on ... [the] grounds of expediency.[81]

The legal system also deprived married women of protection in cases of marital violence. Cobbe saw these issues as inextricably linked with suffrage. 'It is one of the sore grievances of women in particular, that, not possessing representation, the measures which concern them are forever postponed ... .'[82] Women, lacking political rights, became the property of their husbands, a situation which was 'the fatal root of incalculable evil'.[83]

Many women involved in the married women's property campaign were members of other women's rights organisations during the 1860s. In 1865-66, Emily Davies formed the Kensington Discussion Society, which brought together women who were interested in the social, educational and economic advancement of their sex. Cobbe joined the society which, in November 1865, debated the desirability of the extension of the parliamentary franchise to women.[84] Emily Davies was reluctant to organise a campaign for the vote, believing it would damage the campaign for women's education, but by 1866 Barbara Bodichon had gathered 1,499 signatures on a petition for women's suffrage, including Cobbe's, and J S Mill presented it to Commons on 7 June 1866.

The year 1866-7 saw much activity among feminists, as women's suffrage committees were formed in Manchester, London and Edinburgh. As noted above, Cobbe was an active member of the London National Society for Womens' Suffrage and was on its executive in the 1870s. However, her interests at this time were focused primarily on married women's property reform, and, later, on drafting a Bill to protect women who were victims of 'aggravated assaults' by their husbands.

Throughout the 1870s, Cobbe continued to write on moral and theological themes, publishing six more books:

Darwinism in Morals and Other Essays (1872), *Doomed to Be Saved* (1874), *Essays on Life and Death and the Evolution of Moral Sentiment* (1874), *The Hopes of the Human Race* (1874), *The Moral Aspects of Vivisection* (1875), *False Beasts and True* (1876), and a number of her articles for the *Echo* were collected in *Re-Echoes* (1876). Her work increasingly reflected an interest in the anti-vivisection movement, an interest which soon occupied much of her time and eventually isolated her from her feminist friends. However, before devoting the 1880s to the prevention of cruelty to animals, Cobbe turned to the prevention of cruelty to women. This was the part of her work for women on which she would look back with greatest satisfaction.[85]

In 1878, reading in the newspaper of a series of brutal assaults on women, Cobbe resolved to do something. Her approach to her task was characteristically systematic and thorough: she studied the statistics in the Home Secretary's report of 1875, and gathered details of cases of wife-beating. This report clearly indicated that the law relating to such assaults was insufficient, yet no moves had been made to amend it, and women, having no vote, could 'only exceptionally and through favour, bring pressure to bear to force attention even to the most crying injustices under which they suffer[ed]'.[86] Cobbe's statistics indicated that, on average, about 1,500 serious assaults on women were reported every year in England, and, in a widely circulated article, 'Wife-torture in England' (*Contemporary Review*, 1878) she published the results of her research. This article had a dramatic impact on public opinion, and 'was widely recognised as the inspiration for the Matrimonial Causes Act of 1878'.[87]

'Wife-torture in England' indicates that Cobbe believed that society was a gender-based organisation, built on legislation which oppressed women. While she believed in the sanctity of marriage and in 'the potential motherhood in every woman's heart', the marriage laws deprived women of any vestige of individuality and offered virtually no possibility of escape in cases of 'aggravated assault'. Lest her readers did not understand the extent of this problem, she described cases of brutal violence, and explained that 'aggravated assault' meant 'a great deal more than a simple blow. It [meant] knocking out an eye, clogging with hob-nailed boot (i.e. kicking or standing on the woman), setting her on fire, breaking her ribs, throwing a paraffin lamp at her, etc.'[88] She was scathing of those who trivialised the problem of wife-beating:

> [Wife-beating] seems to be surrounded by a certain halo of jocosity which incites people to smile whenever they hear of a case of it (terminating in anything short of actual murder), and causes the mention of the subject to conduce rather than otherwise to the hilarity of a dinner party.[89]

Cobbe's analysis led to the conclusion that, once again, the law could be circumvented by women with money, while working-class women were powerless. Women who could afford it could obtain a judicial separation (on proof of cruelty) under the 1857 Divorce Act.[90] Cobbe demanded

> ... the extension of the privilege of rich women to their poorer sisters, to be effected by an Act of Parliament which should give a wife whose husband had been convicted of aggravated assault on her, the power to obtain a separation order under summary jurisdiction.[91]

She attacked the indifference of politicians to violence against women, pointing out that in May 1874 an appeal had been made to the House of Commons for increased punishment for aggravated assaults on women, and Disraeli had promised an investigation. The resulting report of 1875 had recommended that punishment should be increased and flogging introduced, yet the report remained unheeded by Parliament.

> During the interval scores of Bills, on every sort and kind of question interesting to the represented sex, have passed through Parliament; but this question, on which the lives of women literally hang, has never been even mooted ... . Something like 6,000 women, judging by the judicial statistics, have been in the intervening years 'brutally assaulted' - that is, maimed, blinded, trampled, burned, and in no inconsiderable number of instances murdered outright.[92]

Cobbe did not see flogging as the solution. It relied on the woman testifying against her husband, from whom she might then expect further cruelty. Instead, all women should have the means to obtain a judicial separation:

> A Bill should, I think, be passed, affording to these poor women [the] means ... to obtain from the court which sentences their husbands a protection order, which should in their case have the same validity as a judicial separation. In addition to this, the custody of the children should be given to the wife, and an order should be made for the husband to pay the wife such weekly sum for her own and her children's maintenance as the court may see fit.[93]

Cobbe's proposal, which focused on helping the victim rather than on punishing the offender, was drafted into a Bill and, with a few changes,[94] became the Matrimonial Causes Act of 1878. This amended the Divorce Act of 1857, which allowed magistrates to grant protection orders only in cases of desertion. Additionally, it gave a magistrate discretionary authority to award the mother custody of her children, while the husband was obliged to support his wife and children.

The evidence indicates that the Act did help to reduce crimes of violence against women.[95] It also called into question contemporary ideology which supported the notion that a husband had authority over his wife's body and, together with the Summary Jurisdiction (Married Women) Act of 1895, it marked the partial acceptance by Parliament that the obligations of marriage had to be mutual and reciprocal, rather than enforced by brutality and oppressive legislation. 'Wife-torture' was written as Cobbe was becoming increasingly committed to the anti-vivisection campaign,[96] which she saw as allied to the women's movement. 'Women,' she noted, 'like animals, were subject to the power and the callousness of doctors and scientists and the brutality of many men.'[97]

While Cobbe retained an interest in the women's campaign for the remainder of her life, the 1870s saw her devoting more and more time to the anti-vivisection movement. She expected the support of her feminist friends, but found that not all of them shared her antipathy to animal experimentation. Although an early supporter of Emily Davies and university education for women, Cobbe became involved in a controversy about vivisection at Girton College which brought her friendship with Davies to a bitter end in the late 1870s.

Cobbe's interest in anti-vivisection was evident as early as 1863, when she 'led the English community in Florence against the experiments of Moritz Schiff, Professor of Physiology at the Royal Superior Institute'.[98] Strong connections between the anti-vivisection campaign and nineteenth-century female philanthropic movements have been noted. Richard French's examination of the prospectuses of anti-vivisection societies showed that 'their leadership - patrons, vice-presidents, and executive com- mittee members - was anywhere from 40 to 60 per cent female'.[99] French argues that for Cobbe, the anti-vivisection movement promoted the public image of contemporary feminists because it 'permitted a de-emphasis of the noisy demanding of rights ... while publicly demonstrating female capabilities, and providing women with unprecedented opportunities for administrative and quasi-political experience'.[100] In *The Duties of Women*, Cobbe wrote that every woman 'who works wisely and well for any good (whether the cause directly concerns female interests or not) does her share in thus lifting up the womanhood of the nation'.

Cobbe's aggressive and tireless promotion of the anti- vivisectionist position began formally in 1875, when she attempted to mobilise the Royal Society for the Prevention of Cruelty to Animals (RSPCA) into restricting the practice of vivisection. She drew up a memorial to its committee, which she circulated, together with her two pamphlets, *Reasons for Interference* and *Need of a Bill*, to a large number of influential people. Her reputation as a journalist, and her wide circle of personal acquaintances, including W E H Lecky, J A Froude, James Martineau and many eminent clergymen, assured her of a favourable response. She gathered over 600 signatures, although the movement failed, in the long term, to attract widespread religious support.[101] Cobbe's memorial was signed by such influential men as Martineau, Ruskin, Carlyle, Lecky, Tennyson, Browning, the Archbishop of York and the Archbishop of Westminster.[102] It resulted in Cobbe being invited to the first meeting of the RSPCA sub-committee for vivisection, of which she later wrote:

> On entering the room my spirits sank, for I saw round the table a number of worthy gentleman, most elderly, but ... they were not the men to take the lead in such a movement and make a bold stand against the claims of science.[103]

Impatient with the RSPCA, she again made good use of her connections to have a bill to regulate the practice of vivisection[104] drafted and presented in the House of Lords on 4 May 1875. The anti-vivisection campaign drew oppositon from scientists and medical men, including Charles Darwin, who had refused to sign Cobbe's memorial, and T H Huxley.

Public interest in the controversy continued to swell. A Royal Commission on vivisection began its hearings in August 1875.[105] Cobbe did not testify, causing the movement's historian to write:

> The connoisseur of anti vivisectionist *élan* must always regret that history was deprived of the spectacle of a rotund, forceful, and articulate Frances Power Cobbe lecturing the eminent commissioners on the evils of scientific experiment on living animals. Cobbe would have acquitted herself as well as any witness, and better than most.[106]

In 1876, Cobbe became president of her newly formed Society for the Protection of Animals Liable to Vivisection, soon to be known as the Victoria Street Society. The Society's pre-eminence over other London societies was due to its tireless and articulate president, who is considered to have been 'the most influential of anti vivisection personalities'.[107]

While Cobbe's early endeavours drew widespread praise, she eventually became the object of criticism. In an age of scientific experiment her opinions were often considered narrow and sentimental. Within the movement, some of her contemporaries saw her as domineering and attention-seeking.[108] When she engineered the amalgamation of the Victoria Street Society and the International Association for the Total Suppression of Vivisection in 1883, she retained her dominant position over the new and more powerful organisation.

Conflict within the movement reduced its efficacy. There was little room for fresh ideas whereby the movement might expand its constituency, and her uncompromising stand - that vivisection should be completely outlawed - lost popular support.

In 1892 Cobbe wrote the preface to a Victoria Street publication, *The Nine Circles of the Hell of the Innocent*. It became the subject of much controversy when Victor Hornsley, a neurosurgeon, pointed out its systematic omission of references to the use of anaesthetics in the experiments it cited from research literature. Cobbe's credibility was seriously damaged, although her participation in the publication had been minimal. She had not compiled the offending text and in her preface had clearly stated: 'So far as it has been possible the use or absence of anaesthetics has been noted in regard to all the experiments cited in this book.'[109]

Accused of deliberate falsehood, at a time when popular support for anti-vivisection was waning, her influence over the movement lessened. The *British Medical Journal* carried articles castigating the 'singularly dogmatic and abusive writings' of Cobbe,[110] and arguing that vivisection was 'morally justifiable and ... essential to the progress of knowledge'.[111] By the end of the decade, the Society had decided to accept legislation which would allow experiments to be conducted on animals under anaesthetic. Cobbe, whose refusal to compromise on this issue had caused her to split with the women's movement, resigned from the Victoria Street Society.

In 1884 she and Mary Lloyd moved to North Wales, and the following year her anti-vivisectionist friends gathered the sum of one thousand pounds which, when invested, provided Cobbe with an annuity of one hundred pounds. She returned the annuity to the Society in 1901 when, unexpectedly, she was left residuary legatee by a wealthy widow who supported the anti-vivisection movement. Cobbe found herself 'a rich woman', able to supply the money to maintain Hengwrt, Lloyd's handsome home which they had been obliged to lease out for many years.

Two years after their retirement, Mary Lloyd died. In a letter to Millicent Garrett Fawcett, Cobbe wrote: 'The end of such a friendship - 34 years of mutual affection - is of course almost a mortal blow.'[112] Isolated from many of her friends in both the women's movement and the anti-vivisection campaign, Cobbe spent her last years at Hengwrt working on her autobiography. She died in 1904.

Barbara Caine argues that the nineteenth-century women's movement was for Frances Cobbe 'essentially a philanthropic movement to help women less fortunate than herself'.[113] In this respect Cobbe shared much of the vision of her predecessor Hannah More. Both argued for improvement in the education of women to make them better wives and mothers to the benefit of society as a whole. Both believed that women were particularly suited to philanthropic work and that 'women's mission was the moral and spiritual regeneration of society'.[114]

Cobbe, however, broadened female philanthropy to include 'above all the cause of their own sex, and the relief of the misery of their own sisters'.[115] Where More approved of the patriarchal family, ruled by a father whose benevolence and self-control was a measure of the good influence of his pious and hardworking wife, Cobbe did not believe that women should have to cajole men into good humour, writing of the dreaded atmosphere in the home of the domineering *paterfamilias* in 'Tarry-at-home husbands'.[116]

Although well known in her own lifetime, she did not lead or become identified exclusively with any one feminist campaign. As a consequence, her contribution has been largely ignored. Limits of space allow only an overview of Cobbe's published work here; nevertheless, the diversity of her interests, and the wit and precision with which she constructed an argument, are evident in even a small sample of her writings. These talents were appreciated by colleagues and supporters, including Lady Elisabeth Eastlake, who wrote to Cobbe:

There is no one else who so combines the right thought and the right manner. Few women have the gift of humour, - none, I ever heard of, possess it in the degree that you do. Thus you command the weapons of argument at both ends. No candid mind can fail to be struck with the moral ingenuity as well as humanity and rectitude of your pleas.[117]

Cobbe was very conscious of how her sex limited her opportunities for using her abilities.

> Had I been a man, and had possessed my brother's facilities for entering parliament or any profession, I have sometimes dreamed that I could have made my mark and done some masculine service to my fellow-creatures.[118]

While her contribution to animal and human rights was considerable, contemporary conventions limited a woman's activities, and hers was not in her own eyes, a 'masculine service'. Her love of scholarship, travel, politics and the family estate in Ireland would have had a different and greater scope for expression had she been a man. These interests she shared with her father, and Harriet St Leger once told her, 'You know, *you* are your father's son!'[119] During her visit to Newbridge in the 1860s, she wrote:

> Sometimes it comes over me there in the stately old rooms and beautiful gardens that I was born a gentlewoman and have rather made a downfall in becoming a hack, scribbling for a halfpenny newspaper! But the scribbler is happier than ever the idle lady was (if indeed I ever was), and my regrets end in a laugh.[120]

Nineteenth-century women were defined by relationships to men: their class was that of their father or, after marriage, their husband, and they were either wives, widows or spinsters. Choosing to live with another woman, and earning her living in the public sphere, Cobbe threw off the gendered constraints of nineteenth-century life and virtually re-invented herself. She lived a full life, travelled widely, had a successful career in journalism, and, with the exception of George Eliot and Harriet Martineau, knew 'all the more gifted Englishwomen of the Victorian era.'[121] She had many male friends and colleagues, including J S Mill and Charles Darwin, and enjoyed their company and conversation. Yet she wrote:

... with all their kindly feelings, their good intentions, their
readiness to labour and sacrifice themselves for women,
men give us most rarely that which we really want, not
favour, but - *Justice*.[122]

Cobbe does not appear to have had direct contacts with Irish
feminists, despite the close links between feminist
organisations in Ireland and Britain during her career, and
the fact that virtually all contemporary Irish feminists came,
like Cobbe, from Protestant middle- or upper-class
backgrounds. Nor does the *Life* indicate much interest in
Irish politics. She mentions her dislike of Gladstone,
believing his opposition to the emancipation of women had
adversely affected the suffrage question, and adds that, as a
member of the Anglo-Irish landowning class, she was
strongly opposed to Home Rule. Her autobiography
indicates that, once settled in England, she did not maintain
contact with Ireland, although she took a holiday at
Newbridge at least once during the 1860s.[123]

Yet her legacy was to Irish as well as to British women.
The position of married women under the common law was
essentially the same for both.[124] Her writing contributed an
analysis of the power relationship between husbands and
wives which pivoted on the crucial issue of the financial
dependency of the wife. This left a wife dependent on her
husband's continued good humour for her happiness and
well-being.

Cobbe's examination of the ripple-effect of the
relationship of dependency led her to write on all the major
concerns of the women's movement. She challenged the legal
system which 'subsumed women under the spousal
authority and identity of their husbands';[125] she confronted
the problem of wife-abuse and initiated a change in
legislation (the Matrimonial Causes Act, 1878), and she
supported the suffrage movement and the campaign for
higher education for women. All these contributed to the
cause of Irish as well as British women.

It is also important to place her in Irish history and the
history of Irish women. Her feminist formation was
developed in Ireland during the first thirty-five years of her
life. Also, during the second half of the nineteenth century,

under the Act of Union the campaigns of British and Irish feminists inevitably became linked. This link was more easily recognised and developed by women from the Protestant Anglo-Irish community, whether they worked in Ireland or Britain.

In Cobbe's lifetime the word 'feminist' had not gained currency in England,[126] but it seems unlikely that she would have rejected the label; she adapted for herself the motto: *Mulier sum. Nihil muliebre a me alienum puto.*[127] - 'I am a woman. Nothing concerning the interests of women is alien to me.'

NOTES

1 For a comprehensive selection of the papers of the nineteenth-century women's movement, see Lacey, Candida Ann. 1989. *Barbara Leigh Smith and the Langham Place Group*. London. Important studies of the movement include Strachey, Ray. 1928. repr. 1978. *The Cause: a Short History of the Women's Movement in Great Britain*. London; Rendall, Jane. 1985. *The Origins of Modern Feminism*. Basingstoke; and Levine, Phillip. 1990. *Feminist Lives in Victorian England*. Oxford.

2 Bryant, Margaret. 1979. *The Unexpected Revolution*. London, p.35.

3 Hollis, Patricia. 1979. *Women in Public, 1850-1900*. London, p.33.

4 Emily Davies founded Hitchin College in 1869 and it transferred to Girton, Cambridge, in 1873. The first three 'Girton pioneers' took Tripos in 1873 by private arrangements with the examiners. In 1881 women were admitted to Cambridge University undergraduate examinations on the same terms as men. See McWilliams Tullberg, Rita. 1975. *Women at Cambridge*. London; and Stephen, B 1933. *Girton College 1869-1932*. Cambridge.

5 Bodichon, Barbara. 1854. 'A brief summary in plain language of the most important laws concerning women'. In Hollis, *Women in Public*, pp174, 176.

6 The lives of these and other Victorian feminists have been documented in: Cooke, Sir Edward. 1913. *The Life of Florence Nightingale*. 2 Vols., London; Woodham-Smith, Cecil. 1950. *Florence Nightingale, 1820-1910*. London; Stephen, Barbara. 1927. *Emily Davies and Girton College*. London; Strachey, Ray. 1931. *Millicent Garrett Fawcett*. London; Maurice, Edmund C 1913. *Life of Octavia Hill as Told in her Letters*. London; Manton, Jo. 1976. *Mary Carpenter and the Children of the Streets*. London; Uglow, Jennifer. 1983. 'Josephine Butler: from sympathy to theory', in Spender, Dale (ed.). *Feminist Theorists: Three Centuries of Women's Intellectual Traditions*. London; Burton, Hester. 1949. *Barbara Bodichon, 1827-1891*. London; and Herstein, S R 1986. *A Mid-Victorian Feminist, Barbara Leigh Smith Bodichon*. London.

7 Caine, Barbara. 1992. *Victorian Feminists*, Oxford. See also Caskie, Helen. 1981. 'Frances Power Cobbe: Victorian feminist', unpublished typescript available at Fawcett Library, London.

8 Spender, Dale. 1982. *Women of Ideas and What Men Have Done to Them*. London; Todd, Janet. 1989. *Dictionary of British Women Writers*. London.

9 Cobbe, Frances Power. 1894. *Life of Frances Power Cobbe, 2 vols*. London. Reprinted 1904 with an introduction by Blanche Atkinson. Hereafter, *Life*, (1894) and *Life*, (1904).

10 Cobbe to Lydia Becker, 12 June, no year, Manchester Public Library, NUWSS Collection, M50/1. 2/49, quoted by Caine, p.111.

11 Cobbe, *Life*, (1894), I, p.5.

12 Blanche Atkinson, introduction to *Life*, (1904), p.v.

13 Frances Power Cobbe Papers, Huntington Library, San Marino,

California. Items from these papers are reproduced by permission of the Huntington Library, San Marino, California.

14 Bodleian Library, Oxford: Sommerville Collection; MS. Autog. b. 11; MS Autog. c.18; MS Autog. d.32; MS Acland d.98; Taylor Family Papers; Michael Field Papers. British Library London: MS 39809; MS 46625; BL 45.747; BL 44785; BL 43910.

15 Emily Davies Papers, Girton College Archives. Barbara Bodichon Papers, Girton College Archives. The cooperation of the Mistress and Fellows of Girton College and of Kate Perry, archivist, is gratefully acknowledged.

16 National Library of Wales, Minor Deposits, 1309-1316 15A: seven volumes of the writings of Frances Power Cobbe.

17 See Lesbian History Group (eds.). 1989. *Not a Passing Phase: Reclaiming Lesbians in History 1840-1985*. London.

18 This point is developed in Sylvia H. Myres. 1990. *The Bluestocking Circle*. Oxford.

19 Faderman, Lillian. 1981. *Surpassing the Love of Men: Romantic Friendship and Love Between Women from the Renaissance to the Present*. London, p.121.

20 *Ibid.*, p.122.

21 For a full discussion of the Woods and Pirie trial, see *ibid.*, pp147-54.

22 *Life*, (1904), p.708.

23 For a discussion of lesbian sexuality in history, see Lesbian History Group, *Not a Passing Phase*.

24 *Burke's Landed Gentry in Ireland*. See also *Dictionary of National Biography*; Mant, Richard. 1840. *History of the Church of Ireland from the Reformation to the Revolution*. 2 vols. London, pp637-40; Cotton, Henry. 1847-60. *Fasti Eccl. Hiberniae*. Dublin, ii, 24.iii, 187. iv, 74.

25 *Life*, (1894) I, p.9.

26 Throughout the nineteenth century, the archbishopric of Tuam was held by members of the aristocracy. At one stage three members of the Beresford family were bishops of Tuam, Cork and Kilmore respectively. See McCartney, Donal. 1987. *The Dawning of Democracy: Ireland 1800-1870*. Dublin, p.28.

27 *Life*, (1894) I. p.15.

28 *Ibid.* See also *Report of the Royal Commission to Inquire into Endowments, Funds and Condition of Schools Endowed for the Purpose of Education in Ireland*. HC 1857-1858. XXII. Pt.I. p.160.

29 *Life*, (1904) pp63-4.

30 *Ibid.*, p.25.

31 *Ibid.*, p.168.

32 *Ibid.*, p.207.

33 *Ibid.*

34 *Ibid.*, p.137.

35 *Ibid.*, p.142.

36 *Ibid.*, (1894) I. p.155.

37 *Ibid.*, (1904) p.187.

38 *Ibid.*, p.158.

39 *Ibid.*, pp158, 159.

40 *Ibid.*, p.81.

41 *Ibid.*, pp97-8.

42 Cobbe Papers, CB 657-673. Huntington Library. Cobbe, Frances Power, (ed). 1863. *The Collected Works of Theodore Parker*. London.

43 Caine, *Victorian Feminists*, p.116.

44 *Life*, (1904) p.170.

45 *Ibid.*, p.171.

46 See Astell, Mary. 1694. *A Serious Proposal to the Ladies*; More, Hannah. 1799. *Strictures on the Modern System of Female Education*; and Wollstonecraft, Mary. 1792. *A Vindication of the Rights of Woman*.

47 *Life*, (1894) I. p.114.

48 *Ibid.*, p.220.

49 Cobbe Papers, CB 70-89, Huntington Library.

50 Manton, *Mary Carpenter*, p.148.

51 *Life*, (1894) I, p.197.

52 Manton, *Mary Carpenter*, p.148.

53 Mary Carpenter to Frances Power Cobbe, 6 December 1859. Cobbe Papers, Huntington Library.

54 Cobbe. 1862. 'The education of women, and how it would be affected by university examinations'. In Spender, Dale. 1987. *The Education Papers*. London, p.40.

55 Mary Carpenter to Frances Power Cobbe, 22 January 1865. Cobbe Papers, Huntington Library.

56 *Life*, (1894) I, p.327.

57 *Ibid.*, II, p.29.

58 *Ibid.*, II, p.32.

59 Greg, W. 1862. 'Why are women redundant?' In *National Review* (April), cited in Hollis, *Women in Public*, p.12.

60 *Ibid.*, p.37.

61 Cobbe. 1862. 'What shall we do with our old maids?' In *Fraser's Magazine*, (November), reprinted in Lacey, *Barbara Leigh Smith*, p.355.

62 *Ibid.*

63 Spender, *The Education Papers*, pp37-49.

64 *Ibid.*, p.38.

65 *Ibid.*, p.40.

66 *Ibid.*, p.41.

67 Reports of the London Society for Women's Suffrage, Women's Suffrage Publications, 1868-1879, Girton College, Blackburn Collection 396.3 W84.

68 See Caine, *Victorian Feminists*, p.125. See also Cobbe. 1861. 'Friendless girls and how to help them', *Transactions of the National Association for the Promotion of Social Science (NAPSS) Congress*; 1862. 'The Education of Women', *ibid*; and 1880 'Duties of Women', *Journal of the Women's Education Union*, VIII, 85, 15 January 1880.

69 Cobbe's published books were: *Essays on the Pursuits of Women* (1863); *Thanksgiving* (1863); *Religious Duty* (1864); *Broken Lights* (1864); *The Cities of the Past* (1864); *Italics* (1864); *Studies New and Old on Ethical and Social Subjects* (1864); *Hours of Work and Play* (1867); *Dawning Lights, Secular Results of the New Reformation* (1868);

Darwinism in Morals and Other Essays (1872); *Doomed to Be Saved* (1874); *Essays on Life and Death and the Evolution of Moral Sentiment* (1874); *The Hopes of the Human Race* (1874); *The Moral Aspects of Vivisection* (1875); *False Beasts and True* (1876); *Re-echoes* (1876); *The Duties of Women* (1881); *The Peak in Darien* (1882); *The Scientific Spirit of the Age* (1888); *The Friend of Man, and his Friends, the Poets* (1889); *Health and Holiness* (1891); *Life, by herself* (1894); *Life of Frances Power Cobbe* (posth., 1904).

70 Caine, *Victorian Feminists*, p.104.

71 *Ibid.*, p.126.

72 Between 1861-1863, articles by Cobbe published in *Fraser's Magazine* and *Macmillan's Magazine* included: 'What shall we do with our old maids?'; 'Female charity, lay and monastic'; 'Women in Italy in 1862'; 'The education of women'; 'Social Science Congresses and women's part in Them'; and 'The fitness of women for the ministry of religion'. *Life*, (1904) pp212, 213. Other papers published in the early 1860s included 'Friendless girls and how to help them' (1862); 'Celibacy v. marriage', *Fraser's Magazine* 65 (1862); and 'Woman's work in the church', *Theological Review* 2 (1865).

73 Cobbe to Mary Somerville, 6 September, no year, Somerville Collection, MSFP II (Bodleian Library). The permission of Lady Fairfax-Lucy, owner of the Somerville Papers, to refer to the Cobbe Letters is gratefully acknowledged.

74 Caine, *Victorian Feminists*, p.105.

75 Cobbe, 'Criminals, idiots, women and minors', *Fraser's Magazine* 78, 6 December 1868, pp777-94.

76 *Ibid.*, p.778.

77 *Ibid.*, p.779.

78 *Ibid.*, p.786.

79 Cobbe, *The Duties of Women*, p.156.

80 *Ibid*, p.154.

81 *Ibid.*, p.103.

82 *Ibid.*, p.154

83 Cobbe. 1878. 'Wife-torture in England'. In *Contemporary Review* 32, April, p.62.

84 See Lyndon Shanley, Mary. 1989. *Feminism, Marriage, and the Law in Victorian England, 1850-1895*. London, p.51.

85 *Life*, (1894) II, p.218.

86 *Ibid.*, p.220.

87 Shanley, *Feminism, Marriage*, p.165. In support of her point, Shanley cites the *Englishwomen's Review* 66, 15 October 1878, pp433, 434. See also Bauer, Carol and Ritt, Lawrence. 1983. 'A husband Is a beating animal': Frances Power Cobbe confronts the wife-abuse problem in Victorian England'. In *International Journal of Women's Studies* 6, 2, March/April, p.114.

88 Cobbe, *The Duties of Women*, p.4.

89 Cobbe, 'Wife-torture', pp56, 57.

90 20 & 21 Vict. c.85, Section 16.

91 *Life*, (1894) II. p.221.

92 Cobbe, 'Wife-torture' p.79.

93 *Ibid.*, p.82.

94 See Shanley, *Feminism, Marriage,* p.169.

95 *Ibid.*, pp170-71.

96 The middle of the nineteenth century saw increasing public interest in medical science, and the emerging controversy over vivisection. Richard D French, in *Antivivisection and Medical Science in Victorian England* (Princeton, 1975) noted that the 'leading actors' in the controversy included the Cambridge physiologist Michael Foster, and John Colam, secretary of the RSPCA, yet it was 'the somewhat improbable figure of Frances Power Cobbe who ... became in the public mind the personification of antivivisection', pp61, 62.

97 Caine, *Victorian Feminists*, p.138.

98 French, *Antivivsection*, p.62.

99 *Ibid.*, p.239.

100 *Ibid.*, p.245.

101 *Ibid.*, ch.10.

102 *Ibid.*, p.65. See also 'Memorial against vivisection', *Animal World* 6, (1875), p.38.

103 *Life*, (1894) II. pp577-8.

104 French, *Antivivisection*, p.69.

105 *Ibid.*, p.79.

106 *Ibid.*, pp101-2.

107 *Ibid.*, p.222.

108 *Ibid.*, p.223.

109 Cobbe. 1892. *The Nine Circles of the Hell of the Innocent.* London, p.xi.

110 *British Medical Journal,* 6 August 1892, p.317.

111 *Ibid.*, 3 December 1892, p.1255.

112 Cobbe to Millicent Garrett Fawcett, 11 November 1896, Autograph Collection, vol.8, part 6, Fawcett Library, London, quoted in Caine, *Victorian Feminists*, p.129.

113 Caine, Barbara. 1982. 'Feminism, suffrage and the nineteenth-century English women's movement'. In *Women's Studies International Forum* 5, 6, p.547.

114 French, *Antivivisection*, p.241.

115 Cobbe, *The Duties of Women*, p.160.

116 Cobbe. 1876. 'Tarry-at-home husbands'. In *Re-Echoes.*

117 Elizabeth Eastlake to Cobbe. 18 April, 1889, Cobbe Papers, Huntington Library.

118 *Life*, (1904) pp4-5.

119 *Ibid.*, p.4

120 Cobbe to Mary Somerville, 6 September, (186-?). Somerville Collection, MSFP II, Bodleian Library.

121 *Life*, (1894) II. p.204.

122 Cobbe, *The Duties of Women*, Introduction. (Her italics.)

123 Somerville Collection, MSFP II, Bodleian Library. Cobbe wrote to Somerville on 6 September, no year (186?), that she had visited her brother for a few weeks.

124 Geary, Nevill. 1892. *The Law of Marriage and Family Relations.*

p.568.

125 Levine, Phillipa. 1990. *Feminist Lives in Victorian England.* Oxford.

126 Offen, Karen. 1988. 'Defining feminism: a comparative historical approach'. In *Signs: Journal of Culture and Society,* xiv, i (Autumn) p.126.

127 *Life*, (1894) II. p.237. (Her italics.)

Anne Jellicoe

(1823-1880)

Anne V O'Connor

When Anne Jellicoe, the Quaker educationalist and philanthropist, died in October 1880, the *Freeman's Journal* summed up her life in the following terms: 'She laboured so untiringly to ennoble her sex that the results of her efforts give her a prominent place in the world's list of women's benefactors.'[1]

Who was this woman and why is she largely forgotten outside the college she founded? Part of the answer lies in the fact that, like many other women of the period, she was simply written out of history. Because Anne Jellicoe was not perceived as being of sufficient importance in nineteenth-century history, those personal details which only she, or her contemporaries, could have supplied were never written down. The only material on her early life comes from obituary notices, or the very sparse records in the Friends' Historical Library based on Lydia Goodbody's diaries.[2] Yet while Jellicoe herself appears to be a very shadowy figure, it is clear from her achievements that she was a most successful woman, and a pioneering figure in the provision of education for women in Ireland.

Born in Mountmellick in 1823, Anne Jellicoe was the daughter of a Quaker schoolmaster, William Mullin, who died when she was three years of age.[3] Little is known about her mother, who died when Anne was seventeen years old. Her father had started a school for boys in Mountmellick in 1820. Although there were twelve schools in Mountmellick in the 1820s the only education available for girls was of an elementary nature.[4] Anne Mullin's name does not appear on the rolls of the Friends' Provincial School in Mountmellick, so it is probable that she, like many middle-class girls of this period, was educated privately by a governess. It may have been this experience that made her aware of the low standard of education among women. This awareness is borne out by a personal letter, dating from 1867, which shows that, from an early age, Jellicoe wanted to ensure the possibility of a college education for girls. In the letter she exclaimed: 'Well, I have carried out one dream, the dream that "pleased my childish thought", the founding of a College.'[5] It appears from subsequent developments that what Anne Jellicoe had in mind initially was a training college for governesses.

Anne Jellicoe's pioneering approach to girls' education owes much to the Quaker tradition in education. According to one authority, Quaker schools of this period 'provided a better education for the middle class and lower ranks of society'. Consequently Quakers, it was claimed, were 'more highly cultured, more broad-minded, and more interested in intellectual matters than the people amongst whom they lived'.[6] This eulogy on Quaker education has to be tempered by the history of the Quaker Provincial School in

126

Mountmellick, which, until 1852, was still far behind English Quaker schools such as York and Ackworth.[7] The distinctive aims of Quaker education were, first, that their schools were to be places of religious and denominational training; and, second, that they should give their pupils a good sound education in secular subjects - such a training as would make them useful in later life.[8] No prizes were given, and all that was thought merely ornamental was uniformly discouraged. Most of these ideas were to play their part in Jellicoe's thinking, especially the principle that schools should give a training which would be useful in adulthood.

Her Quaker background, with its well-established business connections and strongly developed sense of involvement in the local community, also helps explain Jellicoe's initial efforts to assist women find paid work in their homes, first in Mountmellick and later in Clara, County Offaly. Quakers were a minority group in Ireland, and in general were self-confident, prosperous and well educated, believing firmly in the virtues of honesty, thrift and hard work. They had founded the town of Mountmellick where Jellicoe was born, and had given it a prosperity which, in the 1820s and 1830s, earned it the title of the 'Manchester of the Queen's County'.[9] In the 1830s it had an ironworks factory and a starch and blue factory, while its bit and stirrup makers exported their products all over the world. This prosperity was short-lived as a result of the coming of the railways and the influx of cheap mass-manufactured goods from England. Nonetheless, Jellicoe was, unusually in Ireland, the product of an industrialised environment, and would therefore have been aware, perhaps more than other women equally interested in girls' education, of the opportunities in business and industry that would be open to women once they had been provided with the key - a better education.

She also showed herself to be deeply aware of the problems of women's employment. This concern first manifested itself in the 1830s when the weaving and spinning industries, on which many women in Mountmellick depended, went into serious decline and created real hardship. An attempt was made to help them by a Quaker woman, Johanna Carter, who introduced a new style of embroidered white work. She used cotton fabrics and thread which were all available locally and therefore reasonably priced. Her invention became known as

Mountmellick embroidery.[10] The young Jellicoe became interested and helped her by drawing some of the designs for the embroidery work. This experience was to prove very useful when she moved to Clara in 1848, two years after her marriage to John Jellicoe, who had acquired a flour mill in that town.[11]

In 1848 Clara had three flour mills on which the town's economy depended. They were not very labour-intensive and employed men as the heavy work involved made them unsuitable for women.[12] The only possibility of employment for women in Clara in the 1840s came from the cottage weaving industry which provided linen sacks for the Goodbody Flour Mills. Anne Jellicoe set about looking for some way to help the women of the town. Using those skills already acquired, she set up an embroidery school for sewed muslin work in the town in 1850.[13] The sewed muslin trade had been started as a cottage industry in the north of Ireland in 1822, where it was a great help to the small farmers and the labouring classes in rural areas. It did not spread south until 1850, but it then took off with great speed, providing work for an estimated 200,000 Irishwomen annually during the 1850s.[14] Local committees of ladies set up schools to teach lace and crochet skills throughout Ireland, with teachers brought from the north to instruct in these crafts. Many convent schools, especially those run by the Sisters of Mercy and the Presentation Order, quickly became involved in spreading these skills, which led to the establishment of industrial schools. Jellicoe's school was, therefore, part of a remarkable movement started by women to help the destitute of their own sex in the immediate aftermath of the famine. Unfortunately, few records of her school survive.[15]

In the Ireland of the 1850s there was little employment for women, apart from low-paid jobs as domestic servants or needlewomen. Even skilled needlewomen could find few outlets for their talents apart from the infamous shirtmaking factories. These 'grinders of the poor' paid their workers the princely sum of 6d for 'a white shirt highly finished with several rows of the finest stitching on the fronts, collars, and sleeves and which took them nearly two days in the making'.[16]

These facts may explain why Jellicoe closed her sewed muslin school in 1853 and switched to lace crochet work. This skilled craft was just then coming into vogue and offered better returns to the workers at 6 to 10 shillings per week.[17] Ironically, many of the girls from areas such as Cork and Clones, where the crochet schools were highly organised, used the money they made from this work to emigrate, so that they and their skills were lost to Ireland.

In the establishment of the lace crochet school, Jellicoe obtained the help of Lewis Goodbody, who, together with his brother Jonathan, had decided to set up a new factory to spin and weave linen in 1853.[18] It seems likely that Jellicoe had persuaded Lewis Goodbody of the advantages to the factory of such a crochet school, with its attendant training and skills. Power looms were installed for the first time in the new factory. They could now spin the yarn in Clara, instead of importing it as before, thus producing the flour sacks more cheaply.[19] In 1865 there were sixty-two women and girls employed out of a total workforce of eighty-two, working ten hours a day for wages ranging from 5d to 11d a day.[20]

The crochet lace school closed in 1856, presumably because most of the girls could now find employment on a more permanent basis in the less exacting work of the factory. Nonetheless, its role in the development of the factory cannot be overlooked. Goodbody family tradition suggests that it was the skills learned in the lacemaking school that were of assistance to Lewis and Johnathan Goodbody when setting up the jute-weaving and sack-making enterprise at the Charlestown Mill.[21]

While Jellicoe could feel that her efforts to improve the lot of women in Clara had met with some success, her experiences both there and in Mountmellick convinced her that education was the long-term solution to better employment opportunities for women. This conviction was reinforced by her experiences in Dublin between 1858 and 1861. She had left Clara in 1858 to live in Harold's Cross, Dublin, where her husband had acquired a flour mill. Once again she came up against great poverty, this time in the Liberties area where John Jellicoe had a corn and flour store.[22] Many skilled needlewomen who worked at home in the area were experiencing a great loss of earnings, due mainly to the introduction of powered sewing machines in the factories. Jellicoe's practical response was to help revive the fortunes of Cole Alley Infant School for poor children of all creeds, run by the Society of Friends.[23] She believed that infant schools struck at the root of the problem of poverty, and she persuaded mothers to send their children to the school as the first vital step on the road to self-improvement.

While Jellicoe indulged her philanthropic nature by helping the poor, she believed 'the means of improvement within reach of this class are few indeed'.[24] Change had to come from the top down. In order to instigate this process of change she opened an institute for the training and employment of educated women.

In August 1861, an invitation to prepare a paper on the condition of young women employed in Dublin factories, for the first Dublin meeting of the National Association for the Promotion of Social Science, provided Jellicoe with the opportunity to put forward her ideas. This association, founded in England in October 1857, opened its membership to women on equal terms with men, and became the forum at which many of the social problems affecting women were first discussed and reforms suggested.[25] This brought her into contact with pioneering English women who were developing opportunities for social activism amongst Victorian women. These included Mary Carpenter, founder of the Reformatory and Ragged School movement; Louisa Twining, founder of the Workhouse Visiting Society; Bessie Parkes, editor of the *Englishwoman's Journal*, the first paper owned by women, and Emily Faithfull, founder of the Victoria Press in London. All of these women had founded their organisations either directly, or indirectly, as a result of papers read at the NAPSS meetings.

The tide of public opinion was beginning to move in favour of educating women for employment. A London Society for Promoting the Employment of Women had been founded by Bessie Parkes as a direct result of the first meeting of the NAPSS.[26] At the Dublin meeting Bessie Parkes referred to the large surplus of women in the British Isles as the immediate problem to be solved. Her society had just begun to organise a scheme to assist well-educated women to emigrate to the Australian colonies. The idea that the function of women was to be wife and mother came up for discussion at the Dublin meeting. Bessie Parkes, in her paper, referred to the vast changes which had taken place in relation to the working women of England and France in the previous ten years. They now had, she claimed, 'the responsibility of earning their own bread'.[27] By 1861, then, it was clear that a new order was emerging, where middle-class women went out to work, and this new order was seen by many activists as the key to their emancipation.

Meanwhile the *Irish Times* was cautioning English businessmen in Dublin for the Social Science meeting against assuming similarities between Dublin and the great manufacturing towns of England: 'We have no very extensive factories in Dublin, and consequently, we have not the vices or crimes which factory life entails. Irish mothers do not drug their children with laudanum for quietness'.[28] Again, in August, its editorial stressed that 'female labour is not so valuable here as to induce the mother to neglect her home and her children's health for wages' sake'.[29] Lectures which would be suitable for the audiences of Sheffield, Bradford and Manchester 'would be inappropriate here'.

It was against this background that Jellicoe now contributed a paper 'On the conditions and prospects of young women employed in the manufactories in Dublin'. She painted a much less complacent picture of life for young girls employed in Dublin factories.[30] Her immediate concern was the urgent need to protect working-class women from exploitative working conditions. She singled out for discussion the new type of factory just then emerging in Dublin, using the newly invented sewing machine and not covered by any of the parliamentary Acts. In each of these were employed between fifty and 200 women, who earned from 2 shillings to 6 shillings per week by working from 9 am to 7 pm The majority of these women had no skills, and simply prepared and finished the work of the machinist, who could earn from 7 shillings to 15 shillings a week, depending on her dexterity.[31] Many of these new factories were overcrowded and lacked the fresh air and space necessary for the health of their workers. The hours of work were long, and in many no time was allowed for dinner; the women brought a piece of bread or some other food, while the long walk to and from work often added to the toil and hardship of the worker. One direct result of Jellicoe's comments was the opening in Harold's Cross of an eating house by the Greenmount Spinning company, for the workers in the cotton factory. There they could obtain their meals, and about a third of the operatives took immediate advantage of this.[32]

Jellicoe noted that as the girls employed in factories were over thirteen years of age, 'schools are not demanded by law for their instruction'. She argued that as the poor and the unskilled workers were among the first to suffer from any trade depression, they should not be denied the right to such training as would enable them more readily to adapt to changes of employment. The 'idle habit' of taking a holiday on Monday, which many Dublin manufacturers complained about, was not, she noted, confined to the working classes but 'prevailed even among children at infant and other schools'.[33]

While the employers fulminated against the 'ignorance, inattention, want of energy and great impatience of restraint exhibited by the generality of the class' who applied for jobs, Jellicoe saw instead unhealthy living conditions and inadequate diet as the prime causes of their listlessness, while their carelessness of order and lack of restraint she put down to the unsettled habits acquired in the street life of their childhood.[34] Her solution for this was education: infant schools for the very young, while for the adolescent girls she suggested evening schools with an industrial element, such as learning how to use the sewing machine, included. Other proposals put forward in this paper included: more penny savings banks to encourage thrift; a home where friendless women could receive shelter at moderate cost, and, ultimately, the establishment of a registry of the various employments open to young working women.[35]

Jellicoe also suggested the employment of women as overseers in all factories where girls were employed. Such a plan 'would be attended with incalculable benefit, both in the moral training of the young women and as affording a healthy stimulus to their exertions to improve themselves, so as to be able to fill such situations'.[36] She hoped in this way to open up more job opportunities for women, and was asked to expand on this idea in a paper read at the next Social Science meeting in London in 1862. It was in London that she made her first public speech, her previous paper in Dublin having been read for her; only her strong belief in the necessity of the case led her to stand before an audience 'as it were at the stake'.[37] She retained this shyness to the end of her life, and remarked once that 'action is more my forte than speech-making'.[38]

In this paper, delivered in London, Jellicoe noted that while women cut out the garments in factories, 'the whole power and control of the workers is exercised by men'.[39] She herself had seen more than one sewing factory where a man occupied a position akin to a slave driver as he tried to meet production targets. She considered that the usual arguments put forward against the employment of women as overseers

- ignorance of machinery, deficiency in arithmetic, inability
to control women workers - could be overcome by classes
such as those which were started in 1861 by the Irish Society
for Promoting the Training and Employment of Educated
Women. Jellicoe had great hopes that a class of designers of
trade patterns would soon be added to these classes, with
lectures delivered by businessmen who recognised 'the full
value of the communion of labour'.[40] Instead of the constant
complaints about the waste of artistic power in designing
patterns totally unfitted for use in factories, Jellicoe asked
why Irish manufacturers did not employ a well-trained,
clever, woman overseer with artistic taste, who could bridge
the gap between the school of design and the factory. She
believed that if women were eligible to hold responsible
positions in society, they should be educated to fill them
successfully. That is why Jellicoe urged that, instead of men
supervising and controlling women workers in factories,
qualified women should be employed to do so.

In support of this contention, Jellicoe prepared another
paper, read at the London Social Science Congress, in 1862,
on 'A Visit to the Female Convict Prison at Mountjoy,
Dublin'.[41] In this paper she noted with approval the success
of an experiment there, aimed at rehabilitating women
prisoners through education. Captain Crofton and Mr
Lentaigne, who had been responsible for this new scheme,
accepted that it could not have been done so successfully
without the appointment of matrons and female officers to
carry it through. Jellicoe believed that the true balance of
power is where 'men and women work harmoniously and
helpfully, combining in due proportion the masculine
element of power and the feminine prerogative of influence
by love'.[42]

These views represent the early stage of the women's
movement, when pioneering women such as Jellicoe realised
that their only hope of achieving anything concrete was
through the power structure controlled by men. The vision
she put forward of women overseers who would win over
the young factory workers to attendance at evening school
and 'implant ideas of self respect, habits of self-reliance and
surround them with humanising influences',[43] did not
become a reality in the nineteenth century. Despite the fact
that her plea to the mill owners and factory proprietors fell
on deaf ears, she showed the capacity of the true reformer to
accept that change must come slowly. In 1862 she stated,

'this idea will not be relinquished, though its development must be a work of time'.[44]

Meanwhile she had succeeded in co-founding, in August 1861 and with the help of Ada Corlett, the first society in Ireland for the employment of women, the afore-mentioned Irish Society for Promoting the Training and Employment of Educated Women. Its committee included twenty-eight men drawn from business, clerical and professional circles in Dublin. There were also thirty-eight women on this committee, including many titled ladies. Out of this enormous group, a managing committee of four men and four women was selected, Jellicoe being among them, while Ada Corlett became one of two honorary secretaries.[45]

From the beginning, this remarkable organisation, which became known in 1864 as the Queen's Institute, set itself to meet the needs of the time by widening the scope of women's work. It went through two distinct stages: a technical training stage between 1861 and 1866, which was one of trial and error and limited success in the employment field; an educational stage between 1866 and 1880, which was much more successful as the Queen's Institute became involved in girls' secondary and higher education. It had many difficulties to contend with initially - shortage of funds, the prejudices of society, the short time spent in its classes, and its limitation to a particular class of women, 'distressed gentlewomen'. This latter weakness limited its effectiveness to middle-class women, and was a far cry from Anne Jellicoe's original suggestion of a registry of the various employments open to young women of the working class. It appears from the earliest reports that Ada Corlett had her own agenda which was to limit the Queen's Institute to middle-class women and thus ensure its respectability. In 1862, Corlett claimed that a considerable number of applications for admittance to classes were rejected 'partly from the persons not reaching the standard of the middle class ... and also as being hopeless subjects for the experiment of teaching'.[46] Again in 1864, Corlett noted that:

> ... almost all the pupils in attendance belong to the higher middle ranks, many being daughters of professional men, whose more successful brethren enjoy positions which confer social importance and in which wealth is commonly

acquired: thus each pupil learns in the company of educated gentlewomen.[47]

The reality behind this facade was that so many of these women were in such impoverished circumstances that they were unable to pay even the purely nominal fees charged for the classes, the committee having to admit forty-seven of them as free pupils.

As a result of the conventions of society, middle-class women with their smattering of accomplishments found themselves unable to compete in the labour market with girls educated in National schools. In 1866 the *Irish Times*, referring to the Queen's Institute, believed such an institute was necessary to counteract the 'solid though limited instruction which has enabled those taught in National schools to displace middle-class earners'.[48] It considered that the National school system was responsible for that revolution in Ireland which was 'rapidly reversing the position of the middle and lower classes'.

However, the biggest obstacle of all to the Institute's plans was the assumption that the 'distressed gentlewomen' who came to them were educated and could therefore be easily trained. In fact it soon became clear that many of these women could not be trained, because they did not have the necessary basic education. The first classes were adult technical training classes, ranging from a sewing-machine class to a commercial French and German class. It was Jellicoe who was responsible for the sewing-machine class, which she hoped would not only bring 'immediate profit to working women' but also be 'useful to matrons in public institutions and overseers in factories'.[49]

The most successful classes were those directly linked to jobs - the sewing-machine class, law writing and the training of telegraph clerks. The law-writing class arose from the fact that many Dublin solicitors complained about the lack of punctuality in returning work shown by the numerous male scriveners in the city. This resulted in the work being sent to London. The Queen's Institute started a law-writing class in February 1862 which had begun to yield dividends by 1866 as it provided work for twenty-nine women, most of whom were daily governesses, on a part-time basis.[50] One of the most successful efforts to find new employment outlets for women workers was the opening in February 1862 of a training class for female telegraph clerks.[51]

Jellicoe's husband, John, died in December 1862 and was 'said to have made a truly happy end', according to an entry in Lydia Goodbody's diary.[52] Their marriage appears to have been very successful - a comment in the *Freeman's Journal* of 1880 noted that Anne Jellicoe 'never ceased to mourn' her dead husband.[53] He had supported her in all her philanthropic endeavours and, in his will, left all his money (£3,000) to 'my beloved Annie'.[54] They had no children, so Anne Jellicoe was now a wealthy woman who could use her money as she wished.

One of the first uses to which she put some of this wealth was as a loan to the Queen's Institute which enabled it to move from hired rooms in Grafton Street to a house in Molesworth Street. While Ada Corlett was preoccupied with the gentility and respectability of its pupils, Jellicoe was aware that the real stumbling-block to advancement for the mature governesses who came to them for help was their lack of a good basic elementary education, and the lack of opportunity to pursue studies in the higher branches of learning. According to Isabella Mulvany, writing later on this subject, Jellicoe found the work of the Institute

> ... crippled by the utter want of mental discipline or habits of reasoning in those who sought to be benefited, and she said that to do good to women she must strike at the root of the evil and give them a sound basis of education as the first step in promoting their mental and moral welfare.[55]

She hoped that the Queen's Institute would now become involved in the training and education of teachers, but failed to win acceptance for the idea when she put it before the committee in 1864. In her 1864 report, Ada Corlett stated that the Institute was not prepared to supply governesses through the registry, as it had 'no organisation to furnish a satisfactory test'.[56] Sir Robert Kane, speaking at the 1864 meeting, wondered why, if this were so, they could not

> ... at least establish some criterion which would afford a just test of the capacity of these ladies for the position which they sought. He found it strange that while every school

mistress was required to go through a course of probation before becoming a teacher, the ladies who taught the middle class were alone exempted from it. [57]

Despite his powerful advocacy of Jellicoe's views, the Queen's Institute refused to become involved in training governesses. One can only speculate as to the reasons for this decision: perhaps differing opinions among committee members, the lack of funds to begin such an undertaking, or the belief that their original brief was to limit their help to those governesses already in distress by training them for other occupations. Whatever the reason, Jellicoe now decided that a separate institution was necessary, and she began canvassing the citizens of Dublin for a training college for governesses. She got nowhere until the arrival of Dr Trench as Archbishop of Dublin from London in 1864. He was known to be interested in the higher education of women, so she decided to put her ideas to him. It took some time and 'some little difficulty' before she obtained an interview with him, as she was not then a member of the Church of Ireland.

Trench was a very cautious man and did not seem at first hopeful that a college for women would succeed in Ireland. Ultimately, 'won over', as he said, 'by her enthusiasm', he agreed, but persuaded Jellicoe to merge her ideas for a training college for governesses into a wider educational scheme for the liberal education of women based on the model of Queen's College, London.[58]

Queen's College, London, established in 1848, was the first college in the United Kingdom to offer higher education to women. It owed its educational vision to the Revd Frederick Denison Maurice, who had been appalled by the problems facing governesses who were desperately looking for employment. In his inaugural lecture at Queen's College, published in pamphlet form in 1848, Maurice put forward a philosophy of education which was to have a profound impact on Jellicoe's thinking and subsequently on girls' secondary and higher education in Ireland. Like Jellicoe, Maurice had at first thought in terms of a training college for governesses, but had come to the conclusion that this would limit the possibility of a better education to those girls preparing for future careers as teachers. In its place he put forward a new ideal for girls' education - the idea of a college which would provide a liberal education for all 'who seek a general not a professional culture'.[59]

This idea of giving girls a better education for its own sake marked a new stage in the development of girls' secondary and higher education. Instead of the usual encyclopaedic approach to girls' education, with a resultant superficial understanding of the many subjects supposedly covered, Maurice stated: 'The teachers of a school may aim merely to impart information; the teachers of a College must lead their pupils to the apprehension of principles.'[60] Study he felt, was not worth much, 'if it is not busy about the root of things'.[61] Thus, drawing and music should be taught as 'pre-eminently useful' subjects instead of as showy accomplishments or ornamental graces. Drawing, for example, should cultivate a habit of observation, a real interest in nature, a power of looking below the surface of things for their ultimate meaning, while music had the ability to awaken the sense of order and harmony in the heart of things.

While the movement for the higher education of women had moved away from Queen's College by the end of the 1860s, it had already fulfilled Maurice's vision by educating many of the women who were to help bring about change in English society. Most of the new pressure groups - for example, the National Association for the Promotion of Social Science, the Society for Promoting the Employment of Women, the women's suffrage movement and the London School of Medicine for Women - were all started or encouraged by a small circle of women who had connections with Queen's College.[62] It also educated many of the future pioneers in the field of education. It could also claim to have contributed to the establishment of Alexandra College, Dublin, founded in October 1866, by Jellicoe with the aid of Archbishop Trench. His intervention ensured that the new college for women would offer a university-type education from the beginning.

An editorial in the *Irish Times* in January 1866 suggests that there was still some debate between Jellicoe and Trench on their differing approaches to the higher education of women.[63] The *Irish Times* editorial expressed its confidence

... that a College where real distinction could be obtained, where depth and breadth would be proportionate, and shallow pretences would be exploded, might accomplish great things for the 'fair girl graduates in their golden hair' ... It should lead the popular views of education instead of being dragged after them ... . We desire not a training school for teachers, but a College for the sound and liberal education of gentlewomen; and we believe that such an institution would strike deep root, if planted by capable hands, and tended while fixing itself in the soil.[64]

These prophetic words were to be borne out to a remarkable degree in the new institution.

Alexandra College was the first institution in Ireland to call itself a college instead of school, and thus the first to aspire to a university-type education for women. Not only did it initiate many of the new movements for the expansion of educational opportunities for women, but it also became a university college during the period 1880-1904, when it prepared girls for the degrees of the Royal University of Ireland. It was also in the vanguard of the movement to persuade Trinity College, Dublin, to open its degrees to women, which, in 1904, it finally did.

Although she had died by 1880, much of the credit for these achievements must go to Jellicoe, who was responsible for most of the educational initiatives which enabled the College to survive during its first twenty years. Yet she was not at the first formal committee meeting to found the College, which took place under the auspices of Archbishop Trench on 2 February 1866. Presumably Jellicoe accepted this situation because she believed that the powerful combination of the Church of Ireland clergy and Trinity College professors, who were at the meeting, would ensure patronage from the highest social circles and thus give the new College a secure start.

This did in fact happen - Alexandra, the Princess of Wales, agreed to allow her name to be given to the new college, a sum of £529 was quickly subscribed, and a house bought in Earlsfort Terrace.[65] A prospectus for the new college stated that its object was 'to supply defects in the existing education of women, and to afford an education more sound and solid .... and better tested, than is at present easily to be obtained by women of the middle and upper classes in this country'. It was to be based on the 'character and work of Queen's College, London', which it was felt would be a sufficient reply to those who criticised such an ambitious project.[66]

Archbishop Trench, in a letter to Dean Plumptre, Principal of Queen's College, London, seems to have been pessimistic about the college's chances of survival: 'Alexandra College', he wrote, 'is to be launched next week ... with what fortune it is impossible to say.'[67] This letter also throws an interesting light on the snobbery and extreme desire for respectability which was deemed essential to the success of girls' schools in this period. Trench asked: 'Have you any arrangement to prevent people from too low a grade in society attending the lectures. We want pupils from the middle class - but how do you keep away pupils who by their manners and associations would deter ladies and such like young women?' For Irish middle-class girls it appears an English accent was also desirable. He asked for an Assistant Lady who should, if possible

> ... have passed through Queen's College and should understand the details of the working of the College in all matters that refer to order and discipline. We have plenty of Irish candidates but the fatal brogue stands in the way of all - even our lady in chief (otherwise an invaluable person) has more than a surfeit of this - of which fortunately she is painfully conscious, and begs for an English helper.[68]

No records survive of Dr Plumptre's reply, but no English lady helper appears to have been willing to make herself available. Instead Jellicoe took the initiative, and during the summer of 1866, visited many schools and colleges in England and Scotland.

From the beginning Alexandra College followed closely along the lines of Queen's College in its structure and organisation. Lectures were given by distinguished professors from Trinity College, Dublin, who also set the Alexandra College examinations. This early association with Trinity College proved to be a vital factor in ensuring the success of Alexandra College as it provided higher levels of teaching at a time when there were no women sufficiently well educated to fulfil this role. The wide range of subjects also raised the new institution above the ordinary level of girls' secondary schools. The first curriculum, which was similar to that of Queen's College, included amongst its subjects theology, history, English language and literature. Students aged fifteen years or over could become compounders, or full-time students, by taking a group of five or seven subjects at fourteen or twenty pounds per annum respectively, or choose whatever subjects they wished as non-compounders.[69]

By calling itself a college, Alexandra aimed to give, as did Queen's College, a liberal education in the best sense. This radical departure from the accepted order must have seemed a very foolish move in the 1860s, when the accomplishments still reigned supreme, and when the difference between what constituted girls' primary and secondary education was still unclear.

The extent of the defects of middle-class girls' education in 1866 was brought home to Jellicoe within a few weeks of starting the college. What came to light was the

> ... inaccurate, vague and fragmentary nature of the education given to girls, the neglect of the rules of spelling and the principles of grammar, the downright ignorance of arithmetic, the absence of any training of the mind, the meagreness of the so-called accomplishments on which so much time and energy had been wasted.[70]

Classes in elementary English, arithmetic, geography, and history had to be started, while the language classes were also sub-divided into several sections. This meant that the College was in fact providing an elementary education to those in need of it.

Educational standards were so low that even those students wishing to take full advantage of the opportunities now open to them could not do so as they lacked the basic knowledge in many subjects. To overcome this Jellicoe submitted a plan to the Council for 'assistant ladies to be chosen by merit from students over eighteen years of age who had attended at least three terms in the college'.[71] This proposal was accepted and a kind of tutorial system of student lady teachers was established in the College. They sat in on the professors' lectures and then prepared the less advanced students for the next lesson. These assistant teachers were allowed to attend up to three free classes and were paid a small salary.[72]

Now that the College had adjusted its courses to the elementary level required for many students, Jellicoe was careful not to lose sight of its wider aims of proving that women were capable of higher study. In May 1868 she suggested that extra lectures should be given in advanced subjects by special lecturers, similar to those in Queen's College, London, and that these classes should be open to all ladies interested in higher education. These lectures in astronomy, Greek literature and English poetry marked the beginning of a course of Saturday lectures in Trinity College, Dublin, in 1869, open to all women. They lasted until 1877 and were highly successful, judging by the numbers who attended: over 200 women each year in the 1870s.[73]

Meanwhile, Jellicoe decided against an entrance examination for Alexandra College because she believed that

> ... even had parents and schoolmistresses generally been contented to relinquish the straining after the phantom of a 'finishing education' and had been willing to enter upon the modest and unattractive ground-work of study which an entrance examination would set forth, many years must elapse before such a radical change could be made widely effective.[74]

Her views were borne out by another educational reformer of this period, Margaret Byers of Belfast.

Byers had founded the Ladies' Collegiate School in Belfast in 1859 in the hope of providing an education for girls similar to that received by boys. Yet records show that in 1873 her collegiate school was still small and privately run, despite the fact that she employed male students from Queen's University and the Presbyterian Assembly's College in Belfast as teachers, and that the Queen's University had extended its examinations to girls. Ultimately Byers' Ladies' Collegiate School was to become, from the 1880s, the highly successful Victoria College, with separate secondary and university departments. Yet, although she was supported by the Presbyterian Church, Margaret Byers was initially less successful than Anne Jellicoe, mainly because she failed to acquire the backing of an influential committee of men, which the far-seeing Jellicoe perceived as being essential to advancing the cause of women in that pioneering period 1860-1880.

The price Jellicoe had to pay was finding herself outside the decision-making process in Alexandra College. She was a member of neither the Council nor the Committee of Education, and therefore could not attend any of their meetings. The Council, made up of eighteen men, including the Provost and Vice Provost of Trinity College and many bishops of the Church of Ireland, had financial control and the final decision on all matters.[75] The Committee of Education, which was in a subordinate position, consisted of the professors who lectured to the students. The only role for women initially was that of Lady Visitors. Fifteen of these were appointed by the Council, including many titled ladies as well as wives and daughters of members of Council. Their role was to 'promote and uphold by their presence and influence, a Lady-like tone and demeanour among the pupils of the College'.[76]

In 1866, Jellicoe became Lady Superintendent, a title she held until her death in 1880. Her duties generally were to oversee the pupils, be responsible for order and discipline within the College, including the conduct of the servants, take charge of the library, and keep the daily accounts. Apart from this enormous workload, she could put forward suggestions only indirectly, through the College Secretary and Bursar. She thus had the unenviable task of trying to organise the College without being able to make any of the major decisions herself. Yet, despite the limitations imposed on her, Jellicoe achieved a remarkable degree of success in carrying out her long-term objectives. The most pressing of these was to found a collegiate school which would act as a feeder to the College, and give teaching practice to women teachers who had been students there. A secondary aim, closely allied to this, was to raise the status of women teachers or governesses by encouraging them to make teaching a profession.

In furtherance of these aims, Jellicoe decided to found the Governess Association of Ireland, formed in April 1869. Its aims were 'to promote the higher education of ladies as teachers' by collecting funds for the foundation of studentships and exhibitions in schools and colleges, all open to women preparing to be governesses and teachers.[77] A general committee of thirty-six members (nineteen women and seventeen men) was set up, with the important decisions being left to the acting committee of six women and five men. On this latter committee Jellicoe had strategically placed TCD professors who were also members of the Committee of Education, and W G Brooke, a member of Council in Alexandra College. This gave her the added support of these men within the college, but also allowed her to act, under the umbrella of the GAI, in an independent capacity outside the college.

Like the Governesses' Benevolent Institution in England, upon whose plan the GAI was largely based, a Registry of Employment was opened at 3 Lower Leeson Street, Dublin. Jellicoe hoped that this registry would play an important role in providing governesses with visiting and resident positions and serve as a source of information on all matters relating to the higher education of women.[78] While, through lack of funds, the GAI never succeeded in reaching its full potential in helping would-be governesses, it did play a major role in furthering the higher education of women by persuading TCD to establish examinations for women.

The minutes of the GAI for 1 June 1869 show that the question of an examining board was discussed, and that Dr Ingram was requested by the Committee to draft a memorial to the Board of TCD, asking them to appoint examiners similar to the Cambridge Syndicate 'in a course to be agreed on afterwards'. The final draft was then approved and presented to the Council of Alexandra College for their signatures.[79] Jellicoe kept discreetly in the background as usual, but notes written by her for a Committee of Education meeting held in Alexandra College on 9 June 1869, reveal (under the heading 'Private Instructions for the Provost') that it was her ideas on the organisation of the TCD examinations for women which formed the basis of the final blueprint. These included:

1. The age for the Junior exams for women to be between fourteen and eighteen years.

2. The Women's Senior Exams should be from eighteen years upwards.

3. The course should be 'about the compass of the curriculum of Alexandra College'.

4. The first exam to take place in 1870.

5. No names or list should be published, the results of the exams to be made known only to parents.[80]

The Board of TCD accepted these suggestions, and the first TCD examinations for women were duly held in 1870. Although these exams were for women and awarded certificates of knowledge only, nevertheless they marked the first stage in the campaign to open up degrees to women by the university. It was not until 1904 that this became a reality, yet this first step was a milestone on the road to the advancement of women in Irish society. The GAI also enabled Jellicoe to express her views on girls' education in a way not open to her previously. In the first annual report of the GAI she was highly critical of the way society had neglected to help girls educationally:

> When it is remembered how much has been done for boys by the foundation of exhibitions and scholarships, and the stimulus which such prizes supply when placed before a boy's fancy - that there is absolutely nothing in a girl's education to quicken her ambition, or excite her to exertion, except the fear of want - that in this respect, as in many others, the woman's cause has suffered neglect - it seems greatly to be desired that those who are really aroused and interested in the cause of education should, either themselves or by a united effort, found exhibitions in Ladies' Colleges attached to girls' schools of known character and respectability through the country.[81]

While she herself helped found two studentships attached to Alexandra College, Jellicoe's hopes of a Provident Fund for teachers, with annuities for the aged and infirm members, never became a reality due to lack of funds. Jellicoe's views were both far-sighted and practical - she wanted long-term remedies not short-term cures - as is clear from the 1878 Report of the GAI:

> The chief difficulty with which they [the Committee] have to

contend in the collection of funds is the idea held by charitable persons, that an association in which money's worth and not money is offered, is not strictly speaking a benevolent organisation, forgetting the economic principle, that the aid given to those who are willing to help themselves, is the only true benevolence, while that which relieves temporary distress, perpetuates, instead of remedying, the evil it seeks to cure.[82]

This latter point was one of the reasons why Jellicoe had been dissatisfied with the Queen's Institute. In 1869, the Institute had begun to move closer to her ideas by extending their classes to cover the more academic subjects such as Latin, Greek, mathematics, French, German, history and English, in preparation for the first Women's Junior Examinations in TCD in 1870, and later the Senior Examination in 1874.

The Queen's Institute could now claim to have contributed to changing public opinion on the subject of 'ladies' earning their own living. By 1870 and its ninth year of operation, it had secured employment for 862 out of its 1,786 pupils. The 1871 report stated that 'even a short time ago it was thought derogatory for a lady to earn money' whereas now women who did so were 'rapidly attaining a place in general estimation which is eminently satisfactory'.[83] However, Margaret Byers, in her evidence before the Intermediate Education Commission in 1899, claimed that it was the Intermediate examination system, established in 1879 which began the real revolution in the employment of women 'as it proved that girls could take the same external examinations as boys and were therefore educationally fit for many of the jobs hitherto denied them'.[84]

Nonetheless, within the narrow framework in which it operated, the Queen's Institute did play an important pioneering role in breaking down barriers and changing public attitudes in relation to the employment of middle-class women. The majority of its pupils were, like those of Alexandra College, members of the Church of Ireland. Both these institutions accepted pupils from different religious denominations, which was most unusual at that time, when the majority of girls' schools were strictly denominational. The comparisons with Alexandra College do not end there. The Queen's Institute started compounders' courses in seven subjects in the late 1870s, and had a council as well as a committee. Both institutions also had pupils in training for the profession of teaching: the Queen's Institute had twenty-three pupil teachers and Alexandra had twelve ladies receiving free education in the College while training in the school.[85]

In her submission to the Endowed Schools Commission of 1879, Ada Corlett claimed that she had founded the Queen's Institute with the aid of a committee of gentlemen: she made no mention of Anne Jellicoe. All its efforts, she said, had been towards creating 'a University for women'. She now prepared a scheme to place the collegiate work of the Queen's Institute on a permanent basis in connection with the Royal University of Ireland, which had opened its degrees to women. She hoped thereby to provide teaching faculties for medicine and 'other chairs which are equally applicable to the capacity of women'.[86] This plan never came to fruition: within a year, the Queen's Institute in Dublin was closed. The immediate reason given for its closure was a legal action taken by the Porcelain Painting Manager against the Institute in 1882.[87] It appears also to have been caused by the failing health of Corlett, who had been personally involved in the running of the Institute, especially after 1866 when Jellicoe had founded Alexandra College. The *Freeman's Journal* commented on the necessity of reviving the Queen's Institute in some form, stating that there was a great need for classes which would prepare girls for the University and Intermediate examinations, and for public clerkships, at low fees. It considered that it would be little short of a national disgrace if 'one of the most practically useful establishments in Ireland were allowed to pass out of existence ... for want of a little timely assistance'.[88]

The Queen's Institute was not revived. A new society, the Irish Association for Promoting the Training and Employment of Women, took its place in 1883, but restricted itself to the original technical aims of the Queen's Institute.[89]

Why did the Queen's Institute fail while Alexandra College succeeded? Part of the answer seems to be that it lacked Jellicoe's vision, which might have ensured its survival at a time of great economic depression in Ireland. In trying to imitate Alexandra College, it followed rather than led. Its emphasis on the utilitarian rather than the liberal view of women's higher education espoused by Alexandra College led it to overreach itself. It tried to cater for every conceivable examination while at the same time striving to retain its technical origins. This diversity weakened its sense of identity and purpose, and may ultimately have been the cause of its final demise.

Meanwhile, Alexandra College had its own problems in the 1870s. In 1871 it was still filled with juniors aged between fourteen and sixteen years, something Jellicoe considered unfavourable to the attendance of students wanting higher education. In November 1871 she asked the Council to consider establishing a preparatory school, as girls of fifteen, sixteen and seventeen were still coming to the College so badly prepared that the short time spent there was of very limited use.[90] She contended parents were unwilling to pay for anything but accomplishments in daughters of those ages.

In June 1872 Jellicoe returned to the attack with a second statement to the Council, urging that the only way to ensure the permanence of Alexandra College was by, first, an endowment of the advanced or unpopular classes (which were a drain on the more prosperous classes), especially mathematics, Latin, moral philosophy, theology and Italian; and second, increased accommodation to allow for a more exact classification of the students.[91]

Jellicoe believed that the long-term solution lay in a school which would act as a feeder to the college, and she reminded the Archbishop that this was no new idea of hers but had been proposed 'on the first day that I had the honour of laying the matter of a College before him'.[92] As a final inducement, she stated that the GAI would give the College £250 if 'this plan be carried out'.[93] The fact that Jellicoe was prepared to make the GAI money conditional on the establishment of a school shows the problems she faced in trying to bring about reforms at such a time.

Her patience and perseverance now paid off. In June 1872 the Committee of Education and the Council formally agreed that a school should be established in connection with the College.

The High School movement was just then beginning in England, and Jellicoe hoped that Alexandra School would be based on its ideas. These included the downgrading of accomplishments, the inclusion of mathematics and Latin, a greater emphasis on external examinations, and close liaison with the universities.[94] The primary moving force behind the High School movement was Maria Grey and her sister, Miss

Emily Shirreff. They had founded the National Union for the Education of Girls of All Classes above the Elementary in November 1871, in the hope of spreading information on the various educational reforms taking place, especially the High School movement. Grey was a skilled propagandist and public speaker, and used these qualities to enlist support for her new movement when she visited Belfast and Dublin in January 1872. This was a critical juncture in the High School movement. Grey feared that her efforts to gain public sympathy and funds for this cause might be endangered by the emerging women's suffrage movement. The 1867 Reform Act, which had granted the franchise to most men, had helped activate the women's suffrage movement in England, and in 1871 the North of Ireland Women's Suffrage Committee was formed by Isabella Tod. She was the most politically minded of her sister reformers on the Irish educational scene and was a speaker at the public meeting in Belfast.

Like Jellicoe, Isabella Tod had gained her first entry into public life through the Social Science Association meeting held in Belfast in 1867. She, too, had advocated the provision of colleges to continue the education of girls at the point where school left off. Yet the organisation which she founded in Belfast in 1867, the Ladies' Institute, was not a college, but rather an institution which gave courses of winter lectures to ladies who had left school. She paid an annual visit to London during the parliamentary session and these political contacts were to prove very useful in behind-the-scenes efforts to procure for girls the same benefits as boys from the Intermediate Education (Ireland) Act of 1878. At a meeting, held in Dublin in 1878 to promote the extension of the franchise to women, Tod paid tributes to the MPs who had helped in their campaign, but pointed out that the task of admitting girls to the benefits of the Act would have been much easier if MPs had owed their votes to women.[95]

Jellicoe, who met Maria Grey in Dublin in January 1872, found in her a kindred spirit, passionately devoted to the cause of reforming girls' secondary and higher education. The 1872 report of the GAI suggests that Jellicoe may have shared Grey's views about the need to keep the movement for the higher education of women a separate issue from the women's suffrage movement. She stressed the great difficulty of enlisting public sympathy and financial support for governesses in Dublin, as they commanded 'little sympathy' as a class. Advocates of a higher education for governesses were

> ... often regarded as amiable enthusiasts ... not only so but by a confusion of ideas, assistance to enable a deserving class to enter more fairly on their allotted task in life is mixed up with the question of women's rights and women's suffrage, with which questions it has nothing whatever to do.[96]

According to Isabella Mulvany, 'in the so-called women's rights movements [Jellicoe] took no active part, the only "women's right" for which she contended was, to quote her own words "their right to be educated".'[97] Mulvany's use of the phrase 'so-called women's rights' gives us some idea of her own views on this subject, and may not represent Jellicoe's position on this question. It is unclear whether Jellicoe favoured a direct political approach as a solution to the problems facing women's education. She never, for example, took part personally in any of the delegations of the 1870s which campaigned for reform of girls' secondary and higher education. But this does not necessarily suggest that Jellicoe did not see direct campaigning as something to be avoided.

As a pioneering educationalist, Jellicoe knew that there was, as she put it in 1872, 'opposition to be conciliated, prejudice to be overcome, and the fear of what is new to be soothed'.[98] She realised the necessity of bringing the conservative elements in society with her, before women could hope to gain even that basic right - the right to be educated. Ultimately that path was proved correct. The women's suffrage movement did not achieve their objectives until after women had been given the right to higher education. Without that, perhaps, they could not have achieved anything of significance.

Jellicoe's final achievement was the establishment of Alexandra School in April 1873. Her view that the college could not survive financially without the school was quickly proved correct. When, in the early 1880s, due to a general depression, the numbers in the college had fallen, it was stated before the Educational Endowments Commission that

'Alexandra College would not be able to remain in existence were it not for Alexandra School'.[99] The school had shown a profit from 1884, onwards and these profits were used to cover the losses sustained by the college.

Jellicoe had now achieved what she had set out to do - a college for higher education with a feeder school ensuring a continuity of pupils and teaching power. As she had hoped, the majority of the women teachers in the school were from Alexandra College or had qualified at the TCD exams for women. Isabella Mulvany was an example of one who had qualified in this way - a product of Jellicoe's vision. She won a GAI Scholarship to the college for two years (1872-74), and became secretary to Anne Jellicoe between 1878 and 1880. Appointed Headmistress of Alexandra School at the early age of twenty-six, Mulvany was a firm believer in the new ideas put forward by the High School movement. She believed that the only way to prove the capacity of women for higher education was by organising the school curriculum on the basis of a future university career, i.e. making Latin and maths the core subjects.[100]

In 1878 Alexandra College took part in the campaign to have the Intermediate Education Bill extended to girls, and a memorial signed by ninety MPs and other influential people interested in girls' education used the success of Alexandra College, the GAI and the University examinations for women as proof of the desire for the higher education of women in Ireland.[101] Thus Jellicoe's creation was, by its very existence, living proof that girls were capable of benefiting from higher education. Both Alexandra College and Alexandra School were ideally placed to take advantage of both the Intermediate Education Act (1878) and the Royal University of Ireland Act (1879).

However, at this time, when the competitive examination system was seen as the panacea for all the ills of the past, Jellicoe sounded a note of warning. While welcoming examinations in general 'as a means of concentrating study, giving mastery to the mind, acting as a step to self-knowledge, often as a check to self-conceit', she viewed with some anxiety their tendency 'to become masters instead of instruments'. Speaking to the Students' Representative Body of Alexandra College in March 1878, she said:

If instead of making the culture and development of the whole human being - soul, mind and heart - our aim, the desire to make examinations a success, or produce what have been derisively called 'mark-making animals' takes possession of us, if we snatch at premature results, and try to condense the knowledge, which it should take half a lifetime to acquire, into pellets, to be swallowed wholesale - a process well described as neither preceded by appetite nor followed by digestion - then, I can but say that our University honours, precious though they are, would be dearly bought at the cost of narrowing and lowering the whole plan of our college life.[102]

Jellicoe was not in favour of prizes or class rewards, as she believed there was no need to encourage the spirit of emulation, when there was a 'very general appreciation on the part of the students of the educational advantages offered to them'.[103] While Alexandra College did not have the traditions of the great seats of learning, it had striven for its own 'tradition', which Anne Jellicoe defined as being 'what is true and womanly in character'. In the context of her age, the 'womanly traditions' meant gentility, refinement and courtesy, but would not be seen as in any way inhibiting the development of all the intellectual gifts.

Her educational philosophy is best summed up in her own words:

By education is not merely meant instruction, but the cultivation of all those faculties - intelligence, affection, will, conscience - such training in short, as will enable each individual to guide herself right through the circumstances of life - to know her duty, and to do it - an education which, if so considered, is as important to women as to men, to poor as to rich.[104]

A student of the 1860s noted later that Jellicoe seemed to 'foresee the possibilities of education for women ... and gave girls the opportunity and incentive they needed'. She gives some idea of the restrictions placed on middle-class girls in the 1860s when she says: 'If it could be avoided, the students did not go to or from College, without an escort, and every class and lecture was attended by a "Lady Visitor" who sat in the classroom to keep order.'[105] Henrietta White, a pupil of Jellicoe's in the 1870s who became Headmistress of Alexandra College in 1890, considered her to be 'one of the remarkable women of our country, and one of those who has most advanced the cause of women's education'. She referred to the 'wonderful power she had of drawing out what was best in every girl by believing in them and loving them. Few women, I think, have ever gained so much of the love, almost adoration, of other women as she did'.[106]

Jellicoe was a very private person, and for insights into her personality we have to rely on the descriptions left by friends and intimates. One who knew her described her as

> ... an admirable woman, full of delightful incongruities which enhanced her charm. Her energy was splendid, her character nobly large - with a delicacy of inner refinement which a commmonplace observer might not have reached. All the lecturing professors adored her, and her rallying of them was a source of wholesome amusement to them! Her habitual seat of government was in the little return room on the stairs, and from that room sounds of merry converse between her and the arriving and departing lecturers would perpetually issue. She was an ex-Quaker, and one of her charming incongruities was her being wont, on gala days or important occasions, to go about, not in garb of drabs or greys, but with a brilliant red shawl which mostly trailed on the ground after her.[107]

Above all, she had a keen sense of humour. Isabella Ferrin-Forbes, writing in 1906 of the early years of the college, considered that Jellicoe 'had more than most women I have known two of the marks of sainthood - *hilaritas* and *sapientia*'.[108]

Circumstantial evidence indicates that she loved the arts, particularly music and literature. In the only personal letter to survive, written to a friend, Jellicoe asks: 'Did you hear Hallé's concert on Saturday? It was exquisite.'[109] Charles Hallé, the founder of the Hallé Orchestra, had given a celebrated piano recital in Dublin for the first time in 1867. Her interest in literature found expression in the College Literary Society - the first society formed in Alexandra College - which she helped establish in 1872. It was for past and present students, all of whom had to be over eighteen years of age. One favourite form of entertainment for the members of a party in the evening, was a reading by Dr Robert Perceval Graves of a scene from Shakespeare or poems by Wordsworth or Tennyson. Earlier in his life, as a curate at Ambleside and a poet himself, he had become the intimate of Wordsworth, Southey, Hartley, Coleridge, the Arnolds and other members of the Lake School of Poetry.[110] He spoke later of the privilege of being associated with Anne Jellicoe: 'That noble woman, to whose high-souled enthusiasm, devotion to the welfare of her sex, and practical genius, Alexandra College is pre-eminently indebted, both for its existence and its successful progress'.[111]

Jellicoe did not live to see the dramatic change in public opinion towards women's role in society which she had done so much to bring about. On 18 October 1880, at her brother's house in Birmingham, she died suddenly at the early age of fifty-seven. Archbishop Trench, in his funeral oration, referred to one particular quality: 'He never knew one in whom there was a more entire absence of self-seeking ... . It never so much as passed through her thought that one of the purposes for which Alexandra College existed was her glorification.'[112] Archbishop Trench also referred to the fact that, while Jellicoe was for many years a member of the Society of Friends, she was 'afterwards led into the fellowship of their church'.[113] As with much of Jellicoe's personal life, no other details are available to throw some light on her conversion and why or when it happened.

In the period 1860-1880, the majority of Irishwomen were not in a position, socially or economically, to bring about change in the position of women. Anne Jellicoe was one of a small number of Protestant middle-class women whose social position and background gave them the opportunity to become agents for social change. Although these groups were small and catered for 'gentlewomen', a necessarily limited class in Ireland at the time, their pioneering work provided the stimulus for the majority of convent schools to spread their ideas gradually throughout Ireland in the late 1880s and 1890s, under the aegis of the Intermediate Education Act and the Royal University of Ireland Act. It was the changes in the employment prospects for women wrought by the Industrial Revolution which had brought Anne Jellicoe into the area of educational reform. These changes have had an important bearing on the growth and expansion of educational opportunities for women during the last one hundred years. No revolution in the way people live or work is possible without a major change in the spread and quality of education. In that sense Anne Jellicoe was a revolutionary. Her major contribution was to increase the spread of knowledge to groups of women, and thus to begin to end gender apartheid in its many manifestations.

In terms of major social change the time span is very short. The effect of the women's movement on gender equality has been equally if not more successful than the abolition of slavery or racial equality over the same time span. It will perhaps take until the next century before these two great social changes will have worked through to a new culture.

NOTES

1 *Freeman's Journal*, 19 October 1880.
2 Archives, Alexandra College (hereafter ACA): document from Friends' Historical Library on Anne Jellicoe, based mainly on Lydia Goodbody's diaries 1841-1886. This typed sheet was prepared in 1965 for the Alexandra College Centenary of 1966. (Hereafter Centenary Document.)
3 *Ibid.*
4 Brenan, M 1835. *Schools of Kildare and Leighlin AD 1775-1835.* Dublin, p.298.
5 Letter from Anne Jellicoe to a friend dated 1867. ACA.
6 Bell, S Hilda. 1919. Ms Notes on Friends' Education in Ireland 1919. Friends Historical Library, Dublin. (Hereafter, FHL.)
7 *One Hundred Years of Mountmellick School.* 1886. Dublin, p.38.
8 Bell, Notes on Friends' Education.
9 Houston-Almquist, Jane. 1985. *Mountmellick Work.* Dublin, p.10.
10 *Ibid.*
11 Centenary Document.
12 Stewart, Margaret. n.p, n.d. *The Goodbodys of Clara 1865-1965*, p.5.
13 Centenary Document.
14 *Englishwoman's Journal 1858-59*, 1, p.334.
15 Lydia Goodbody's diary entry for November 1850. FHL.
16 *Englishwoman's Journal, 1858-9*, 1, p.336.
17 *Englishwoman's Journal, 1862-3*, p.307.
18 Diary of Lydia Goodbody, Clara, July 1853. FHL.
19 Stewart, *The Goodbodys*, p.5.
20 *Ibid.*, p.7.
21 Letter from R E Goodbody, Clonmullen, Clara, 30 March 1892. ACA
22 Centenary Document.
23 *Englishwoman's Review*, November 1880, p.519.
24 *Transactions of the National Association for the Promotion of Social Science*, 1861, p.645.
25 Borer, M C 1976. *Willingly to School.* London, p.270.
26 *Englishwoman's Journal*, 8, 1862, p.56.
27 *Ibid.*, p.57.
28 *Irish Times*, 2 July 1861.
29 *Irish Times*, 14 August 1861.
30 *Englishwoman's Journal*, 8, 1862, pp107-11.
31 *Ibid.*, p.110.
32 *Ibid.*, p.108.
33 *Ibid.*, p.109.
34 *Transactions of the National Association for the Promotion of Social Science*, 1861, p.644.
35 *Ibid.*, p.645.
36 *Englishwoman's Journal*, 8 February 1862, p.110.
37 *Ibid.*, 10 October 1862, p.119.
38 Jellicoe, Ann. 1878. *A Few Words Addressed to the Students,*

Representative Body, Alexandra College Dublin. Dublin.

39 *Englishwoman's Journal*, 10, October 1862, p.116.

40 *Ibid.*, p.118.

41 *Transactions of the National Association for the Promotion of Social Science*, 1862, pp437-42.

42 *Ibid.*, p.440.

43 *Englishwoman's Journal*, 10, October 1862, p.118.

44 *Freeman's Journal*, 7 April 1862.

45 *Englishwoman's Journal*, 8, February 1862, pp226, 228.

46 *Transactions of the National Association for the Promotion of Social Science*, 1863, p.699.

47 *Irish Times*, 10 December 1864.

48 *Irish Times*, 26 January 1866.

49 *Freeman's Journal*, 7 April 1862.

50 *Daily Express*, 22 December 1866.

51 *Irish Times*, 1 February 1862; *Freeman's Journal*, 7 April 1862; 8 February 1868.

52 Diary of Lydia Goodbody, December 1862. FHL.

53 *Freeman's Journal*, 22 October 1880.

54 Copy of John Jellicoe's Will dated 9 July 1850, National Archives, Dublin.

55 *Englishwoman's Review*, 15 November 1880, p.518.

56 *Irish Times*, 10 December 1864.

57 *Ibid.*

58 *Alexandra College Magazine*, 28, June 1906, p.4.

59 Maurice, F D 1848. *Inaugural Lecture on Queen's College*. London, p.8.

60 *Ibid.*, p.10.

61 *Ibid.*, p.13.

62 Kay, Elaine. 1872. *A History of Queen's College, London 1848-1872*. London, p.86.

63 *Irish Times*, 26 January 1866.

64 *Ibid.*

65 First Minute Book of Alexandra College Committee, February-October 1866, ACA.

66 First Printed Prospectus, October, 1866, ACA.

67 Letter dated 27 September 1866 from Archbishop Trench to Dr Plumptre, Principal of Queen's College. Queen's College Archives, London.

68 *Ibid.*

69 Printed prospectus of Alexandra College, Dublin, 1866. ACA.

70 Alexandra College Calendar. 1874. Printed return by Anne Jellicoe dated 1873.

71 Lady Superintendent's Book, October, 1867. ACA.

72 Endowed Schools Commission 1879-1880. Questionnaires filled in by Schools National Archives, Dublin.

73 O'Connor, Anne V and Parkes, Susan M 1983. *Gladly Learn and Gladly Teach: A History of Alexandra College and School*. Dublin, p.19.

74 Alexandra College Calendar 1874.

75 *Rules for the Constitution and Government of Alexandra College 1866*,

p.4.

76 Prospectus of Alexandra College 1866; *Rules 1866*, p.8.

77 Minute Book of the GAI containing 1st Annual Report, February 1870. ACA.

78 *Ibid.*

79 *Ibid.*, 1 June 1869.

80 Lady Superintendent's Book, 9 June 1869. ACA.

81 1st Annual Report of the Governess Association of Ireland, 1870.

82 8th Annual Report of the Governess Association of Ireland, March 1878.

83 *Freeman's Journal*, 22 September 1871; 9th Annual Report of the Queen's Institute, Dublin, 1871, p.10.

84 *Evidence to the Commission on Intermediate Education (Ireland)*. HC. 1889. (C. 1952), xxiii, p.259.

85 Endowed Schools Commission 1879-80: Questionnaires filled in by schools, National Archives, Dublin.

86 *Ibid.*

87 *Freeman's Journal*, 23 November 1882.

88 *Ibid.*, 5 August 1882.

89 Blackburn, Helen (ed.). 1888. *A Handy Book of Reference for Irishwomen*. London, p.80.

90 Lady Superintendent's Book, to Council, 1 November 1871. ACA.

91 *Ibid.*, 26 June 1872.

92 Committee of Education Minute Book, 26 June 1872. ACA.

93 Lady Superintendent's Book: statement by Anne Jellicoe for Council meeting, 26 June 1872. ACA.

94 *Englishwoman's Review*, January 1872, p.193.

95 See chapter on Isabella Tod in this book.

96 Third Annual Report of the Governess Association of Ireland, 1872.

97 *Englishwoman's Review*, 15 November 1880, p.519.

98 Third Annual Report of the Governess Association of Ireland, 21 April 1872.

99 Evidence of Revd H H Dickinson, a member of the Council of Alexandra College. *Educational Endowments (Ireland) Commission 1886*. H C. 1886, xxvi, 143-4.

100 *Alexandra College Magazine 69*, December 1927, p.2.

101 *Englishwoman's Review*, 15 August 1878, p.357.

102 Jellicoe, Anne. 1878. *A Few Words Addressed to the Students Representative Body, Alexandra College, 5 March 1878*. Dublin.

103 Calendar, 1874, ACA.

104 Third Annual Report of the Governess Association of Ireland, 1872.

105 *Alexandra College Jubilee Record, 1866-1916*, pp12-13.

106 Manuscript by Henrietta White, dated April 1881, called, 'My Life', ACA.

107 *Alexandra College Jubilee Record, 1866-1916*, pp11-2.

108 *Alexandra College Magazine*, 28 June 1906, p.5.

109 Letter from Anne Jellicoe to a friend, dated 1867. ACA.

110 Graves, Revd R.P. 1893. Obituary. In *Irish Times*, 7 October.
111 Address to the Revd R P Graves, MA, Dublin 1886.
112 *Freeman's Journal*, 22 October 1880.
113 *Ibid.*

Anna Maria Haslam

(1829-1922)

Mary Cullen

Anna Haslam, 'one of the giants of the women's cause', as her colleagues described her[1], became a legend in her own lifetime and the symbol of the women's movement, in particular the suffrage campaign, for a younger generation of Irish women in the early years of the twentieth century.

While much of her life's work was completed by the end of the nineteenth century both her personality and her continuing vigour made a strong impact on the younger women and their descriptions bring her to life for us. Their affection and respect is the more telling since many of them strongly disagreed with her position on the conflict between nationalism and unionism. We know she took part in virtually every campaign for women's rights during the second half of the nineteenth century, and that her organisational and leadership qualities were widely recognised. Yet, with the exception of women's suffrage, detailed information on her life and work is tantalisingly scarce. The sources so far available are largely public records such as minutes, speeches, leaflets and newspapers. This is the more frustrating since she and her husband, Thomas Haslam, arranged for the preservation of their papers, but few of these have been located.[2]

She was born Anna Maria Fisher into a middle-class Quaker family in Youghal, County Cork, in April 1829, the second youngest of the seventeen children, nine girls and eight boys, of Abraham Fisher of Youghal and Jane Moore of Neath in southern Wales. Anna's great-grandfather, Reuben Fisher, had come from London to Youghal where he set up as a druggist in 1695, and married Margaret Shute of Youghal in 1705. Their grandson, Abraham (1783-1871), Anna's father, ran a corn milling business in Youghal.[3]

She herself saw both her religion and her family as significant influences in her formation as a future activist in the cause of women. The more a religious denomination emphasised individual conscience, the more favourable it appears to have been to the development of feminist consciousness. Where Roman Catholicism stood at the authoritarian extreme, the Religious Society of Friends, or Quakers, stood at the other, the most positive of the Protestant denominations. The central Quaker belief in the 'Inner Light', the voice of individual conscience which overrode every other authority, encouraged 'an attitude of individuality and responsibility'.[4] Quakers valued hard work and self-support above inherited ease and had a strong record of philanthropic activity. They also had a tradition of civil disobedience, such as refusal to take oaths or to bear arms, on grounds of religious principle.

In practice Quakers do not appear to have given women quite the same autonomy and authority they accorded to men. Quaker women, like women in other Protestant minority sects, did take leadership roles in the early days, in the case of Quakers after the foundation of the Society in the aftermath of the English civil war in the 1640s, but in all the sects women were later relegated to more subordinate and stereotypical female roles.[5] Yet, by comparison with women in other denominations, Quaker women were active and autonomous. Travelling ministers, who could be of either sex, kept groups in contact. There were both men's and women's monthly, quarterly and provincial meetings. While only the men's had executive authority, the women's dealt with such matters as the relief of the poor, and of widows and orphans, good behaviour, marriage and female dress, and the 'interaction between meetings and the idea of spiritual, if not executive, equality gave women important roles to play in this distinctive community'.[6] Haslam herself undoubtedly saw her religion as a training in sex equality. She noted that, like 'my dear friend, Susan B Anthony,[7] I was brought up a member of the Society of Friends, and was accustomed to see women working side by side with their brothers, as Ministers, Elders, and Overseers, upon the footing of undisputed equality'.[8]

As a Quaker she also received an education superior to that available to most contemporary middle-class girls. She attended the Quaker boarding school at Newtown in County Waterford from 1840-42, and then went to England to the famous Quaker School at Ackworth in Yorkshire which she left in 1845. Thus she was away from home at school for five years from age eleven to sixteen.

Quakers attached considerable importance to education for both boys and girls. Their schools aimed both to develop a sense of individual responsibility and to mould the pupils' wills through strict discipline and regulated lives.[9] Boarding schools were preferred to day schools as being more conducive to both objectives. Newtown, founded in 1798, was one of three Quaker provincial boarding schools in Ireland, the others being in Lisburn in Ulster and Mountmellick in Leinster. Originally intended to educate children from poorer Quaker families, girls for domestic service and boys for apprenticeships, at first they had a limited and practical curriculum. By the time Anna Fisher went to Newtown the provincial schools were also educating children from better-off families and expanding the curriculum to prepare students, or at least the male students, for careers in trade and commerce.

Many Quaker schools, including Newtown, were co-educational. However, the sexes attended separate classes, and girls had additional domestic tasks, learned spinning and other domestic skills, and received a more limited academic education.[10] Nevertheless, Quaker education for girls was highly rated by comparison with that available elsewhere, and Haslam herself was later described as one of 'the many workers whom the Society of Friends, with its solid and equal education for boys and girls', had given to the suffrage movement.[11]

Philanthropy is also seen as a nurturing ground of feminist consciousness. Haslam's parents engaged in a wide range of philanthropic activity.[12] The young Anna helped in the soup kitchen in Youghal during the Great Famine of 1845-9, and, like many other middle- and upper-class women, she and her sister started an industry, teaching poor girls fancy knitting and crochet, and arranging for the sale of their products. With what they earned many were able to emigrate. When the Fisher sisters left Youghal the Presentation nuns took over the industry and extended it to include embroidery and lace-making.[13]

Her parents also introduced her to the more political forms of philanthropy which are particularly linked with feminist activism. Abraham and Jane Fisher were involved in the anti-slavery movement, the temperance movement led by Fr Theobald Mathew and the international peace movement.[14] They 'entertained representatives of [the various philanthropic causes] at their home', so the young Anna would have met a number of these. She herself was certainly active in the peace movement, and in 1849 helped to start an Olive Leaf Circle and acted as its secretary.[15] These Circles grew from the Quaker London Peace Society founded in 1816. As the movement developed it stressed a connection between women, especially women as mothers, and peace. By the 1840s Olive Leaf Circles, inter-denominational groups of fifteen to twenty women, had emerged with monthly meetings and activities including discussions, correspondence with other Circles, and writing didactic stories for children. There was a strong link between peace movements and feminism in Britain, with early women peace polemicists championing women's rights.[16] Haslam saw a causal connection between her family upbringing and her feminism. She 'could not remember any time when she was not a believer in women's equality. It came to her naturally, and was always taken for granted in her household - a Quaker household, where nothing that was produced by slaves was allowed to be worn or eaten'.[17]

It is highly probable that she was aware of the leading role played by Quakers in the developing women's movements in both Britain and the United States. The American Quaker minister and feminist Lucretia Mott (1793-1880) was in London for the 1840 anti-slavery world convention at which the Amercian women delegates were refused full participation. This rejection led Mott and Elizabth Cady Stanton (1815-1902) to organise the famous Seneca Falls convention on women's rights held in New York state in 1848. Mott visited Dublin and Belfast after the 1840 convention and Irish Quakers must have heard her account of what happened in London.[18]

In 1853 Anna Fisher returned to Yorkshire as a teacher at Ackworth School where another Irish Quaker, Thomas Haslam, had been teaching for some years. They came back to Ireland where they married in Cork in 1854 and then came to live in Dublin where Thomas Haslam worked as a book-keeper or accountant. Thomas Haslam was born in 1825 in Mountmellick in Laois (then Queen's County) and educated at the Quaker Leinster Provincial school in the town where he became an apprenticed teacher. By the time he met Anna Fisher he was already interested in 'the women's question', an interest he dated to his reading the British philosopher Herbert Spencer's aphorism: 'Equity knows no distinction of sex'.[19] Throughout their lives together he was to be his wife's co-worker and colleague in all the campaigns around women's rights.

The earliest description of Haslam comes from 1870 when she was in her early forties, and 'full of perseverance and buoyant energy'.[20] Most other descriptions date from her later years, and energy and vigour combined with vivacity and good-humour are the characteristics that keep recurring. Margaret Cousins, co-founder of the Irish Women's Franchise League in 1908, met the Haslams in 1906. They were, she wrote,

> ...a remarkable old pair, devoted to one another and dedicated to the cause of the advancement and enfranchisement of women. They were nearly seventy [in

fact Anna had her 77th birthday and Thomas his 81st in 1906] when I met them; always in the best of health; she a dynamo of energy, small and sturdy; he intellectual, tall, rather like a university don, a good speaker, very refined and kindly.[21]

At the celebrations for the Haslams' sixtieth wedding anniversary in 1914 she was still making the same impression. She replied to the tributes 'in a very touching manner, and then most characteristically and amid applause, made a stirring appeal for further whole-hearted endeavour in the suffrage cause'. She went on to recite, 'by special request, and with surprising vigour', a poem she had learnt over seventy years earlier.[22] The report of another reception noted 'the inexhaustible verve and gaiety of Mrs Haslam, who concluded the evening by dancing Sir Roger de Coverley with Mr Haslam as her partner'.[23]

Extant photographs are all of the couple in their later years, their seventies or eighties, while the Sarah Purser portrait in the Municipal Gallery of Modern Art in Dublin was painted for their fiftieth wedding anniversary in 1904. In all of these she looks alert and vigorous, while he looks tall and thin, more serious and somewhat frail.

Accounts of their partnership in the cause of women speak of him as her assistant and helper and never the other way around. She herself said that marriage brought her 'a most valuable helper in her husband. She could never have undertaken what she did in later years if it were not for his sympathy and help.'[24]

Though he was the one who wrote feminist pamphlets and was in demand as a public speaker on feminist questions before she was, neither of them, nor anyone else, ever suggested that she was not the leader. At the anniversary celebrations in 1914 Thomas Haslam himself was explicit. For himself,

...the most I can say is that, from time to time, I have rendered my wife some little help in her various efforts to raise her sex out of the many disabilities from which they are everywhere suffering.... for nearly sixty years she has lost no opportunity of promoting that object in whatever way it has come within her power.[25]

Their relationship experienced another reversal of accepted sex-roles when Anna Haslam became the family breadwinner. In 1866 Thomas Haslam's health broke down and he never again worked in paid employment. It is not clear what the nature of his illness was, or whether it was the reason the Haslams, both of whom came from large families, had no children. Whatever it was, Thomas Haslam lived a life which was active by most standards until his death at the age of ninety-two in 1917. A reader, writer and scholar, he was a member of the Rathmines Public Library Committee over many years and a 'great figure' at the weekly meetings of the Dublin Friends' Institute where he frequently read papers.[26] In the Dublin Women's Suffrage Association he attended all the committee meetings over the years, often spoke at its open meetings with three of his addresses being published as pamphlets, and was regularly a joint delegate with his wife, or accompanied her, to women's conferences in Britain.

When her husband's health broke down Anna Haslam opened a business described as a stationer's and 'fancy repository'[27] at 91 Rathmines Road, there 'maintaining her home and her invalid husband'.[28] True to Quaker principles she had no inhibitions about going into trade. She ran this business, which 'required her almost undivided attention', for the next forty years until the assistance of friends made it no longer necessary.[29] That she still managed to take an active part in so many campaigns and a leadership role in some is a testimony to the energy noted in descriptions of her. The other side of this, of course, was her husband's contribution to her activism. Without at least the sympathy of a husband it was difficult for a married woman in the mid-nineteenth century to play an active political role, and Haslam enjoyed a support from her husband, a feminist in his own right, that went beyond sympathy to active collaboration.

As a young married woman in Dublin, 'already alive to the questions of higher education and employment for women'[30], Haslam began her long career as a campaigner. Organised action was developing in Great Britain and Ireland on a number of issues; married women's property rights; improved female education and access to higher education; access to better paid and a wider variety of employments for middle-class women, including the professions; opposition to double sexual standards in the response to prostitution; and participation in political life, where the first step was the acquisition of the vote in central and local government. The early women's rights activists in Ireland had a close working relationship with their English counterparts. While the position of women was not identical in both countries, Irish women and English women shared the same general disabilities under English common law, and largely similar discrimination in education, employment and political life. Most reforms in either country required laws to be passed by the all-male parliament at Westminister. Lobbying members of that parliament was of necessity a central focus of feminist political action in both countries. On some issues there was joint action and on other quite separate campaigns. Irish nationalists tended to view women's rights campaigns with suspicion as an English importation.

As yet we do not know much about the first networks in Ireland, but it is clear that in all of these areas of action Haslam was among the pioneers, although, as noted, information about most of her work is frustratingly scanty.

Education was linked to women's self-development and self-esteem, as well as to widening employment opportunities for all women, and particularly for middle-class women. One major objective was to establish the principle of education as mental training for girls as well as boys, and to raise the content and quality of female education to the level of that of males.

Haslam was one of the group led by Anne Jellicoe[31] which founded the Irish Society for the Training and Employment of Educated Women, later called the Queen's Institute, in Dublin in 1861.[32] The Institute was a pioneering venture in the technical training of women and led in turn to Jellicoe's foundation of Alexandra College for the Higher Education of Women in 1866 and Alexandra High School for Girls in 1873. Haslam, though not one of the most prominent leaders, saw her work in education as one of her major activities.[33] She also played a part in the successful efforts to have the provisions of the Intermediate Education Act of 1878 and the Royal University Act of 1879 extended to girls and women. These Acts respectively opened public competitive school examinations to girls as well as boys and allowed women to take the degrees of the Royal University.

When these achievements were mistakenly attributed solely to Haslam's efforts she disclaimed the unmerited laurel, incidentally confirming her contribution. Regarding the 'removal of some serious blots on the original drafting' of both Bills, she wrote, she was only 'a co-worker with several others - and, more especially, Miss Tod, of Belfast, and Mrs Jellicoe of the Alexandra College - both of whom did admirable service in all questions affecting the educational and industrial interests of girls'.[34]

In 1882 she was involved in setting up the Association of Schoolmistresses and Other Ladies Interested in Irish Education as a network to monitor and protect the educational interests of girls and women. It aimed to build on what had been achieved while combating attempts to undermine it by such stratagems as the introduction of separate lower-level programmes for girls in the Intermediate examinations.[35]

During the 1860s and 1870s Haslam also made some input into the campaign to gain access for women to medical degrees and into the founding of the London School of Medicine for Women in 1874[36], though again we do not have details of her contribution.

Under the Medical Registration Act of 1858 only registered persons could legally practice medicine in the United Kingdom. Since registration required the holding of a qualification from one of the specified British examining bodies, and since the latter barred women, women were effectively excluded from the practice of medicine. Women's accepted role as primary health-carers in the family and the local community and their long association with healing and medicine made the exclusion keenly felt.

A vigorous campaign resulted in an act of parliament in 1876 which allowed medical degrees to be conferred on women. The 'well-known sympathy of some of the leading members of the medical profession in Ireland' led to the King's and Queen's College of Physicians in Dublin being the first in the United Kingdom to allow women admission to medical degrees and thus to practise as physicians.[37]

Also during the 1860s and 1870s Haslam took part in the married women's property campaign.[38] The English common law, operative in Ireland, gave husbands full legal rights to the control and disposal of their wives' inherited or earned income, with the limitation that they could not actually dispose of property in land. Property rights for married women were a central issue for women's emancipationists. They affected the lives of women of all social classes. Lack of control drastically curtailed married women's power to make decisions about their own lives, and encouraged the education of middle-class girls to aim at the acquisition of accomplishments which maximised their chances of marriage to the wealthiest available male, rather than at self-development and economic independence.

The property of wealthy women could be protected by the system of trusts developed by the courts of equity to circumvent the common law. But this merely empowered trustees to 'protect' a woman's property against her husband. It did not give control to the woman herself and did not disturb the principle of patriarchal marriage. In any case the legal expense made trusts feasible only where fairly substantial property was involved.

Isabella Tod[39] of Belfast, a leading figure in the campaign, explained that the 'educated', by which she meant middle-class, women in Belfast and Dublin involved in the campaign were primarily concerned about the position of the many poor married women working in the linen mills in the Belfast area. The law left their earnings, and those of their children, at the mercy of their husbands. The only satisfactory solution was a woman's full legal right to her own earnings. Middle-class women of limited means also needed this right since it was difficult for them to pay for a protective settlement or to find suitable trustees. A women's committee had been established in Dublin and petitions in favour of an act had been organised in both Dublin and Belfast.[40] Haslam was probably a member of the Dublin committee and one of the organisers of the Dublin petition.

The campaign succeeded by forcing one limited legislative reform after another in successive Acts between 1870 and 1907 by which time the principle of spouses' separate property was fully established.

More is known about Haslam's work in the campaign to repeal the Contagious Diseases Acts. She later said that this campaign held up suffrage activity for years because

...we were all so caught up in it. When it began, I remember one old friend saying, it was such an obviously just demand, that the moment people understood it, it would be granted;

it could not be possible that such things should endure more
than a few months. It took us eighteen years.[41]

Her comment highlights how small the number of activists
was and how the same people were involved in all or most
of the campaigns on different issues.

Passed during the 1860s, due to fear that venereal disease
was undermining the British army, the acts provided for
state regulation of prostitution in certain designated areas,
including three in Ireland, the Curragh, Cork and
Queenstown (Cobh). They introduced compulsory medical
examination of any woman supected of being a prostitute
and compulsory medical treatment if she was found to be
suffering from a venereal disease.

The National Association for the Repeal of the
Contagious Diseases Acts and the Ladies' National
Association (LNA) were founded in England in 1869 and
had branches on Ireland. Isabella Tod in Belfast and Anna
Haslam in Dublin were again involved from the start. Tod
first, and after her Haslam, were members of the executive of
the LNA. Membership in Ireland appears to have been small
with subscribers never numbering more than forty-nine. The
members appear to have been exclusively Protestant, with
Quakers as usual to the fore.[42]

Work with prostitutes had always been high on the
agenda of philanthropic women. Their opposition to the Acts
was based first on the belief that state regulation gave
recogniton, and hence approval, to prostitution which they
saw as a threat to family life. Feminists also rejected the
double standard which did not interfere with the men
involved, but treated the women as commodities to be
periodically cleansed and recycled as 'clean harlots for the
army and navy'.[43]

In 1870 Thomas Haslam published a vigorously argued
eleven-page pamphlet[44] which, in view of the couple's close
collaboration, it appears reasonable to see as representing his
wife's views as well as his own. The thrust of the pamphlet,
issued at an early stage of the campaign, was to place the
blame for prostitution, 'one of the deadliest evils of our time',
firmly on male injustice and licentiousness. It saw prostitutes
themselves as women seduced and then abandoned by some
man. Thomas Haslam argued that the law should concern
itself with these guilty men, both the original seducers and

the men who availed of prostitutes' services. The man who seduced 'a virgin girl' should be legally forced to marry her. If already married his guilt was worse as he betrayed two women, his children and society, and stringent penalties were called for. Turning to the 'compulsory celibates', soldiers and sailors, largely recruited from 'the dregs of our population', he suggested it might be better to have a volunteer force or attract a 'higher class of men' by better pay and encourage them to marry. Total suppression of brothels was not immediately feasible until 'the public conscience' had been better educated about the issues. In the meantime the Contagious Diseases Acts, by removing one of its 'natural penalties', venereal disease, encouraged rather than deters prostitution. The Acts, he argued, must be repealed or radically amended.

Apart from seeing prostitutes as the victims of male seducers, the pamphlet said little about why women become prostitutes except to mention the lack of remunerative employment for all single women. This is probably because the immediate political purpose was to challenge the sexual double standards underlying the Acts.

Middle-class women had to breach many social and sexual taboos to campaign and speak at public meetings on an issue explicitly related to women's sexuality. As a result women's committees co-existed with mixed-sex committees. Anna Haslam, typically, took part in both, being secretary of the mixed-sex committee set up in Dublin in 1870, and treasurer of the women's committee set up a year later.[45] Thomas Haslam, for his part, collected the signatures of over one hundred doctors for a petition for repeal.[46]

The campaign continued with meetings and demonstrations in Belfast and Dublin over the years. In 1878 the English leader of the campaign, Josephine Butler, addressed a public meeting at the Rotunda in Dublin, which was disrupted by heckling medical students. Butler planned to return to England 'in chagrin', but Haslam and her husband promptly organised another meeting which Butler addressed and where she 'moved to tears some of the people who would not listen to her at the first'.[47] The Acts were eventually repealed in 1886. Haslam then became secretary of the Women's Vigilance Committee which was part of the Social Purity campaign which succeeded the Contagious Diseases campaign and worked for the 'health and safety of women and girls and the purification of the moral atmosphere of society.'[48]

The 1860s and 1870s also saw action on women's suffrage get under way. Participation in the making of laws was essential for women's citizenship. In 1866 the emerging circle of activists in Britain organised a petition to parliament to have women included on the same terms as men in the impending act to extend the male franchise. In the space of a fortnight the signatures of 1,499 women were gathered, and among the fifteen names with Irish addresses was that of Anna Haslam, who dated her involvement in the suffrage campaign from that time. The petition was followed a year later by a proposed amendment to the bill to replace the word 'man' by 'person'. When the amendment was rejected organised action began.

In England the National Society for Women's Suffrage was founded in 1867 and in Ireland the Northern Ireland Society for Women's Suffrage was established in 1871.

In the Dublin area Anne Robertson of Blackrock, County Dublin, was the first leading figure. She organised and spoke at meetings from 1866, and lobbied candidates in the 1868 general election urging support for women's suffrage. Anna Haslam recalled what she said at the first public suffrage meeting in Dublin in 1870, organised by Robertson, at which Millicent Garrett Fawcett, the English suffragist leader, spoke

'I well remember,' says Mrs Haslam,' seeing Mrs Fawcett, a mere girl, leading her blind husband [F.C.Fawcett MP] on to the platform. I can see her now. That was the best meeting that ever was held in Dublin - no such names have been got together for any meeting since'. And she showed me the list of names on the platform - Sir Robert Kane, Sir William Wilde (father of Oscar Wilde), and his famous wife 'Speranza', Sir John Gray M.P. of the *Freeman's Journal*, whose statue stands in O'Connell Street, Provost Lloyd of Trinity College, Dr Ingram, Dr Shaw, Dr Mahaffy, and a host of other notabilites.[49]

Haslam herself was among the organisers of a suffrage meeting in Dublin in 1872 at which Isabella Tod was one of the speakers. It was in connection with this meeting that Helen Blackburn noted Haslam's 'perseverance and buoyant energy'. She added that the meeting led in 1876 to Haslam's founding the Dublin Women's Suffrage Association (DWSA), the first permanent suffrage organisation in Dublin.[50]

Meanwhile, in April, May and July 1874 Thomas Haslam wrote and published three issues of a periodical, *The Women's Advocate*. The first issue gives an insight into the Haslams' thinking on the suffrage question. It argued the case for women's suffrage as 'the moral right of properly qualified women to some share in the enactment of the laws which they are required to obey'. Women's claims are just in themselves, he asserted, and no convincing counter argument has appeared. Women demanded political and educational rights and 'to be treated as reasonable beings, who are personally responsible for the talents which have been confided to their care'. The second issue gave practical advice on how to organise local groups for effective political action. This advice was deemed so valuable that Lydia Becker, the English suffrage leader, ordered 5,000 copies for distribution.[51] The advice also corresponded closely to the methods adopted by the DWSA under Anna Haslam's energetic leadership.

Haslam was secretary of the DWSA from its foundation in 1876 until 1913 when she stood down and was elected life-president. Throughout that entire period she did not miss a single meeting and was clearly the driving force in the organisation. The membership was predominantly Quaker, including men as well as women, though as the years went by women increasingly outnumbered the men. It worked to educate public opinion by writing to the newspapers and organising drawing room and public meetings, the latter whenever the opportunity of high-profile women speakers presented itself. It maintained contact with the movement in England and sent delegates, regularly both Haslams, to suffrage and other feminist conferences, and later to suffrage demonstrations and parades. It followed political developments in Ireland and Britain to avail of every favourable opportunity for lobbying in support of its objective. It organised petitions to the House of Commons. It sent deputations and letters to Irish MPs urging them to introduce or support bills or amendments to bills to enfranchise women. It exhorted 'influential' women in various parts of the country to lobby their MPs. It noted with approval advances in the various feminist campaigns, not surprisingly since Haslam was involved in all or most of them.

In 1884 women were yet again excluded from a reform act. This one extended the franchise to male agricultural labourers by making male household suffrage the basic vote, though a property qualification for lodgers still excluded a substantial proportion of men. After this private members' bills for women's suffrage were regularly introduced. These often received substantial support from MPs including the Irish members, who, according to Thomas Haslam, 'as a general rule ... voted preponderately upon our side in all questions relating to the interests of women'.[52] This support never translated into legislation both because the Conservative Party, generally opposed to women's suffrage, was in government almost continuously from 1885 to 1906, which enabled the leadership to use parliamentary procedures to dispose of unwelcome bills, and also because the Conservative majority in the House of Lords could quash any measure which passed the Commons.

The DWSA, like most suffrage organisations in the United Kingdom, demanded the vote for women on the same terms as men. In the mid-nineteenth century 'on the same terms as men' meant on a property qualification which also excluded most men. As the vote was extended to more categories of men by reducing the property qualification the demand for women's suffrage correspondingly extended to more women. Every extension of the franchise to new groups of men while still excluding all women increased the grievance felt by the latter. Haslam wrote in 1886 that it 'is not easy to keep our temper when we see the most illiterate labourer, with no two ideas in his head, exercising the very important function of self-government while educated women capable in every way of giving a rational vote are still debarred'.[53]

Socialist feminists challenged suffragists as bourgeois women looking for votes for their own class. Taken in historical context neither the demand for parity with men nor the exasperation expressed by Haslam and others necessarily implied opposition to universal suffrage - so long as this included both sexes, and we may note that in 1916 Thomas Haslam's last pamphlet argued for universal suffrage for all women and men. Undoubtedly, some suffragists did see political participation as the preserve of the better-off, who had a corresponding duty to look after the poorer classes. Others may have simply made what they saw as being the only achievable demand in the social and political realities of the time. For similar reasons early suffrage demands applied only to unmarried women and widows, since married women did not control property and could not qualify for a property-related vote on the same terms as men. As married women gained property rights the suffragists demanded the removal of disqualifiation on the grounds of either sex or marriage.

Related issues emerged regarding the protection of women's interests in employment. Some middle-class philanthropic feminists moved beyond attempts to ameliorate the conditions of working-class women's employment to help in the organisation of women's trade unions which would be run by the workers themselves.[54] As with so many other aspects of feminism there was not a clear dividing line between the philanthropic and the self-help approaches, and Anna Haslam, who earned her own living, and whose Quaker principles gave her a respect for others who did the same, was involved with both. In the aftermath of the Trade Union Congress held in Dublin in 1880, two women's trade unions, were established, the Dublin Tailoresses' Society and the Bookfolders and Sewers' Union. Both were branches of British unions and neither survived for long.[55] Haslam actively supported the venture, and also appears to have tried to link it to the suffrage campaign. With Rose McDowell, joint secretary of the DWSA, and acting against a decision of the DWSA committee[56], she organised a public meeting in Dublin in support of women's suffrage where she was on the platform with women from the English Weavers' Union and the Shirt and Collar Makers' Union.[57]

Later in the 1890s Halsam entered a long association with the British-based National Union of Women Workers (NUWW), later the National Council of Women. The NUWW, which emerged during the 1880s, was not a trade union but a forum where women working for women could liaise and exchange information. Its first members were mainly middle-class women involved in philanthropic and religious work. By the end of the century it was promoting women in local government and on public bodies[58], and women's trade unions were becoming affiliates.

Haslam and other DWSA delegates attended NUWW conferences over the years. Haslam was an enthusiastic supporter of the NUWW. In an account of the NUWW conference in Croydon in 1898, she emphasied the value she saw in the interchange of ideas at these meetings, and their particular benefit for Irish women who were 'so largely excluded from direct participation in the *mainstream* of human progress'.[59]

Meanwhile the numbers involved in the Irish suffrage campaign remained small. As late as 1896 the DWSA had only forty-three members.[60] As noted already, activity was sometimes interrupted by suffragists' participation in other feminist campaigns. At others unrest caused by the Land War and Home Rule agitation did the same. No executive meeting was held between April 1882 and June 1883 and the association 'did not feel that in the recent very excited condition of the country that the time was favourable for much action'.[61]

The Land War, while interrupting suffrage activity, gave a group of nationalist, and mostly Catholic, middle-class women the unique opportunity of running a nation-wide political movement composed largely of men. Their experience in the Ladies' Land League[62] pushed many towards feminist consciousness. For Anna Haslam the possibility of Home Rule for Ireland was far from welcome and she became involved in counter-action. Around this time she helped to found a Dublin branch of the Women's Liberal Unionist Association and was also a member of both the Rathmines Liberal Association and the Central Unionist Committee. As was typical of Haslam she held office as secretary in the first two of these.[63]

To judge by a speech she made to a meeting of women in Dublin in 1888, she feared for the political and civil liberties of unionists under a Home Rule parliament. Ireland's present government, she claimed, while not perfect, was 'probably as good as that of any other great nation' and was improving rapidly. As evidence she pointed to Catholic Emancipation, the National Schools, the Poor Law System, the Royal University and the Intermediate Education System, the Industrial and Reformatory Schools, 'our admirable police force', and the extension of the vote to male householders, though she stressed the 'male'. She believed that all the main political leaders were committed to giving justice to Ireland, even if some made temporary mistakes, and that, with over one hundred Irish MPs to 'set them right', any serious injustice was impossible. The one threat to 'reasonable liberty' was the 'tyranny of the National League, - the most unscrupulous body of men, I suppose, that have ever attempted to seize the reins of power in our land'. Home Rule would mean putting government in their hands, and they have 'refused to permit *one single Loyalist* to represent us in either of the three southern provinces', and the danger is that the Loyalists of Ireland 'will be politically extinguished'.[64]

Despite these views Haslam was committed to crossing barriers of religion and politics. The DWSA was explicitly non-party and Haslam consistently tried to widen its membership. She rejoiced in 1898 when the evidence of the polls showed that many women voters in Dublin had risen 'above all sectarian prejudices' and voted for a woman candidate of a different religion to their own, 'simply because ... she can be absolutely trusted to do her duty' by the poor.[65] In the early decades of the twentieth century, when Home Rule was becoming an imminent probability, she actively encouraged women of nationalist sympathies and Catholic religion to become members. To the end of her life she was respected and held in real affection by feminists of very different political opinions. Indeed, in this speech her defence of the United Kingdom is based on what she sees as its record of justice to Ireland. She may also have been reassured by what the Haslams saw as the relatively good record of Home Rule MPs on women's interests.

In the later 1880s Irish suffragists turned their attention to local government. In England women had won the vote in municipal elections in 1869 and in 1887 the Northern Ireland Suffrage Society did the same for Belfast. The poor law system, which had become an important part of the structure of Irish local government, was also under scrutiny. In England and Ireland women could vote in elections for Poor Law Guardians on the same property qualification as men, while women in England were also eligible for election as guardians. The office of Poor Law Guardian had obvious potential for women philanthropists as a move to participation in policy making. Haslam explained the failure of Irish suffragists to move on it earlier as due to the fact that election to the boards had almost from their establishment become an arena for political contest between male nationalists and unionists. It was conducted 'so on party lines and with so little regard for the well-being of our destitute poor that we were fairly excusable for taking little interest'[66]. Now the DWSA asked the Belfast MP, William Johnston, to introduce a bill and lobbied vigorously in support.[67] Participation by women in local government did not meet as strong opposition as did their access to parliament, and the Women Poor Law Guardian Act passed in 1896, providing that 'no person otherwise qualified ... shall be disqualified by sex or marriage' from being elected or serving as a guardian.

The DWSA moved at once to consolidate this success and build on its potential. Haslam wrote to the newspapers and published leaflets explaining how women should ensure they were properly registered to vote and to stand for election, as well as writing to individual women around the country exhorting them to seek out suitable candidates and urge them to go forward. By 1898 there were seventeen women Poor Law Guardians, and by 1900 nearly one hundred.

This year of success, 1896, saw the death of Isabella Tod, the formidable Belfast campaigner for women's rights. Haslam considered Tod to have been 'one of the most effective speakers we have ever had in either Great Britain or Ireland, and her premature decease, in 1896, has been a serious loss to the cause of women in the northern province'. Tod and Haslam filled complementary roles as leaders in a number of campaigns. Haslam saw Tod as her 'great ally and co-worker in all the early fights'[68], and recognised a geographical divide, with Tod operating in Ulster, while Dublin activists were responsible for organising and inspiring women in 'our three southern provinces' as she often expressed it. While it was Haslam who later became a legend and inspiration to the next generation, Tod during her lifetime had the higher public profile as a speaker and writer while Haslam's talents lay more in organisation. While both women supported the union of Ireland with Great Britain, Haslam never saw herself as anything but Irish, and she saw the cause of women as crossing the boundaries of political and religious differences.

Eligibility as Poor Law Guardians was quickly followed by the achievement of all remaining local government franchises and eligibility for election to most local government bodies. The DWSA was again active in a campaign to include women in the forthcoming reorganisation of Irish local government, lobbying Irish MPs to support the relevant amendments. The Local Government

(Ireland) Act of 1898 set up county councils and urban and rural district councils. It gave women all local government franchises on the same qualification as men, as well as making women eligible for election as urban and rural councillors, though eligibility as county councillors was withheld until 1911.

Again the DWSA published letters and leaflets to explain what had been achieved and how women could avail of it. In Anna Haslam's words the Act was 'the most signal political revolution that has taken place in the history of Irishwomen. We have, in round numbers, somewhere about one hundred thousand women ratepayers who are now invested with powers which they never possessed before'. As well as opening to women unprecedented opportunities of participation in public political life, the Act had an important psychological impact. The DWSA and Haslam saw it as a significant step to the parliamentary franchise. 'For the vast majority of our countrywomen in all our rural districts', Haslam wrote, 'their political education commences with the present year.' The experience of participation in local government 'will make them not only desire the Parliamentary vote, but willing to take some little trouble in order to obtain it'. She anticipated the spread of the suffrage movement which so far had 'never penetrated much beyond the outskirts of Dublin, Belfast and one or two other towns'[69]. This expansion had already begun and by by 1898 the DWSA had branches in Tralee, Sligo, Skibbereen, Strokestown and Miltown Malbay.[70] In line with these developments the Association now changed its name, first to the Dublin Women's Suffrage and Poor Law Guardian Association, then to the Dublin Women's Suffrage and Local Government Association, and finally to the Irish Women's Suffrage and Local Government Association (IWSLGA). The parliamentary franchise remained its core objective. However valuable in itself, the local government vote was not, insisted the Association, 'and never can be, a substitute for the parliamentary vote, to which all duly qualified women are morally as indubitably entitled as any male voters'.[71]

Anna Haslam's prophecy was proved true as the suffrage campaign grew internationally in the early years of the new century. In Ireland this expansion took place in the atmosphere of action and self-help that characterised the cultural and political renaissance of the late nineteenth and

early twentieth centuries. Many of the new recruits to the
suffrage cause were educated young women who had
benefited by the earlier women's campaigns. Many were
active in the cultural revival, some were nationalists and
some sympathetic to the labour movement. Catholic women
became involved in greater numbers than heretofore.

The long-established IWSLGA introduced many of the
new suffragists to the movement. Anna Haslam continued to
encourage educated women of all political and religious
affiliations to join. Among IWSLGA members with well-
known nationalist sympathies were Hanna Sheehy
Skeffington and Margaret Cousins, the future founders of
the Irish Women's Franchise League, Jennie Wyse Power,
formerly of the Ladies' Land League and now on the
executive of Sinn Féin, and Mary Hayden, professor of Irish
History in University College Dublin.

In 1906 Thomas Haslam published another pamphlet on
the suffrage question. Again his basic argument was that
there is no sustainable argument against the principle of
women's right to suffrage. He listed and rejected those which
were usually trotted out; that women did not serve as
policemen or soldiers; that the vote would lead to family
disputes; that, because women outnumbered men in the
United Kingdom men would be driven to forcibly prevent
women from exercising their franchise; that women's
delicacy and refinement would be put at risk. He proceeded
to a succinct statement of the philosophy which permeated
the thinking and statements of both Haslams on women's
rights. 'Women', he wrote, 'have been brought into the
world, like men, to cultivate their whole nature, physical,
intellectual, moral, spiritual, political, and so on, in the way
most conducive to their happiness, and the well-being of the
world at large.'[72]

As the suffrage movement grew internationally it began
to employ new methods to use its size to political effect.
Large scale street demonstrations with banners, slogans and
colours became popular. Some suffragists moved further to
what were called 'militant' methods, first to forms of passive
civil disobedience such as refusal to pay tax, then to heckling
and disrupting public meetings, and finally to physical
violence such as damaging public property. This final level
of militancy emerged in Britain and Ireland where suffrage
had so long appeared just within reach but had never
actually materialised. The name 'suffragette' was coined to

designate the militants. In England the Women's Social and Political Union (WSPU), founded in 1903 by Emmeline Pankhurst and her daughters, was an explicitly militant organisation.

In June 1908 nine IWSLGA committee members, including both Haslams, 'under two appropriate banners', were among the Irish participants in a major suffrage demonstration in London.[73] However, the Association remained committed to action strictly within the law. Ireland's principal militant suffrage organisation, the Irish Women's Franchise League (IWFL), was established in 1908. The aim was a society on the model of the English WPSU but completely independent of any English society. Its founders, Hanna Sheehy Skeffington and Margaret Cousins, both members of the IWSLGA, were impatient for more assertive action. In recognition of the position Haslam held in the Irish suffrage movement, in November 1908 the founders of the new group went to

...the dear old leader of the constitutional suffragists, Mrs Anna Haslam, to inform her that we younger women were ready to start a new suffrage society on militant lines. She regretted what she felt to be a duplication of effort. She was also congenitally a person of peace, non-violent, law-abiding to the finger tips. But she sensed the Time Spirit, and we parted as friends, agreeing to differ on means, though united in aim and ideals.[74]

The IWFL, like the IWSLGA, demanded the vote for women on the same terms as men, and both organisations were non-party and open to members of all religions and political affiliations. Their constitutions differed in that the IWSLGA was committed to staying within the law while the IWFL was committed to breaking it if necessary. In practice there was another difference in that the leadership of the IWSLGA was unionist in sympathy and that of the IWFL was nationalist.

Other new suffrage societies were established in Ireland and by 1912 there were over three thousand active women suffragists, and the movement had attained a numerical strength far beyond any earlier feminist campaigns. The largest groups were the IWFL with over 1000 members, the

IWSLGA with 700-800, an Irish branch of the Conservative and Unionist Women's Suffrage Association with 660, and the Irish Women's Suffrage Society, Belfast, originally a branch of the IWSLGA but now independent, with 'several hundred'.[75] The majority of suffragists were still middle-class and Protestant but the Catholic presence was much larger than before with the Catholic to non-Catholic ratio about one to two. Irish working-class suffragists appear to have remained few in number. A range of smaller organisations were affiliated to an umbrella network, the Irish Women's Suffrage Federation (IWSF) established in 1911. By 1913 it had fifteen affiliated societies, including nine from Ulster as well as the Munster Women's Franchise League (MWFL), which itself had branches.[76]

Home Rule for Ireland by now posed problems for suffragists. Once the Parliament Act of 1911 removed the power of the House of Lords to veto legislation the passing both of a women's suffrage act and a Home Rule act became more likely. In 1912 one of a number of what were called 'Conciliation Bills', women's suffrage bills agreed by members of the main political parties, failed to pass its second reading because the Irish Parliamentary Party did not support it. Its leader, John Redmond, himself an opponent of votes for women, feared that if the Bill passed it could lead to the fall of the Liberal government and so endanger Home Rule, and his party fell into line. The failure of this Conciliation Bill infuriated many suffragists in both Ireland and Britain. Interestingly, the IWSLGA, while sharing the anger, made some allowance for 'the tergiversation' of Irish MPs in the light of their fears for the Home Rule Bill[77], an attitude which may reflect the presence in the IWSLGA of members like Mary Hayden who supported the Irish Parliamentary Party.

The suffrage organisations strove to remain united in action despite the contrary pull of nationalist and unionist loyalties and commitments to constitutional or militant action. The general policy was to support all measures of suffrage, whether a franchise bill for the whole United Kingdom or the inclusion of women's suffrage in a Home Rule Bill. However, some nationalist women argued that to ask the Westminster parliament for the vote was to recognise its authority over Ireland. They also claimed that there was no need to demand the inclusion of women's suffrage in a Home Rule Bill since this would be freely granted by nationalist men in a free Ireland.

When the third Home Rule Bill began its course through parliament in 1912 Redmond refused to endanger its passage by insisting on the inclusion of women's suffrage. Suffrage organisations of all political affiliations joined forces to demand its inclusion at a mass meeting presided over by Mary Hayden of the IWSLGA.[78] Redmond did not move and the IWFL turned to militancy. This was largely symbolic and publicity-directed. Members broke windows in a number of public buildings with the aim of being arrested, refusing to pay the fines imposed by the court and going to prison. Between 1912 and the outbreak of the First World War in 1914 thirty-five women had been convicted for suffrage militancy in Ireland.[79]

Haslam was in London at the time of the window-breaking. On her own initiative she wrote to the newspapers to publicly express the IWSLGA's disapproval of such action. She had been unable to summon her committee,

> ...but I know that I am embodying their sentiments when I express my strong disapproval of the breaking of windows as a means of advancing our cause. It is my conviction that the adoption of such action by a section of our supporters was one of the chief contributory causes of the defeat of the Conciliation Bill, and I do not believe that it will promote the passing of a women's suffrage amendment to our Home Rule Bill, if carried. Our Association, which has been in existence since 1876, has always consistently disapproved of what are called militant methods in the advancement of our cause.[80]

Although the IWSLGA subsequently approved her action (although three members resigned in protest).[81] the attitude of both Haslam and her organisation was not one of blanket condemnation of militancy. Many suffragists who were themselves committed to constitutional methods could empathise with militancy provoked by the long denial to women of one of the basic rights of citizenship, and were angered by the hypocrisy of condemning actions by suffragists which, if carried out by male members of a political movement, would hardly have raised an eyebrow. Constitutional suffragists also conceded that miltant methods sometimes succeeded where theirs did not. A few years earlier both Haslam and her friend and colleague in the IWSLGA, Lady Dockrell, had expressed sympathy and even approval of methods they would not themselves adopt. After clashes between some suffragists and police at a demonstration at Westminster in 1907, Dockrell admitted that she both sympathised and approved of militant action and that she thought it was the only way 'by which women will ever get anything'. Haslam smiled, said they could not really blame them, 'they are our sisters, after all', and gave it as her opinion that 'on the whole the campaign will do more good than harm'.[82] In 1910 the IWSLGA wryly noted that militancy had persuaded the Chief Secretary, Birrell, to receive a deputation when he had refused its own 'courteous request'.[83] Finally, we can note Hanna Sheehy Skeffington's account of Haslam's visit to her in Mountjoy Prison after the IWFL's window-breaking:

> Mrs Haslam came, with a difference: 'Don't think I approve - but here's a pot of verbena I brought you. I am not here in my official capacity, of course - the Irish Women's Suffrage and Local Government Association strongly disapprove of violence as pulling back the cause. But here's some loganberry jam - I made it myself'.[84]

In 1913, at the age of eighty-four, Haslam resigned as secretrary of the IWSLGA, becoming life-president instead. This, however, was far from signalling the end of her active role in the feminist movement. The outbreak of World War 1 in August 1914 made it difficult to maintain active suffrage campaigning. Irish organisations most closely associated with English groups tended to suspend suffrage action temporarily and turn to work in support of the British war effort. The *Irish Citizen*, the suffrage newspaper founded in 1912 in association with the IWFL, insisted, under the headline 'Votes for Women Now - Damn Your War', that suffragists must continue their campaign.[85] Both it and the IWFL took a pacifist position to the war itself. Other nationalist women, believing that England's difficulty was Ireland's opportunity and that for the time being the rights of the nation took precedence over women's rights, joined Cumann na mBan, the women's organisation set up in 1914 to work with the Irish Volunteers. The IWSLGA started a fund for the relief of Belgian refugees in Ireland[86], and endowed a bed in the Dublin Castle Red Cross Hospital.[87] At the same time it initiated a Joint Committee, under Haslam, of delegates from women's societies in Dublin to co-ordinate efforts on women's issues other than suffrage.[88] One of the Joint Committee's activities was the setting up of patrols. The introduction of women police was a long-standing feminist objective and voluntary women patrols, working in conjunction with the police, were part of the campaign for professional women police.

Haslam, who, with Mary Hayden, was joint president of the Patrol Committee, reported in 1915 to the annual meeting of the Council of the Women's National Health Association of Ireland that there were twenty patrols, authorised by the police, in action in central Dublin. The patrols worked in couples, a Catholic and Protestant where possible, and needed more Catholic volunteers, as well as Catholic and Protestant clubs to which the patrols could direct girls who were walking about the streets.[89]

The *Irish Citizen* was uneasy about aspects of the patrols. While not disputing the need for women police in the exclusively male law-enforcement system, it feared that the patrols' method of removing women from the streets would in effect repeat the sexist method of policing women to protect men, and ignore the problem of rough treatment of women by the police.[90] It also queried the implications of such voluntary amateur services for demands for full entry by women into all the professions.[91] *The Irish Worker* challenged the middle-class composition of the Joint Committee and called on working-class parents to resent these 'well-to-do snobs'.[92]

1915 also saw the fulfilment of Anna Haslam's long-time aim to establish in Dublin a branch of the English-based National Union of Women Workers, of which the IWSLGA was already an affiliate.[93] This drew criticism from the *Irish Citizen* on the grounds it was unlikely to 'unite women of every shade of opinion' since the vice-presidents and committee appeared to be 'restricted practically to women of precisely the same shade of opinion', and expressed its disapproval of setting up Irish branches of British organisations.[94] Yet the nationalist Hayden was a member of the committee and the same issue of the *Irish Citizen* printed the full text of Thomas Haslam's address to a meeting of the IWFL.[95]

1916 brought the Easter Rising and the Proclamation of the Irish Republic which included full citizenship for all Irish men and women In the following years, through the War of Independence to the Treaty and the establishment in 1922 of the Irish Free State, the IWFL, with Cumann na mBan and the Irish Women Workers' Union (IWWU), concentrated much of its attention on pressing Sinn Féin to include women in its own leadership and on ensuring that the citizenship of the 1916 Proclamation was delivered on in a future independent Ireland. This was an area where Haslam and the IWSLGA could have little input. What Haslam thought of the 1916 Rising is not recorded and the IWSLGA report for 1916 made no mention of it, instead focusing on the anticipated concession of women's suffrage by the UK government at the end of the war, and deciding to urge the inclusion of women in the new electoral register.

In 1916 Thomas Haslam, at the age of ninety, published his final suffrage pamphlet, *Some last words on women's suffrage*. In this he continued to argue that the essential for success was that enough women actively wanted it. He noted that the prime minister, Asquith, was committed to some measure after the war and that the extent of the suffrage then granted would depend on the attitude of women in the meantime. He called for full adult suffrage for both sexes, claiming that people with no property needed the protection of the vote more than people with property and that there was no justification for the present position which excluded all married women with the exception of those who were property owners in their own right. Women needed the vote more than men, he asserted, because generally they were poorer, paid less, victimised by inheritance laws, physically weaker, and their interests are also those of their children. He rejected the argument that it would be dangerous to give women the vote because women were constitutionally unable to take the broad view in national emergenices, though he conceded that in the short term women would follow their husbands and brothers until they acquire political experience which would give a sense of personal responsibility.

A year later, in 1917, Thomas Haslam died and was buried in the Friends' Cemetery at Temple Hill, Blackrock, County Dublin. What the breaking of this partnership of sixty-three years meant to Anna Haslam can only be imagined. If he had lived for another year he would have seen the culmination of their work for women's suffrage when his wife at last cast her vote in a parliamentary election.

In January 1918 the Representation of the People Act, a compromise between the Liberal and Conservative parties, gave a limited measure of female suffrage, confined to women over thirty, who themselves or whose husbands were householders or occupiers of land or premises of a minimum yearly value of £5. The restriction reflected the fears of all the parties as to how they would fare when women voted in the coming election. Even with these limitations both the Irish Party and the Unionists tried to prevent its extension to Ireland. In view of their past attitude to women's suffrage both had reason to feel apprehensive. Later in the year another Act made women eligible to stand as parliamentary candidates.

The general election was not held until November after the end of the war and, in the meantime, women's organisations were active on two main issues. In April 1918 the attempt to extend conscription to Ireland began, and in August a new government regulation of prostitution, similar to the Contageous Acts of the 1860s, was introduced in the Defence of the Realm Act (DORA). The IWSLGA took part in the campaign against DORA but not in the anti-conscription campaign, though members like Hayden did so in an individual capacity, while Cumann na mBan, the IWWU and the IWFL all took part in both.[96]

In November 1918 the first general election in which at least some women could vote and stand for election took place. The *Irish Citizen* noted that the declared voting intentions of some prominent feminist women refuted predictions that all women would vote the same way, all conservative or all radical. In Rathmines in Dublin, Mary Kettle, sister of Hanna Sheehy Skeffington, and Mary Hayden supported the Irish Party candidate, Anna Haslam the Conservative candidate, and Hanna Sheehy Skeffington the Sinn Féin candidate.[97] That these differences did not undermine the unique position Haslam held in the esteem and affections of Irish suffragists is shown in the IWFL's account:

On Election Day the League was represented with its banners and colours at joint demonstrations organised by the various suffrage and women's organisations for Mrs Haslam, the veteran Irish suffrage leader. She recorded her vote in the midst of an admiring feminine throng to cheer her, was presented with a bouquet in suffrage colours for the occasion ... It speaks well for the broadmindedness of the new women voters that women of all parties - Unionist, Irish Party and Sinn Féin - joined heartily to honour Mrs Haslam and suffrage.[98]

In the same month the IWSLGA changed its name to the Irish Women Citizens and Local Government Association to continue to work for sex equality in all franchises and opportunities for public service, to further the registration of women voters and the election of women at parliamentary and local levels, as well as the appointment of women to public offices.[99] It continued its efforts to promote combined action by the suffrage organisations at a series of conferences, but the IWFL reported that, 'owing to the disturbed state of the political atmosphere no common basis of agreement could be reached.'[100] The War of Independence, which began early in 1919, and the succeeding Treaty negotiations and debates dominated the following years. Haslam died at the age of ninety-three in November 1922, the year when the constitution of the new Irish Free State gave the vote and full citizenship to all women and men over twenty-one years of age.

Assessing Anna Haslam's contribution to Irish history is difficult. The energy and enthusiasm which made an impact on everyone she met brings her alive as a personality in a way that contrasts with the scarcity of information on most of her work, with the exception of women's suffrage.

One aspect that stands out is the sheer quality of her work. This is evidenced in particular by the thoroughly-researched pamphlets she wrote for the IWSLGA explaining in careful and accurate detail what women had gained in the poor law and local government legislation and how they could avail of this.

Her leadership qualities were also impressive. She had the ability both to inspire others and to work with them, as shown by her effective guidance of the suffrage association she founded in 1876 throughout her long tenure of its secretaryship. That the IWSLGA was not a one-woman show was demonstrated by its active survival when Haslam retired and after she died. Under its new name, the Irish

Women Citizens and Local Government Association, it was quickly in the field in the early 1920s and played a leading role in feminist opposition to attempts by successive Free State governments to renege on aspects of women's full citizenship as established in the 1922 Constitution. This role continued until 1947 when the Women Citizens emerged with a new and vigorous group, the Irish Housewives' Association.[101]

In their claims for women's equality the arguments of both Anna Haslam and her husband are based mainly on the concept implicit in European Enlightenment thought that, on the basis of shared rational human nature, all persons had the right to autonomy and full citizenship. Both Haslams did at times speak of women's contribution as differing in some ways to that of men. For example, Anna refered to the need for women Guardians to improve the diet, the nursing and the training of children in many Poor Law Unions,[102] while Thomas saw women's participation in politics needed to solve the social problems of temperance, pauperism, prostitution and aggressive wars.[103] But neither urged these as the basis of their claims for equal rights.

Both placed much more emphasis on the equality of the sexes as persons. As has been seen, Thomas Haslam developed these arguments in his writings, both in *The Women's Advocate* and in his various pamphlets. While Anna Haslam did not expound her thinking as fully the same ideas permeate her speeches. In 1898 she spoke of the parliamentary franchise as '*a matter of the barest equitable right.*'[104] In 1907 she explained that 'we are still battling for a constitutional right which Mr Gladstone's government should have conceded to us when they passed their Reform Act of 1884'.[105] In the following year she emphasised that , in her opinion,

> ...the elevation of women, the whole world over, to their rightful position in the social and political organism, is one of the most important problems, if not, indeed, the *most* important, that is confronting us at the present day. Our parliamentary enfranchisement is only the first step in its practical realisation; but it is the first, and the *most indispensable* to the realisation of the rest.[106]

The thinking of both Haslams on women's rights can be summed up in the quotation from Herbert Spencer which was printed under the title of each issue of *The Women's Advocate*: 'Equity knows no diffference of sex. The law of equal freedom applies to the whole race - female as well as male', and in Thomas Haslam's comment: 'Ethically speaking, that principle covers all that needs to be said upon the subject'.[107]

Research on Irish feminist organisations has tended to concentrate on the relationship between feminism and nationalism in the early decades of the twentieth century. The work of Haslam and her contemporaries extends our perspective, backwards to at least the mid-nineteenth century and forwards with the organisation she founded into the inter-War years and after. The feminism-nationalism nexus is then seen as one aspect of a multi-faceted engagement of feminism with unionism and with nationalism, with Catholicism and with Protestantism, and with socialism and the Labour movement. A more complex picture emerges, within which feminism actively influenced other movements and ways of seeing the world as well as being in turn influenced by them.

Haslam and her Protestant middle-class colleagues created the first organised Irish feminist campaigns and changed the legal position of women in Irish society in a number of significant ways. The specific contribution of Haslam herself included her clarity of thinking and expression, her long presence as an articulate and confident voice steadily and consistently asserting the self-evident truth of women's claims, and, perhaps most of all, her inclusive concept of Irishness. This last quality, allied to her warm and lively personality, must have been a major factor in encouraging the participation of Catholic and nationalist women in organised feminist action, particularly the Irish suffrage movement, in the early twentieth century. It was to this quality that a leading Irish feminist paid tribute in 1913, when she wrote:

[T]he Society of Friends is as prominent in the history of suffrage in Ireland as it is in every other good work. Many have sought to help Ireland and have only earned the distrust of the Irish: to the Friends alone it has been given to win the trust and love of the Catholic south and the Protestant north, and so we find the name of Mrs Haslam in the list of suffrage work.[108]

NOTES

1 *Report of the executive of the Irish Women's Suffrage and Poor Law Association for 1917.* (Hereafter *IWSLGA Report*), Dublin, 1918, p.4.

2 Thomas Haslam's obituary stated that the Haslams had deposited their collected papers in the National Library, Dublin, but the National Library has no trace of them. A few items are in the custody of the Irish Housewives' Association (hereafter IHA).

3 Geneological information from the Religious Society of Friends' Historical Library, Swanbrook House, Dublin. (Hereafter FHL).

4 Brannigan, Cyril G 1984. 'Quaker education in 18th and 19th century Ireland', in *Irish Educational Studies* iv, 1, p.57.

5 Kilroy, Phil. 1991. 'Women and the Reformation in seventeeth-century Ireland'. In MacCurtain, Margaret and O'Dowd, Mary (eds). *Women in Early Modern Ireland*. Dublin, p.192; Hempton, David and Hill, Myrtle. 'Women and Protestant minorities in eighteenth-century Ireland', *ibid.*, p.198.

6 Hempton and Hill, 'Women and Protestant minorities', p.200.

7 The American Quaker feminist, born in 1820, and for many years co-leader with Elizabeth Cady Stanton of the US women's movement. She visited Ireland in 1884.

8 Typescript of speech given by Haslam, no date. IHA.

9 Brannigan, Cyril Gerard. 1992. 'Quaker eduation in Ireland 1680-1840'. Unpublished MA thesis. St. Patrick's College, Maynooth.

10 *Newtown School Centenary Record*. 1898. Waterford, passim and p.76.

11 Blackburn, Helen. 1902. *A Record of the Women's Suffrage Movement in the British Isles*. London, p.129.

12 MS note, IHA.

13 *Irish Citizen*, 21 March 1914, p.347 and 28 March 1914, p.355.

14 *Ibid* and newspaper cutting, 5 April 1909. FHL.

15 Typescript of speech 1886. IHA.

16 Liddington, Jill. 1989. *The Long Road to Greenham: Feminism and Anti-militarism in Britain since 1820*. London, p.16.

17 *Irish Citizen*, 21 March 1914, p.347.

18 Tolles, Frederick B.(ed.). 1952. *Slavery and 'the Woman Question': Lucretia Mott's Diary 1840*. London and New York. Mott made a pithy comment on Quaker education in one Dublin school; 'his boys forward in arithmetic - girls sampler work - stitching and other nonsense -', p.64.

19 *Irish Citizen*, 21 March 1914 , p.347.

20 Blackburn, *Record*, p.129.

21 Cousins, J H and M E 1950. *We Two Together*. Madras, p.129.

22 *Irish Citizen*, 4 April 1914, p.366.

23 *Ibid.*, p.361.

24 MS note, IHA.

25 *Irish Citizen*, 4 April 1914, p.366.

26 Obituary of T J Haslam by Professor C H Oldham, FHL.

27 *Slater's Commercial Directory of Ireland*. 1870. London , p.120.

28 Obituary by Oldlam. FHL.
29 Speech by Thomas Haslam at function in honour of Anna Haslam's eightieth birthday. Newspaper cutting, 5 April, 1909. FHL.
30 Blackburn, *Record*, p. 129.
31 See chapter on Anne Jellicoe in this volume.
32 *Final Report of the Royal Irish Association for Promoting the Training and Employment of Women*, Dublin. 1904. p.10.
33 *Irish Citizen*, 12 March 1914, p. 347.
34 *Ibid.*, 28 March 1914, p.355.
35 O'Connor, Anne V and Parkes, Susan B 1983. *Gladly Learn and Gladly Teach; a History of Alexandra College and School, Dublin 1886-1996*. Dublin, pp46-7
36 MS list of campaigns in which Haslam had been involved. IHA.
37 *Englishwoman's Review*, 15 March 1877, p.132 and 14 April 1877, pp150-1.
38 *Irish Citizen*, 21 March 1914, p.347.
39 See chapter on Tod in this volume.
40 *Special report from the select committee on married women's property Bill*, H.C. [4417] 1867-8 339, pp74-5.
41 *Irish Citizen*, 21 March 1914, p.347.
42 Luddy , Maria. 1993. 'Irish Women and the Contagious Diseases Acts', in *History Ireland* i,1 (Spring), pp32-4.
43 Evidence of Josephine Butler to the *Select Committee on the Contagious Diseases Acts*, H.C., p. 440, (323),viii,397.
44 Haslam, T J 1870. *A few words on Prostitution and the Contagious Diseases Acts*, Dublin.
45 *Annual Report of the National Association for the Repeal of the Contagious Diseases Acts 1870-1*, p.4.
46 *Irish Citizen*, 21 March 1914, p.347.
47 *Ibid*.
48 *The Shield*, 5 June 1886.
49 *Irish Citizen*, 21 March 1914, p.347.
50 Blackburn, *Record*, p.129.
51 *Irish Citizen*, 21 March 1914, p.347.
52 Haslam, T J 1906. *Women's Suffrage from a Masculine Viewpoint*. Dublin, p.15.
53 Typescript of speech 1886. IHA.
54 Mappen, Ellen. 1985. *Helping Women at Work: the Women's Industrial Council 1889-1914*. London, p.13.
55 Moriarty, Theresa. 1994. *Work in Progress: Episodes from the History of Irish Women's Trade Unionism*. Dublin and Belfast, p.2.
56 Minutes of DWSA executive committee, (hereafter DWSA Minutes), 4 November 1880. IHA.
57 *Women's Suffrage Journal*, 1 October 1880.
58 Hollis, Patricia. 1987. *Ladies Elect: Women in English Local Government 1865-1914*. London, pp25-6.
59 Ms notebook, IHA.
60 Cullen Owens, Rosemary. 1984. *Smashing times; a History of the Irish Women's Suffrage Movement 1879-1922*, Dublin, p.25.

61 DWSA Minutes, 27 June 1883. IHA.
62 See chapter on Anna Parnell in this volume.
63 MS list of societies Anna Haslam was connected with IHA.
64 MS text of speech. IHA.
65 *Ibid.*, p.222.
66 *Englishwoman's Review*, 10 October 1898, p.221.
67 *Report of the Executive Committee of the Dublin Women's Suffrage and Poor Law Guardians Association for 1896*, (Dublin, 1897), p.3. (Hereafter *IWSLGA Report*.).
68 *Irish Citizen*, 28 March 1914, p. 347.
69 *Englishwoman's Review*, 15 October 1898, pp223-5.
70 *IWSLGA Report for 1898*, p.8.
71 *IWSLGA Report for 1900*, p.11.
72 Haslam, *Women's Suffrage*.
73. *IWSLGA Report for 1908*, p.7.
74 Cousins, *We Two Together*, p.164.
75 *Irish Citizen*, 25 May 1912, p.7.
76 Cullen Owens, *Smashing Times*, p.43.
77 *IWSLGA Report for 1912*, p.5.
78 Cullen Owens, *Smashing Times*, pp51-3. While the IWSLGA is not mentioned among the organisations represented, Hayden presided and Anna Haslam sent a message.
79 *Ibid.*, p.64.
80 *Irish Citizen*, 22 June 1912, p.39.
81 IWSLGA minutes, 12 September 1912. IHA.
82 *Evening Mail*, 15 February 1907.
83 *IWSLGA Report for 1910*, p.12-3.
84 Sheehy Skeffington, Hanna. n.d.(1975) 'Reminiscences of an Irish suffragette', in Sheehy Skeffington, Andree and Owens, Rosemary. *Votes for Women*. Dublin, p.21.
85 Cullen Owens, *Smashing Times*, p.95.
86 *IWSLGA Report for 1914*, p.7.
87 *IWSLGA Report for 1915*, p.5.
88 *IWSLGA Report for 1914*, p.4.
89 *Irish Times*, 15 April 1915.
90 *Irish Citizen*, 2 January 1915, p.253.
91 *Ibid.*, 9 January 1915, p.258.
92 *Ibid.*, 16 January 1915, p.267.
93 *IWSLGA Report for 1915*, p.8.
94 *Irish Citizen*, 20 November 1915, p.165
95 *Ibid.*, p.171.
96 Cullen Owens, *SmashingTimes*, p.76.
97 *Irish Citizen*, December 1918, p.633.
98 *Ibid*, January 1919, p.643.
99 Meeting 12 November 1918, pp8-9, *IWSLGA Report for 1918*.
100 *Irish Citizen*, April 1919, p. 655.
101 Tweedy, Hilda. 1993, *A Link in the Chain: The Story of the Irish Housewives' Association 1942-1992*, Dublin, p.22.
102 *Englishwoman's Review*, 15 October 1898, p.222.
103 Haslam, *Some Last Words on Women's Suffrage*, p.17.

104 Speech to the National Union of Women Workers, Croydon, October 1898. IHA.

105 Typescript of speech delivered at Manchester. IHA.

106 Typescript of speech to International Suffrage Congress meeting in England, 1908. IHA.

107 Haslam, *Last Words*, p.4.

108 Dora Mellone, quoted in Murphy, Cliona. 1989. *The Women's Suffrage Movement and Irish Society in the early Twentieth Century.* New York and London, p.17.

Isabella M S Tod

(1836-1896)

Maria Luddy

To write the life of Isabella Maria Susan Tod is to write a history of feminist activism in Ireland from the 1860s to the time of her death in 1896. Tod was the outstanding advocate of women's rights during this period. She initiated, organised and managed a range of societies while simultaneously theorising and writing justifications for the demands these organisations made. Tod is particularly interesting in a number of ways. She was unusual in the context of late nineteenth-century Irish society for the diversity of her political and social activities. The only other comparable figure who campaigned around women's issues was Anna Haslam,[1] and she did so on a much smaller scale than Tod. Tod had more in common with English activists, such as Lydia Becker, Josephine Butler and others, than her Irish counterparts. She also viewed herself as British, rather than Irish, an identification which found its fullest expression in her campaign against Gladstone's first Home Rule Bill.

Like many other women in this book, the information available on Tod's private life is scanty and can be outlined in a few short paragraphs. Her public life is a different matter. Tod wrote numerous articles, a number of which were reprinted as pamphlets, and countless letters to the newspapers of the period. Her speeches were widely reported in suffrage journals and daily newspapers in both Ireland and England.

It is possible to see a clear development in her thinking during the thirty-odd years of her public activism. Like many other women who became political activists, Tod's interests in issues relating to women were first developed in charity work. Further involvement in the areas of education and temperance led to her belief that it was only by gaining the franchise that women, and here she meant women of the middle and upper classes, could influence and bring about change in society. Her interests ranged from philanthropy and temperance, to the issue of girls' secondary education and women's access to universities. She was involved in the campaign to reform the married women's property laws and to repeal the Contagious Diseases Acts. She organised the first suffrage society in Ireland and campaigned to ensure that women were granted the municipal franchise and could be elected as Poor Law Guardians. A staunch Unionist, she used her energies to campaign vigorously against Gladstone's first Home Rule Bill. This indeed was the campaign she saw as her most important work.[2] During the period of her public activism there was no organised campaign with women's interests to the fore with which she was not involved. Tod was the best known Irish women's activist of her day. She shared platforms with, and was friend of many leading English suffragists including Helen Blackburn, Josephine Butler, and Lydia Becker. She has been all but forgotten.

Tod was born on 18 May 1836, in Edinburgh. Her father James Banks Tod, was a Scottish merchant, and her mother, Maria Isabella Waddell, was a native of County Monaghan. The family returned to live in Belfast, apparently in the 1860s, though the date and cause of this return remains unclear. Tod was always proud of her Scottish blood, and frequently alluded to the fact that one of her ancestors signed the copy of the Solemn League and Covenant at Holywood, County Down, in 1646. Another proud recollection was the fact that her great-grandfather was a colonel in the Volunteers of 1782. She came, she said 'of fighting stock'.[3] Another of her ancestors was the Rev. Charles Masterton, a leading Presbyterian minister of Belfast in the seventeenth century.[4] Her attachment to the Presbyterian faith was a strong one and her religious beliefs were to influence her political activism. From the scant information that remains on Tod's personal life, it appears that she lived with her mother, who died in 1877, and to whom she was particularly devoted. 'I always feel I am my mother's mouthpiece,' she was to state in an interview many years later.[5] Tod also had at least one brother, Henry, a merchant who lived in London, and a niece, a Mrs Groffier, who also lived in London.[6] Tod does not appear to have had a permanent residence in Belfast, and in various committee reports her addresses vary. This suggests she lived in rented accommodation, or stayed at times with friends.

From the available evidence it seems that Tod had no formal education. She claimed she was a voracious reader. Her interest in the affairs of women was apparently fostered by her mother whose encouragement led her to 'careful private study'.[7] Her initial means of raising the status of women was through writing, and in the 1860s and 1870s she contributed pieces anonymously to the *Dublin University Magazine* and the *Banner of Ulster*. Until the early 1880s she also wrote leaders for the *Northern Whig*, and it is more than likely that she earned her living through her journalism.

Once her public life began, Tod travelled extensively between Ireland and England. She remained unmarried and had a personal assistant, Gertrude Andrews, who acted as her companion and secretary for many years.

It was not until 1867, when Tod was 31 years old, that she

entered public life, prepared to express her views in person. In that year the National Association for the Promotion of Social Science held its annual meeting in Belfast. This society had developed from the British Association for the Advancement of Science in 1857. In an era when science was pre-eminent, the founders of the association felt that if scientists, economists, political theorists and social reformers were brought together, and their ideas and theories examined, it would be possible to develop a 'social science' of society. Change could then be brought about in a scientific and controlled way.[8] The NAPSS provided an important platform for activists, many of them women, who wished to reform society. Over the course of her early public career, Tod was a regular contributor to the annual meetings of the society.[9] On the occasion of the meeting in Belfast, Tod prepared a paper entitled 'On advanced education for girls of the upper and middle classes', which was read to the public, not by Tod, but by a male friend.[10] It is clear that she had not yet acquired the confidence she was later to develop through public speaking. The meeting in Belfast marked her auspicious entrance into public life and political activism.

The Belfast of Tod's adulthood was a hive of social, political, cultural, economic and philanthropic activity.[11] Along with Tod, the most notable women activists in the city were the formidable Mary Hobson, founder of the Belfast Association for the Employment of the Industrious Blind, and Margaret Byers, headmistress of Victoria College, who became a very close friend of Tod's.[12] She, like Tod, was both a leading advocate of education for girls and a strong temperance activist. It was in the cities of Belfast and Dublin that women's rights were first publicly debated, and it was the inhabitants of those cities who were to provide their most fervent supporters. The advancement of women's rights was advocated by middle-class women, many of whom had, by mid-century, spent a number of years in philanthropic work. Like many other women of the period, Tod had been active in charity work for a long period before her entrance into public political life. From that work developed her ideals of social change for the poor, and also for women in general.[13]

The education of women was Tod's first interest, spurred no doubt by her own lack of formal education. Two issues relating to women's education interested Tod, the provision of secondary education and women's higher education. The campaigns waged over these educational issues were conducted simultaneously, and Tod operated by organising committees, petitions and meetings with MPs, and also by writing articles and speeches which lent theoretical weight to the campaigns.

A brief outline of the situation regarding women's education in Ireland is necessary to explain the action which she felt needed to be taken. Secondary education for girls, where it was available in nineteenth-century Ireland, tended to prepare them for their future role as wives and mothers, and was more concerned with the acquirement of feminine accomplishments than with intellectual attainments.[14] From the 1860s, a number of changes occurred which helped shape and develop the type of education provided for girls at second level. Anne O'Connor argues that the two major influences affecting secondary education were the impact of French teaching orders, and the establishment of a number of schools concerned with a pragmatic and liberal education.[15] The second development was one in which Tod played a major role. The lack of educational provision for girls of the middle classes which would equip them for some form of employment was first addressed in England in 1841, with the establishment of the Queen's Institute in London. Debates on women's education took place within the meetings of the NAPSS, and led from 1859 to the founding of four establishments initially similar to the Queen's Institute in London: the Ladies' Collegiate School, Belfast (1859); the Queen's Institute, Dublin (1861); Alexandra College, Dublin (1866), and the Ladies' Institute, Belfast (1867). The establishment of these institutions paved the way for demands in legislative reform in girl's secondary education, and also for women's entrance into university.[16]

An attempt to improve the Irish education system resulted in a proposal for an Intermediate Education Act, which would provide for the organisation of examinations and award prizes based upon the results of these examinations. As originally introduced in 1878, the Bill referred only to boys' education, but Margaret Byers and Tod quickly organised a delegation to London to pressurise for the inclusion of girls. The Belfast Ladies' Institute fully supported the women's action. The delegation consisted of Tod, Byers, the local Belfast MP, J P Corry, a supporter of women's education, and an influential group of Irish men and women from London. They met with Lord Cairns, the

Lord Chancellor, and James Lowther, the Chief Secretary for Ireland. Having presented evidence of the successes already achieved by Byers in her school, they persuaded Cairns that girls must be included in the Act.[17] The Intermediate Education Act, when implemented, awarded amongst other benefits 'results fees' to schools for students who passed exams, whether those students were male or female. 'One thing I am very proud of,' Tod was to state in later life, 'and that is getting girls included in the Intermediate Education Act of 1878.'[18] The inclusion of girls was an important step toward making university education available to women.

The campaign to allow women access to university education in Ireland began at the same time as women reformers were bringing about changes in secondary education. In 1845 the Queens' Colleges had been established in Belfast, Cork and Galway. They were intended to provide a non-denominational education for Irish men. The colleges were strongly opposed by the Catholic hierarchy, whose opposition ensured that enrolment remained low. The provision of university education remained a vexed problem until 1879, when the government attempted to provide a solution to some of the issues which had surfaced. In the meantime women reformers had begun to campaign for women's access to university education. Alexandra College in Dublin aimed to provide higher education for women, and a number of the staff of Trinity College gave lectures to the female students. These students were not, however, eligible to be awarded degrees from the Queen's Colleges, nor indeed were they allowed to enter for degrees at TCD.[19]

In Belfast, the Ladies' Institute helped to pave the way for change. The original function of the Institute was to provide classes for young women interested in improving their education and hence their employment prospects. Tod acted as the Institute's secretary and it is quite clear from the minutes which survive that it was she who was the main force in drafting petitions and letters, and meeting representatives of the University and MPs. Lectures were organised on, amongst other subjects, modern languages, history, astronomy, chemistry and Latin. The Institute also petitioned the Queen's University of Ireland in Belfast to allow girls to take their examinations. It was as a result of the requests made by the Institute in 1869 that a scheme of examinations for women was drawn up by Queen's University.[20]

In March of 1873, when the House of Commons was debating the University Education (Ireland) Bill, which eventually failed to pass, the committee of the Ladies' Institute forwarded a petition to the house deploring the fact that there were no endowments available to girls for any education, other than primary, in Ireland. The timing of the petition was considered important and the discussion taking place on this Bill was seen as an opportunity for advancing the cause of higher education for women.[21] In their petition the ladies of the Institute noted the many obstacles which had to be overcome in the pursuit of their aims. Among them were 'the diffidence of candidates unaccustomed to such an ordeal [examinations], the uncertainty of teachers in regard to the fitness of their pupils, and the want of appreciation of the value of such tests on the part of parents'.[22]

While little notice was taken of the petition in parliamentary circles, it was closely followed by Irish education reformers, and the petition, along with a speech given by Tod on the subject, provoked the Queen's Institute in Dublin to petition Trinity College for women to be allowed to sit for degrees. In September of that year the Ladies' Institute in Belfast wrote to the Senate of Queen's University requesting that women be allowed entrance to their degrees. Both petitions were rejected.[23]

The Ladies' Institute petition argued that

... a feeling has been gathering strength that more might be done by the University for the education of women than the institution of special examinations, valuable as they are, as long as the means of good teaching are so scanty, and so irregularly distributed, tests of instruction are only applicable to a very limited number.

The Institute suggested a way forward: 'the only and efficient remedy for this situation is to admit ladies to share the best teaching, that of the universities themselves.' The women noted that: 'so far as we have been able to ascertain there is nothing in the constitution of the Queen's University to prevent it from being opened to women'. They argued that if the university were to open its doors to women it

would be 'an immediate boon to ladies, and a future benefit
of inestimable value to Irish women of every rank'. It would
also enhance the university's reputation.[24]

Although the request failed, changes were on the way. In
1879, after years of debate regarding university education in
Ireland, the government introduced a new University Bill
which dissolved the Queen's University of Ireland and
instituted in its place the Royal University of Ireland. As
soon as the Bill was announced, Tod formed a committee to
fight to ensure that women were included in any benefits
that would result from the Bill.[25]

Under the new Act the Queen's Colleges at Belfast, Cork
and Galway remained in existence, with the Royal
University of Ireland acting as an examination body.
Students enrolled in the Queen's Colleges were
automatically entered for its degrees. Since it was to be an
examining body only, students could prepare themselves in
any way they saw suitable for the examinations, either
through private study or by attending classes. The degrees
and scholarships of the RUI were open to both men and
women. But in spite of the fact that women could now sit for
degrees, their actual educational needs were not addressed.
Female students, as Eibhlín Breathnach notes, did not have
the same facilities as male students and tended to receive
their education in any establishments that would take
them.[26] In 1882 the Ladies' Institute approached Queen's
College in Belfast and requested that women be admitted to
their arts degree courses. The request was granted.[27]

Along with her active involvement in these campaigns,
Tod wrote a number of articles and pamphlets on
educational matters to support the cause. As previously
mentioned, her first public paper delivered at the annual
conference of the National Association for the Promotion of
Social Science in 1867 had been on this subject. Later
published in the proceedings of the conference, her paper
argued for the complexity of the educational process. There
were, according to Tod, three main branches of education:

> the religious and moral training which form the most
> essential part can be begun by parents only, and must be
> carried on by the pupil herself. But the other two great

divisions of education, intellectual instruction, and mental discipline, come within the province of the school or college; and they largely subserve the purpose of the first two.[28]

Tod argued that women needed intellectual discipline in order to properly assume the responsibilities they were expected to take up as adults. Adult women were bound to have an impact either directly or indirectly on society. Without a proper and fitting education, one that would develop their intellectual capacities, women could not play their proper role in society. A 'wise and wide course of education not only teaches much absolutely, but, what is of far more importance, so enlarges and strengthens the mind, so instructs it how to learn, as to prepare it for all the contingencies of life'.[29]

Tod called for the development of a college system of education for girls. Such a system offered 'an orderly and complete curriculum of study'. It would also allow scholarships to be awarded and would provide access to the best of teachers. A high standard in collegiate education must of necessity raise the standard of all education provided for girls and its benefits would seep through the secondary sphere. Tod also anticipated some of the arguments which might be made against organising such an education for girls, '[that]... girls might find associations hurtful to their refinement', and the fear among parents that daughters so educated might '... shape a novel path in life for herself', but she cast these aside as unnecessary fears. College education for girls would benefit society in many different ways. It would strengthen the religious and moral aspects of a woman's life. Equality of education for men and women would 'allow different but harmonising modes of action' on social problems. Such education for women would also benefit women of the lower classes. 'Who can tell,' Tod argued, 'how great an amelioration may take place in the painful conditions of women of the lower classes, when not merely a few, but most of those in the classes above them have not only the will, but the power and the knowledge how to help them?'[30] Not only was education necessary to develop the full intellectual and spiritual potential of an individual, but it was also to serve a social purpose.

The ability of the middle classes to help those less fortunate than themselves was a theme which constantly appeared in Tod's writing, a theme developed from her philanthropic and temperance work and her religious beliefs.

In a pamphlet entitled *On the Education of Girls of the Middle Class* published in 1874, Tod continued the arguments outlined above. She recognised that many women had to enter the world of work in order to survive. Middle-class parents had expectations

> ... [of] all their daughters marrying, to all these marriages being satisfactory, and to the husbands being always able and willing to take an active management of everything. We shall not stop to discover whether such a state of things is even desirable. It is sufficient to point out that it does not and cannot exist.[31]

Here she also stressed the need for a practical education for girls, one that would allow them to work and support themselves, and that would cater also for the needs of both married and single women. On other occasions Tod noted the 'unreasonableness of the prejudice against change', whether in relation to the secondary or higher education of women. 'Before an argument of any kind is offered to us', she noted in 1874, 'we are met with an advanced guard of horrified ejaculations.'[32] In answer to the arguments that higher education would damage women's health or refinement, she observed that 'the great features of the human mind are the same in both men and women, and that they need the same nutriment, though the development of the natures so fed will differ according to their capabilities'. Against the charge that women were presumptuous in looking for higher education she stated it to be a '... nonsensical charge ...[for] if self-preservation be the first law of savage nature, self-improvement is the first law of civilised nature, and we have no notion of disobeying it'.[33]

Throughout the 1870s and 1880s, Tod continued campaigning and writing to support further improvements in girls' and women's education. She was also the main influence behind the establishment of the Ulster Head Schoolmistresses Association, which was founded in 1880.[34] This association worked closely with the Central Association for Irish Schoolmistresses and other Ladies interested in Irish Education, (AISLIE), established in Dublin in 1882. During the 1880s and 1890s, both were extremely influential in exerting pressure for the rights of women in education.

The aims of the Association of Irish Schoolmistresses and other Ladies Interested in Irish Education were the same as those of the Ulster Society:

> ... promoting the higher education of women in Ireland, by affording a means of communication and co-operation between schoolmistresses and other ladies interested in education, and of watching over the interest of girls, especially with regard to Intermediate education and the Royal University.[35]

Margaret Byers and Tod represented the Ulster schoolmistresses at meetings of the AISLIE. The organisation forwarded letters and memorials to the Board of Intermediate Education, suggesting improvements that would be beneficial to girls. In 1883, when proposed changes in the Intermediate syllabus threatened to affect girls adversely, the committee forwarded a petition with almost 3,000 signatures, requesting that no rules should be made which could 'in any way make the examinations unequal in value to girls as compared with boys, either in regard to their educational or their pecuniary importance'.[36] The Association continued to send letters and memorials on the subject throughout 1884 and 1885.[37] Individual members of the Association also lobbied anybody with political influence. In March of 1882 Florence Arnold-Forster, niece and adopted daughter of the influential liberal MP and Irish Chief Secretary, William Edward Forster, noted in her journal two visits from Tod. On 16 March Florence's mother had 'a long visit ... from Miss Tod of Belfast on women's education, and a forthcoming bill of Mr O'Shaughnessy's'. Five days later Tod had returned 'to breakfast to talk about Intermediate education - more money needed'.[38] Tod's concern with women's education remained a strong interest throughout her life even when other subjects seemed to take up all her time.

It was through the Social Science conference in Belfast in

1867, at which Tod's paper on education was read, that she became involved in the campaign to amend the Married Women's Property Laws. This campaign gave her what she later described as her first experience 'of direct political effort for a social purpose, and was also first led by it to speak in public'.[39] As an active member of the Presbyterian Church, Tod was a regular visitor of the poor in parts of Belfast, and thus became aware of the economic exploitation of women. Being asked at a committee of inquiry how long she had been interested in the question of women's property, she replied, 'For a considerable time; I began to take an interest in it as soon as I was old enough to visit at all among the poor'.[40] She believed that women must have control over their own property and earnings. Much of the distress she witnessed in the households she visited was, she felt, brought about by the idle and loutish habits of husbands. Tod told of women who could not maintain themselves and their families because their husbands took their wages from them or, more frequently, '[ran] up debts at the public houses which the women must discharge, at least under the threat of having their furniture and other property taken to pay it, and the consequences are very bad for all the family'.[41] Enabling women to keep their own wages, she argued, would help to ensure that the family was fed, and would also improve their moral welfare. Tod felt that granting women control of their finances would bring immense benefit to their families and particularly to their children, since children's wages were also liable to be seized by a father, and their education disrupted by the necessity of working to help support the family.[42]

Tod was the only woman called to give evidence to an 1868 Select Committee inquiry on the Married Women's Property Bill. The Bill, which had been introduced into the Commons in April of that year, had been sponsored by the NAPSS, and doubtless Tod's involvement with this association and her organisation of a Married Women's Property Committee in Belfast, suggested her as an appropriate witness. She advocated that any changes which were to be made in the law must cover both working- and middle-class women. She was adamant also that any changes which were to come about must move beyond protecting women's right to their wages to include their rights to property.

Tod was not the only Irish woman fighting for this cause. Helena Pauline Downing, a niece of McCarthy Downing, MP for Cork from 1868 to 1879, was noted for her activity on behalf of women's property, and she was later to become a leading suffragist.[43] Besides Tod's committee in Belfast, there was also an independent organisation formed in Dublin to campaign for reform in the law. These organisations do not seem to have had much contact with each other though their work was clearly similar. Both groups organised and sent petitions to the House of Commons on the subject. Tod was also to serve on the executive of the Married Women's Property Committee which was based in London.[44] This Committee found it difficult to keep its organisation intact over the long number of years in which campaigns were waged. Membership declined in the early 1870s, and in 1874 Tod ceased to serve on the executive of the Committee. Through her activities on this Committee, Tod came to know a number of reformers, including Frances Power Cobbe, Lydia Becker, Elizabeth Wolstenholme and Josephine Butler. She went on to work with Butler in the campaign to repeal the Contagious Diseases Acts.

Tod's lifelong interest lay in the temperance activism. 'I was,' she stated in an interview in 1893,

> interested in the temperance question long before I joined any temperance association, when as a member of the Presbyterian church, I visited among the people of a mission district connected with it. My work soon taught me that drink is the main cause of poverty, and that in a yet larger measure it is the cause of domestic discord and misery.[45]

There were few women's temperance associations operating in Belfast at this time. Among those that did exist was the women's auxiliary of the Irish Temperance League. This had developed from a male-run organisation, but a number of women, including Margaret Byers, dissatisfied with their secondary status within that organisation, got together and decided that it would be as well for them to organise a society of their own. To this end the Belfast Women's Temperance Association was formed in 1874. In order to become a member of this organisation it was necessary to be a total abstainer. Tod became a committee member, and she undertook a number of speaking engagements to further the cause. By 1875 the BWTA had opened in the city three 'refreshment houses ... where there can be no temptation to drink', one of which offered 'nutritious dinners to girls engaged in factories'.[46] The women of the BWTA were also aware of the work being done for the temperance cause in America and in 1876 invited the famous temperance activist Mrs Stewart, or Mother Stewart as she was known in her homeland, to speak to the Association.[47]

In one of the leaflets produced by the Association, women as a group were recognised as suffering most from the evils of intemperance. It was to women as wives that this society looked to help remedy the situation. 'Is it not,' they asked, 'the duty of women in the spirit of meekness, by the power of a strong personal and womanly influence, to endeavour to help men to overcome the tyrannical drinking customs of society?'[48] It was through her influence in the home that the wife was to stem the intemperance of her husband. One means of doing this, according to the society, was to place a ban on all alcoholic spirits in the home. Here, once again, is echoed the belief in the moral and domestic influence of women. The BWTA saw temperance as God's work, a unification of the moral and religious dimensions of female benevolence. Margaret Byers, secretary of the BWTA, spoke particularly of the need for women in the field of temperance. 'She who founds a temperance society at her own hearth, who imbues her sons and daughters with a hatred of intemperance and its kindred vices, and trains her children in habits of self control, is doing good work for the nation,'[49] she stated. Temperance was to be inculcated in the home, the 'power' sphere of women, and women's involvement in temperance was a reflection of a desire to protect the home and women's place in it.

The Belfast Ladies' Temperance Association branched out from supporting temperance to initiating schemes for social reform. They concentrated on working with women. To this end they established a Prison Gate Mission, and a home for inebriate women. 'The world is unspeakably harder to a woman who falls than a man, and [the] doors of escape which stand open to him are closed to her,' wrote Tod in

1881.[50] The woman drunkard was also seen as a 'fallen woman', and needed the protection of an organisation which would cater specifically to her needs. As well as providing homes for these women, the WTA also gave lectures to the poor, as a major cause of alcohol abuse among the working classes was seen to be '... untidy homes, insufficient diet [and] weak health.'[51] To combat these problems they began classes in cookery and hygiene, and attempted to bring the moral and social standards of their own class into the homes of the poor.

In 1882 the BWTA opened a home for girls. Tod commented that the children of the upper stratum of the 'poor class' were thought to be adequately looked after by their parents, but the children of a 'lower and vagrant class ... where the children cannot possibly grow up sober and industrious'[52] needed looking after. The home was to prevent these children falling into vice. At the end of its first year of operation it catered for twenty-one children, and the committee also boarded out infants. Tod hoped that '[the] Prison Mission and perhaps this new departure [the home for destitute children] may prove the beginning of a widespread movement among Christian women in battling against corruption and vice'.[53]

By 1889 the BWTA claimed to have forty branches organised around the country. By 1894 all the branches of the WTA had merged into one organisation called the Irish Women's Temperance Union, whose motto was 'United to Win Ireland'. Their first annual conference was held in Dublin in May of that year.

In addition to her temperance activities in Ireland, Tod also acted as the vice-president of the British Women's Temperance Association, from 1877 to 1892. In 1893 the WTA split, and Tod left to become vice-president of the Women's Total Abstinence Union, a position she held until her death in 1896. The WTA developed a policy of fighting for a number of issues, while the WTAU pressed only for reform on the temperance issue.[54]

It appears that Tod was wary of legislation in this field. In a talk she gave on the methods to be used to cure drunkards, Tod stated that government initiatives in this area would lead to interference in the liberty of the individual. She believed in the duty of each individual to practise their own moral judgement, and felt that government interference would only coerce people, thus removing them from their duty to practise right. 'To supersede the conscience,' she stated, 'is to weaken it.'[55] It was only through example and the concern of individuals in the moral and religious welfare of drunkards that any changes should be brought about. Through these means inebriates would be led to an understanding of their duty and responsibility to themselves and to society. Philanthropic and temperance activists such as Tod felt that their homes and refuges, their preventive and reformative work, were the surest means which could be used to initiate change.

Through temperance work, women such as Tod hoped to influence the social and moral world of the poor. Women's work in this field was to be used by Tod as an argument for the granting of women's suffrage. 'The whole temperance movement,' she wrote, 'is based upon the acceptance of social responsibility by the individual for herself ... that acceptance is caused by the conviction of the existence of mighty evils all around her ... and which she has some power to lessen.'[56] The power to reduce evil lay within the woman's practice of her innate goodness, and Tod urged that the granting of the franchise would extend women's power for good. She urged women to seek the vote because 'no vote is a vote, and is a vote inevitably on the side of evil'.[57] Politics were part and parcel of everyone's life, and affected not only women's material and intellectual circumstances but, much more importantly for Tod, their moral choices. Women's involvement in charity and temperance work had proven women's true value, the '... addition of women to the electorate would mean a far larger proportionate addition to the ranks of good'.[58]

Tod's work in the cause of the reform of married women's property, her fight for women's education, and her temperance work convinced her that only by the exercise of the electoral franchise could women really make an impact for good on society. Her involvement in another campaign, that to repeal the Contagious Diseases Acts, added to her conviction that social reform was a vital concern of women, and that only they could ensure its successful implementation.

In 1864 Parliament passed the first of three statutes which

permitted the compulsory inspection for venereal disease of prostitutes in certain military camps in both England and Ireland. The three Acts of 1864, 1866, and 1869 were introduced to control the spread of venereal disease among the soldiery.[59] In Ireland the areas designated 'subjected districts' were Cork, Cobh and the Curragh Camp. In effect, the Acts subjected women who were on the street to arbitrary and compulsory medical examination. If the woman inspected was infected, she was forcibly detained in a Lock hospital, where such diseases were treated, and registered as a prostitute.

Opposition to the Acts arose for a number of reasons. Their implementation was seen by some groups as an interference with civil liberties, and by others as the recognition and support of vice by the state. The National Association for the Repeal of the Contagious Diseases Acts had a large and active female membership in England, and one of the chief reasons they opposed the Acts was because they applied solely to women, leaving men untouched. For them the implementation of the Acts marked the legitimisation of the double standard of sexual morality which existed in society.

A number of associations were established in England to enforce the repeal of the CDAs. These included the National Association for the Repeal of the Contagious Diseases Acts (NARCDA), formed in 1869, and the Ladies' National Association (LNA), formed also in 1869 by Tod's friend, Josephine Butler. Both of these organisations had branches in Ireland. By 1871 three branches of the LNA had been established in Belfast, Dublin and Cork. Both Isabella Tod and Anna Haslam were involved in the campaign from the beginning, and Tod also served on the executive committee of the London-based LNA until 1889, when Haslam took her place. Tod also served on the general council of the NARCDA, although this society was run by men, and women council members had little impact on policy.[60]

The LNA, in Ireland, was a small and localised affair.[61] Its function was to support the aims of the parent body in London. In practice this meant raising funds, organising petitions to Parliament against the Acts, attempting to alter public opinion by distributing pamphlets and papers on the subject, and by holding meetings. Although Belfast was not a 'subjected district', the campaign to repeal the Acts was very strong in the city. In 1870 a ladies' meeting was held in the Ulster Hall to condemn the Acts. Those present formed a branch of the LNA, and Tod was elected secretary.[62] Tod was certainly the most active worker on this subject in Ulster, but she was supported by other non-conformist Church members. The General Assembly of the Presbyterian Church totally opposed the Acts, and a number of Church meetings in the 1870s and early 1880s registered their strong revulsion at what they considered to be the legitimisation of sin.[63]

Tod's importance to the cause can be seen clearly in the words of Butler herself who hailed her '... as one of the ablest, and certainly the most eloquent, of our women workers'.[64]

The Belfast branch of the LNA was active in trying to ensure that the Acts would not be extended to that city. Tod claimed that their efforts in bringing the operation of the Acts to the attention of the public had averted '... the terrible danger and degradation of being subjected to the direct operation of the Acts'.[65] She saw the implementation of the Acts as an affront '... to the decency and purity of society - the dignity and independence of every woman in the land'.[66] In 1877 the Belfast branch of the LNA claimed that the enlargement of the Lock hospital in that city, which patients entered voluntarily since the city was not one of the 'subjected districts', had resulted from the committee's attempts to improve the treatment of women afflicted with venereal diseases. They were thereby proving that individual action, always a strong argument in Tod's arsenal, could prevent the spread of such diseases and that the CDAs were essentially unnecessary.

The recognition and articulation of the operation of a sexual double standard was fully expressed in this campaign, and a higher moral standard for men was demanded. Women, it was believed, possessed this high standard, and it was the ideal which they felt should be expected of men. Tod, in a speech to the Christian Women's Union, articulated the problem, and proposed the solution:

... the greatest and most consistent force at work, both in

lowering the moral tone throughout all classes, and in bringing about not only individual acts of vice, but in degrading a number of women into a class where occupation is vice, is that unspeakably wicked idea that most men may be expected so to sin, and that in them it is a venial offence ... We must utterly refuse ... to acknowledge the existence of any such class of men, in any rank, as inevitable; or any class of women to meet their horrible demands ... We owe a duty to men ... to awaken their consciences to pull down the selfish screen which society has set up ... We have the power of the newly awakened conscience of women, as to their duty to protect their poorer and weaker sisters, and to withstand and enlighten those who would seek to assail them.[67]

Again Tod used the work of the women in the LNA to support women's claim to the vote. The success of the repeal movement - the Acts were suspended in 1883 and repealed in 1886 - had, according to Tod, shown how effective women's activism could be:

It was not only for the help which women must give to women, but even more, for the discharge of their special duty to the whole state - a duty which God has entrusted to them, and which no man can do - women are bound to demand their immediate admission within the electorate.[68]

As in many of her campaigns, her zeal was almost evangelical in both word and action. Overcoming the evils of the CDAs, intemperance and other vices was always an individual choice, but for Tod women were strengthened in their 'goodness' by a highly developed conscience and 'the power of prayer'. 'We can try,' she stated, 'to awaken the individual sinner, whether man or woman, and show them the place of repentance which is open alike for both.'[69]

There is no doubt that Tod's involvement in these various campaigns, and her activism in philanthropic societies, had an impact on her suffrage beliefs. Tod established the Northern Ireland Society for Women's Suffrage in 1871, and linked it to the London Women's Suffrage Society. She remained secretary of the NISWS until the 1890s. It was generally Tod who organised their annual meetings and who invariably read the annual reports at those meetings.[70] She travelled the country tirelessly speaking at public meetings on the suffrage issue. For example, between 6 and 14 February 1873, she spoke at meetings in Belfast, Carrickfergus, Coleraine, Armagh and Dungannon.[71] One week in May 1874 found her speaking from platforms in Cork, Limerick, Bandon, Clonmel and Waterford. She also appeared regularly at suffrage meetings in London.[72] During this time she was still active in the campaign for educational rights for women, was organising petitions to support the reform of property laws and was also active in the campaign against the Contagious Diseases Acts.

She argued for the vote on the basis of justice and on women's right to citizenship. Like most suffragists of the period she sought a relatively restricted franchise, based on property requirements which would qualify women to vote on the same terms as men. She based her argument on what she claimed were inconsistencies in the laws between Ireland and England. In 1875 she noted that some Irishwomen could vote for Poor Law Guardians, for Harbour and Water Board Commissioners, and in towns which were not incorporated they could vote for Town Commissioners, but they could not vote for Municipal Councillors. These, she argued, were 'capricious' arrangements. She referred to the necessity of aiding middle-class women's constructive work of philanthropy in 'elevating the classes who naturally come under their care'.[73] It was also right to grant women the vote in view of their domestic responsibilities.

> Not only in the details of management of a workhouse (which needs an experience in housekeeping), but in the care of the sick, of the old, of the children, and the training of girls to earn their bread, no less than in the discrimination between honest poverty and imposture, there is work which must be shared by women to be done efficiently.[74]

Tod argued in 1884 that the care of the poor had always been women's work, and women had a special understanding of that work which men could never have. Just as mothers, she asserted,

> ... must inculcate in their children, day by day, truth and purity, and the thought of all that is due to others, so also with different machinery but the same end, must women feel it their task to uphold truth, purity and justice to all, in the legislation and administration of the realm.[75]

For Tod, the acquisition of the vote would allow women to participate, as individuals, directly in society. Women must not be perceived as being subordinate to men but as their equals. Women, she stated,

> ... are citizens of the state, inheritors with men of all the history which ennobles a nation, guardians with men of all the best life of the nation; bound as much as men are bound to consider the good of the whole; and justified as much as men are justified in sharing the good of the whole.[76]

With the vote women would regenerate society from a new power base:

> Women would be in all respects the better for these direct privileges; that by her many things that were now wrong could by her be put right; that woman would have to lead a freer and more useful life; and that the change would conduce to the welfare of the whole of the country, as the influence of women would be good as promoting all sorts of wise reforms, social and moral.[77]

Implicit in Tod's speeches and writings is her belief that women were morally and spiritually superior to men. On one occasion she argued

> [that] ... experience showed that they [women] felt a deeper sense of responsibility resting upon them, and that they attempted to carry their religious principles into the

common things of life to a greater extent than men did.[78]

Later she insisted that the 'addition of women to the electorate would mean a far larger proportionate addition to the ranks of the good'.[79] On another occasion she declared that often men's interest in politics stemmed from selfish motives while 'Women', she noted,

> ... never gather together in this way only for themselves. They fight for others; and it is because we have so much work to do that we fight so hard as we do, and we will not give up the fight to please mortal man.[80]

Women's involvement in charity work, and in temperance work, had proven women's true value. Using her temperance work as an example, Tod argued that:

> The whole temperance movement is based upon the acceptance of social responsibility by the individual for herself ... that acceptance is caused by the conviction of the existence of mighty evils all around her ... and which she has some power to lessen.[81]

Like many of the early suffragists, Tod's demand for the franchise did not extend in practical terms to all women, but all women would benefit from even a limited suffrage. The benefits to be conferred on all women were not just legislative but would improve the quality of relationships between men and women. Poorer men, whom Tod considered had little regard for women, would, with the granting of the franchise, recognise immediately the importance of all women, even their own wives, daughters and sisters. 'Women who suffer,' she stated, 'need the franchise for protection, and women who work for others need the franchise for efficiency.'[82] Tod believed in the reciprocal dependence of the social classes. She wanted not only political power for women but, much more importantly, their admission as citizens. In the nineteenth century, she noted, 'neither the humanity of women nor their citizenship is acknowledged by a large proportion of uneducated men'. Granting the vote could teach men that 'women are citizens of the state'. Even more importantly, the acquisition of the vote would allow women to exercise 'moral responsibility and freedom of action'. Suffragists such as Tod expected to gain concrete powers with the acquisition of the vote. By strategic and moral use of their vote, women would be able to transform society into their own vision of moral and spiritual rightness.

In campaigns to gain formal political rights for women Tod played a key role in three areas: there was, first of all, the fight for the parliamentary suffrage; secondly the issue of municipal voting for women; and finally the attempts to have women elected as Poor Law Guardians. The first area was not resolved in Tod's lifetime, but the success gained by women in the other two issues owed much to her efforts. None of these campaigns was left to chance, and each was carefully orchestrated and prepared.

The granting of the municipal franchise to women in Belfast was quite a coup on the part of Tod. The campaign to win this franchise for women had been started in 1873,[83] and in Belfast women householders finally gained the vote in 1887 as the result of a local Act, concerned with drainage plans for the city, introduced by the Belfast MPs Sir James Corry, William Ewart and William Johnston. During the progress of the Bill through Parliament Tod organised a group to press the claims of Irish women to the municipal franchise, a privilege which their sisters in England had enjoyed since 1869. The North of Ireland Women's Suffrage Committee approached Corry and other supporters of the bill and persuaded them to substitute the word 'person' for 'man' in the clause defining qualified voters. To make absolutely certain that the Bill would include women, an amendment was moved in the Lords by Lord Erne adding an explanatory clause showing that the word 'person' was intended to include women. Tod was delighted with the passage of the Bill, and in a letter to the *Northern Whig* in July 1887 she welcomed the admission of women to the 'most important of local franchises'.[84] Tod expressed the hope that in casting their votes the women of Belfast would:

... care less for mere party politics than men do, and more for the great social and moral questions which ought to be the end for which party politics are only the means. As they will now have a share in choosing the policy of the town and the men who are to carry it out, they can influence efficiently all matters concerning the peace and good order of the streets, the progress of sanitary reform, the cause of temperance, and other questions in which they have a vital interest.[85]

It is from 1881 that we find Tod publicly interested in ensuring women could be returned as Poor Law Guardians. In an article published that year on 'The place of women in the administration of the Irish Poor Law', she argued that women must share in the administration of the Poor Law system because 'the economy of the workhouse is the economy of a house ... the management of officials ...needs the same kind of wisdom as the management of servants ... the care of the poor ... the care of children ... the prevention and cure of sickness ... are all women's duties'.[86] In 1882 she became a subscriber to the Society for Promoting the Return of Women as Poor Law Guardians, a London-based organisation.[87] It remains unclear what function Tod played in this society, but she was certainly interested in promoting its cause in Ireland. On the many platforms from which she spoke in the 1880s, Tod claimed the right of women to act as Guardians. It was not, however, until 1896, the year of Tod's death, that the Belfast MP William Johnston introduced a Bill to enable women to act as Guardians. There were, as always, many members of Parliament who believed that being a Poor Law Guardian was not a suitable occupation for women. The Bill was passed not because it conferred rights on women, but rather because it brought the situation in Ireland into line with that of England.

The year 1886 proved to be a momentous one for Tod. At that stage she was well known throughout Ireland and England as an eloquent speaker on issues pertaining to women. She had spent over twenty years in public life advocating and organising for change. She had been successful in a number of her endeavours, particularly in the educational field. The introduction of Gladstone's first Home Rule Bill for Ireland seemed to Tod to threaten the destruction of all her work. In later years she was to note:

I can scarcely write of the sickening shock of the Home Rule proposal of 1886. Knowing Ireland thoroughly, I knew that all the social work in which I had taken so prominent a part for twenty years was in danger, and that most of it could not exist for a day under a petty legislature of the character which would be inevitable ... . I shrank in horror from the revival of the religious and racial difference which was certain to ensue.[88]

Tod threw herself into a campaign against the Bill. The resulting crusade not only lost her a number of friends in the suffrage movement, but also seriously damaged her health.

Immediately on the announcement of the Bill, Tod organised a Liberal Women's Unionist Association in Belfast, shortly after a similar society was organised in Birmingham. On 14 April (Gladstone's Bill had been introduced on 8 April) a letter to the *Northern Whig* stated her position clearly. At this stage Tod raised a number of arguments against the granting of Home Rule, 'They [the Government]', she wrote,

have literally no idea of the large numbers of the population opposed to Home Rule ... they suppose that this opposition arises from religious bigotry and need to have it brought strongly before them that this is not the case, but that what we dread is the complete dislocation of all society, especially in regard to commercial affairs and to organised freedom of action. They suppose that Home Rule is a democratic movement and therefore unavoidable ... it is needful to point out that the conditions of a free democracy do not exist in Ireland. Before they can exist the two great training influences of widespread education and large local government must have room to be fairly brought into operation.

She continued by suggesting that Ulster should perhaps claim:

... a separate jurisdiction. If we can keep some degree of political freedom, such as is totally impossible for Ulster in a Parnellite parliament, we can continue to do some good for the rest of Ireland. But no conceivable good for any created being could come from our being crushed under such a parliament.[89]

Tod spent most of the period from April to July, when polling took place, in England campaigning on behalf of the Liberal Unionists. She spent some time on the campaign trail with Leonard Courtney,[90] an old friend and staunch supporter of the suffrage cause. She spoke on platforms in Devon, Cornwall and London. She penned letters to MPs and local newspapers, she wrote pamphlets, she threw all her energies into the campaign.[91] Throughout Tod argued that Home Rule would destroy Ireland's economic base, not only would there be a '... withdrawal of capital ...[but] many skilled artisans would come over to England which would not tend to raise wages'.[92] She spoke, she felt, for all Ulster Liberals, and had little time for the handful of Liberals who supported Home Rule.

During her months in England, Tod became a friend of Millicent Garrett Fawcett, another opponent of Home Rule and a leading light in the Women's Liberal Unionist Association, and they spoke on platforms together.[93] While Tod campaigned in England, her organisation in Ireland had raised a petition, signed by 30,000 women, which was presented to Queen Victoria asking her not to give her assent to the Bill, if it should be passed.[94]

By the time the campaign ended with the election of a Conservative government and the dropping of the Home Rule legislation, Tod had exhausted herself. It was from this period that her health deteriorated, and she blamed this deterioration on the stresses of the campaign. Another outcome of the campaign, and one that pained her deeply, was the loss of a number of friends in the suffrage movement. Many of the British suffrage organisations were sympathetic to Home Rule, as was Josephine Butler, a friend of Tod's from her earlier campaigns. When, in 1887, Butler and a number of other women presented a memorial of sympathy to a number of 'Parnellite MPs', Tod immediately disassociated herself from Butler in a letter to the *Northern*

Whig, in which she asked to be allowed

> ... to assure those ladies throughout Ulster with whom I have worked for so many years for the repeal of the late Contagious Diseases Acts and who have been in the habit of admiring Mrs Butler's efforts in that cause, that she does not by any means represent the feeling of the religious and philanthropic workers here, but only of the Gladstonian section. That section is just as intolerant and intolerable within the committee rooms of religious and philanthropic societies as on political platforms ...they will not succeed in driving us out of the good work in which we have borne our full share.[95]

Tod's interest in the Home Rule issue remained strong. For the remainder of her life she organised meetings and petitions whenever the spectre of Home Rule appeared on the horizon. In 1892, she was organising an anti-Home Rule meeting in Aughnacloy and requesting the presence of H. de F. Montgomery. 'Every meeting,' Tod declared, 'does good, in one way or another.'[96] In June of the same year she helped organise, with other Unionist ladies, a meeting in Belfast's Ulster Hall. Banners placed around the hall displayed the mottos 'Keep our noble kingdom whole' and 'British freedom, British laws, and British citizenship'.[97] When Gladstone introduced his second Home Rule Bill in February of 1893, Tod organised further campaigns, demonstrations and petitions, though her health at this stage was not good.[98]

The last ten years of Tod's life were afflicted by illness, but throughout she remained active in a variety of causes. The Home Rule issue was to the fore, but she continued to organise the annual meetings of the suffrage society, and lobbied for the election of women as Poor Law Guardians.

Tod's work was much appreciated by many individuals in both England and Ireland. A number of presentations were made to her during the period of her public life. In 1884 she was presented with a testimonial of £1,000 contributed mainly by her 'English fellow workers in various philanthropies'.[99] In November 1886 she was presented with a full-length portrait as a token of appreciation for her work in Ireland. Another testimonial some years later consisted of a gift - it appears it may have been money - and an album which contained '120 signatures - many of them of the front rank of the Unionist party'.[100]

Tod's last public appearance, just before her death, was at a meeting on behalf of distressed Armenians. She died at her home in Belfast on 8 December, 1896. The cause of her death was given as pulmonary illness - an illness, it was claimed, that had been brought on and exacerbated by the stress of her campaigns against Home Rule. She was buried in Balmoral Cemetery in the city of Belfast. Her death was widely reported in the press and many obituaries were written. Her funeral was a large one and there were representatives from all the groups to which she had been attached, amongst them the British Women's Temperance Association, the Irish Women's Temperance Union, the Ulster and London branches of the Women's Liberal Unionist Association and various Irish and British suffrage organisations.

A memorial service organised by her friends was held a few days after her death. On 12 December a large group meeting in the Albert Bridge Hall in Belfast were addressed on 'Lessons from the life of Isabella M. Tod'.[101] In October 1898 a memorial portrait of Tod was unveiled in the Free Public Library of Belfast. Also in that year two scholarships were made available in Tod's memory. The first was a scholarship worth £15, offered by Victoria College and to be held by a student of that college; the second amounted to £300 and was to be awarded every third year to the woman candidate achieving the highest marks in the first-year examinations of the Royal University of Ireland.[102]

It seems strange that someone of Tod's importance to the political and social life of Ireland could be so completely forgotten. Her contribution to society did not affect the interests only of women, and her fight to oppose the various Home Rule Bills placed her on a par with many male politicians of the period. The fact that she was a woman has clearly played some role in her disappearance from Irish history. Perhaps too the fact that she was a Unionist has made her less appealing to historians writing on Irish history.

During her period of public activism Tod filled lecture halls in Ireland and England. She set no boundary to the limits of her activities. Her commitment to so many causes was clearly made possible by her single and financially independent status. She was well versed in the use of all means of propagating her causes. Her most effective means of disseminating her ideas was through the letters that were regularly published in the newspapers, particularly the *Northern Whig*. It is clear that she dominated the societies she organised. Kate Courtney, wife of Leonard Courtney for whom Tod had canvassed in the 1886 election, visited Ireland in 1890. While in Belfast she attended a meeting of Unionist women organised by Tod. While she admired Tod immensely, Courtney noted that

> ... Miss Tod is wonderful herself but she is constantly ill, and she does not seem to have the gift and perhaps not quite the inclination to insist on these ladies working apart from her...she [Tod] probably does not see that she overpowers others and prevents them doing much.[103]

To have engaged in such extensive activity over such a long period of time demanded a strong character and also a strong sense of purpose. Tod proved to be uncompromising in many of her views and was prepared to lose friends rather than change those beliefs she held most deeply. Her audience was an English audience, her writings, letters and pamphlets were generally published in England. Ireland, for Tod, was an integral part of the Empire, and all benefits to Ireland would come through the Imperial Parliament. Her religious convictions, the evangelical spirit in which she wrote and worked, gave her a sense in the justness of her causes. She was without doubt a formidable character: her energy, enthusiasm, organisational abilities and political skills made her a force to be reckoned with during her public life.

It is unfortunate that we have little information on Tod's private life. There are a number of portraits and photographs available which show her to have a kind face, a direct gaze, and the barest hint of a smile. Few of her letters seem to have survived, but those that do show her to be a warm individual with a lively sense of humour. There is no doubt that she won the friendship of many individuals through her hard work, commitment and genuine talent for friendship. She believed profoundly in the importance of her work and also in her own ability to bring about change in society.

NOTES

1 See article on Haslam in this volume.
2 For general information on Tod's life, see *Women's Penny Paper* 51, (12 October 1889), pp1-2; *Wings*, July 1893, pp217-9; *Englishwoman's Review*, 15 January 1897, pp58-63, (hereafter *EWR*); Dewar, James. 1900. *A History of Elmwood Church*, Belfast, pp174-6; *Belfast Newsletter*, 9 December 1896; *The Witness*, 11 December 1896.
3 *EWR*, 15 January 1897, p.58.
4 *Ibid.*
5 *Ibid.*
6 *Belfast Newsletter*, 9 December 1896.
7 *EWR*, 15 January 1897, p.59.
8 McCrone, Kathleen E. 1982. 'The National Association for the Promotion of Social Science and the advancement of women'. In *Atlantis* 8, 1 (Autumn), pp44-66.
9 She delivered papers in 1867, 1869, 1870 and 1879.
10 *EWR*, 15 January 1897, p.59.
11 Jordan, Alison. c. 1992. *Who Cared? Charity in Victorian and Edwardian Belfast*. Belfast.
12 Jordan, Alison. n.d., c. 1991. *Margaret Byers*. Belfast.
13 Luddy, Maria. 1995. *Women and Philanthropy in Nineteenth-Century Ireland*. Cambridge, chapter six.
14 O'Connor, Anne. 1986. 'Influences affecting girls' secondary education in Ireland, 1860-1910'. In *Archivium Hibernicum*, xli, pp83-97; *idem.*, 'The revolution in girls' secondary education in Ireland, 1860-1910'. In Mary Cullen (ed.). 1987. *Girls Don't Do Honours: Irish Women in Education in the 19th and 20th Centuries*, Dublin, pp31-54.
15 O'Connor, 'Influences'.
16 See article on Anne Jellicoe in this volume.
17 *Ibid.*
18 Interview with Tod in the *Women's Penny Paper*, 12 October 1889, p.1.
19 Breathnach, Eibhlín. 1980. 'Women and higher education in Ireland, 1879-1914'. In *The Crane Bag* 4, pp47-54; *idem.*, 'Charting new waters: women's experiences in higher education, 1879-1908', in Cullen, *Girls Don't Do Honours*, pp55-78.
20 MS Ladies' Institute Minute Book, 1867-97, Victoria College, Belfast (hereafter Minute Book). See also Moody, T W and Beckett, J C 1959. *Queens Belfast, 1845-1945*. London, p.267.
21 O'Connor, 'Revolution'.
22 Minute Book, 25 August 1873.
23 Breathnach, 'New waters', p.62.
24 Minute Book, 22 September 1873.
25 Breathnach, 'Women', pp79-80.
26 Breathnach, 'New Waters', pp69-70.
27 *Ibid.*, p.60.
28 Tod, Isabella M S 1867. 'Advanced education for girls of the upper and middle classes'. In *Transactions of the National Association*

for the Promotion of Social Science. London, p.369.

29 Tod, Isabella M S 1874. *On the Education of Girls of the Middle Class.* London.

30 Tod, 'Advanced education', p.372.

31 Tod, *On the Education of Girls*, p.9.

32 *Journal of Women's Education Union*, 15 December 1875, pp183-4.

33 *Ibid.*

34 Breathnach, 'New waters', p.62.

35 Association for Irish Schoolmistresses and other Ladies Interested in Education, leaflet 1883.

36 Minute Book, 1883.

37 *Ibid.*

38 Moody, T W and Hawkins, R A J (eds.). 1988. *Florence Arnold-Foster's Irish Journal.* Oxford, pp409, 414.

39 *EWR*, 15 January 1897, p.59.

40 *Special Report from the Select Committee on the Married Women's Property Bill*, H.C. 1867-8 (441), vii, 339, pp74-6.

41 *Ibid.*

42 *Ibid.*

43 Holcombe, Lee. 1983. *Wives and Property: Reform of the Married Women's Property Law in 19th Century England.* Oxford, p.141.

44 *Ibid.*, pp141,167, 184.

45 *Wings*, July 1893, p.218.

46 *EWR*, June 1875, p.273.

47 *EWR*, May 1876, p.219.

48 Anon., n.d. *Will You Help Us? The Story of the Women's Temperance Association and Christian Worker's Union.* Belfast, p.3.

49 Quoted in *ibid.*, p.5.

50 Tod, Isabella M S 'Prison Mission and Inebriates' Home'. In *EWR*, 15 June 1881, pp247-8.

51 *EWR*, 15 May 1883.

52 *Will You Help Us?*, pp7-8.

53 *Ibid.*

54 For the split see Lewis Shiman, Lilian. 1986. 'Changes are dangerous: women and temperance in Victorian England'. In Gail Malmgreen (ed.). *Religion in the Lives of English Women, 1760-1930.* London, pp193-215; *idem.* 1988. *The Crusade Against Drink in Victorian England.* London, chapter seven.

55 Tod, Isabella M S 1875. 'On the principles on which plans for the curative treatment of habitual drunkards should be based'. In *Statistical and Social Inquiry Society of Ireland Journal*, vi, 7 (May), pp408-10.

56 *EWR*, 15 March 1888, p.105.

57 *Ibid.*

58 *Ibid.*, pp106-7.

59 See Luddy, Maria. 1993. 'Women and the Contagious Diseases Acts in Ireland'. In *History Ireland* 1, 1, pp32-4.

60 Walkowitz, J R 1980. *Prostitution and Victorian Society: Women, Class and the State.* Cambridge.

61 Luddy, 'Contagious Diseases Acts'.

62 Jordan, *Philanthropy*.

63 *Ibid*.

64 Butler, Josephine. 1910. *Personal Reminiscences of a Great Crusade*. London.

65 *To the Members of the Belfast Committee for the Repeal of the Contagious Diseases Acts* (Belfast, 1878), p.1.

66 *Ibid*., p.2.

67 *EWR*, 15 October 1883, pp438-40.

68 Tod, Isabella M S c.1885 'The new crusade and women's suffrage', reprinted from the *Pall Mall Gazette*.

69 *Ibid*.

70 See the annual reports of the Northern Ireland Women's Suffrage committee published in the *Northern Whig*.

71 *Women's Suffrage Journal*, March 1873 (hereafter *WSJ*).

72 *WSJ*, 3 June 1873.

73 *WSJ*, 1 March 1875, p.29.

74 *WSJ*, 1 March 1886, p.38.

75 *EWR*, 15 December 1884, p.550.

76 *WSJ*, 1 March 1875, p.31.

77 *WSJ*, 1 August, 1882, p.121.

78 *WSJ*, 1 March 1883, p.45.

79 *EWR*, 15 March, 1888, p.105.

80 Tod, Isabella M S n.d., c. 1878. *The Necessity of Stronger Representation in Parliament of the Religious Feeling Against the State Regulation of Vice*. London.

81 *EWR*, 15 March 1888, p.105.

82 *WSJ*, 1 March 1875, p.30.

83 *WSJ*, 1 March 1873, p.35.

84 *Northern Whig*, 23 July 1887. For the background to issues in local government, see Crossman, Virginia. 1994. *Local Government in Nineteenth-Century Ireland*, Belfast.

85 *Ibid*.

86 *EWR*, 15 November 1881, p.486.

87 See *Annual Report of the Society for Promoting the Return of Women as Poor Law Guardians*, 1883.

88 *Queen*, September 1892.

89 *Northern Whig*, 17 June 1886.

90 See reports of her campaigning in the *Western Morning News*, June 10, 14, 16, 18, 24, June 10, 1886.

91 See reports in the *Northern Whig*, 13, 21 May; 10, 17, 29 June 1886. Amongst her writing was 'Some Historical Fallacies', in the *Liberal Unionist*, 1 August 1888.

92 *Northern Whig*, 17 June 1886.

93 *Northern Whig*, 6 July 1886.

94 *Northern Whig*, 13 May 1886.

95 *Northern Whig*, 26 May 1887.

96 Letter to Mr Montgomery from Isabella Tod, 12 October 1892. D627/428/196/ Public Record Office, Northern Ireland.

97 *Belfast Newsletter*, 7 June 1892.

98 *EWR*, 15 April 1893.

99 *The Witness*, 11 December 1896.
100 *Ibid.*
101 *Northern Whig*, 1 December 1896.
102 *EWR*, 15 January 1898.
103 Kate Courtney, diary of a trip to Ireland written in the form of a letter to Margaret Courtney, 3 September-19 October 1890, vol. xxv, Courtney papers, British Library of Political and Economic Science, London School of Economics.

I would like to thank the Research and Innovations Committee of Warwick University which provided a grant that allowed me to conduct the research for this paper.

Charlotte Grace O'Brien

(1845-1909)

Anne O'Connell

Charlotte Grace O'Brien, a Protestant and a member of the landlord class, single-handedly fought to abolish the degrading and demeaning practices associated with the female emigrant trade towards the end of the nineteenth century. As a result of her efforts, conditions in steerage on transatlantic vessels were radically improved, a mission for immigrant women was established in New York, and a temporary refuge was set up in Queenstown (now Cobh). Her activities received support from neither the Catholic church, nor the institutions of the State; and while neither body was openly hostile towards her, their collective silence meant that she was obliged to work alone and with limited resources. Her story starts in Cahirmoyle, near Ardagh, County Limerick and spans just 64 years, coming to a close in Ardanoir, Foynes, where she spent most of her adult life.

During the 1880s the political stage was dominated by Parnell, the battle for Home Rule and the settlement of the land question. In spite of the intensity of the political climate, access to public life for women, although more common, was still limited. In O'Brien's youth, leisure was extolled for the wives and daughters of the gentry, both as a virtue in itself and as a status symbol. The notion of paid employment, or even a university education, for girls was completely alien to the beliefs of her class. However, women of the upper classes functioned as mistresses of great homes, accomplished hostesses, and often as philanthropists throughout the eighteenth and nineteenth centuries. In nineteenth-century Ireland philanthropic activity was widespread amongst Protestant ascendancy, and middle-class women.[1] A small number of women also became involved in male-dominated organisations such as the Young Irelanders and the illegal Fenian movement.[2] As the century progressed the various campaigns around women's education, the fight for the repeal of the Contagious Diseases Acts, the formation of the Ladies' Land League and the suffrage campaign allowed for the creation of distinctly female associations which provided an outlet for women's voices at a political level.

Interestingly, Charlotte Grace O'Brien never became a member of the Ladies' Land League, although she was appalled by the suffering of the small tenant farmer and the thousands of labourers who were without holdings, and voiced admiration for its work and political convictions on many occasions. Instead, she felt compelled to try to improve the lot of the emigrant, and, in particular, that of the young, single girl who, from 1880 onwards, was a common sight on the wharf at Queenstown. On the question of her membership of the Ladies' Land League, she once remarked:

Well, the fates led me to the emigration instead, otherwise I should have probably joined it, as I sympathised with it - I lost £8 today through the means of it, having to accept my mortgage interest short (owing to the no rent agitation). I am not less the land leaguer though.[3]

The only organisation to which she ever belonged was the Gaelic League which, after her retirement from public activity, was to provide an important outlet for her unbounded support of cultural nationalism. As the first organisation to admit women on the same terms as men, the Gaelic League attracted her individualism, while at the same time promoting the revival of the Irish language and support for Irish industries - causes which she embraced with great enthusiasm.

O'Brien's illustrious background set her apart from her contemporaries. The O'Briens of Dromoland, although now Protestant and assimilated into the ascendancy, could trace a direct line of descent from King Brian Boru and the Kings of Thomond, and it was more as an Irish chief than as a member of a colonial elite that Sir Edward O'Brien, Charlotte's grandfather, was regarded by the masses. Over the years, the family greatly endeared itself to its tenants by its benevolence and sense of fair play. An early role model for the young O'Brien was her grandmother and namesake, Lady Charlotte O'Brien. In 1819 she became actively involved in philanthropic work when she tried to improve conditions for the Irish peasants who lived on the land surrounding her stately home at Dromoland, County Clare.[4]

Charlotte Grace O'Brien was born on 23 November 1845, the second youngest in a family of seven children - two girls and five boys - of William Smith O'Brien and Lucy Gabbett. Her childhood was dominated by her father's political activities.[5] His involvement in O'Connell's Repeal Association caused his immediate family, all staunch Unionists, considerable pain and embarrassment. It was greeted with horror by his mother, Lady O'Brien, a fervent Evangelist with a deep mistrust of Rome, who pleaded with her son on many occasions to give up what she termed 'this unsuitable ... this unholy ... this wicked alliance'.[6] The final disgrace - his leadership of a motley band of insurgents in the 1848 rising - was hard to bear. While those closest to him opposed his activities as a betrayal of everything his class stood for, family solidarity was not threatened in any serious way by these events, and after his arrest the O'Briens were present in large numbers during William Smith's trial, providing moral support as well as legal assistance.[7] Lucy, Charlotte Grace's mother, was deeply hurt by her husband's exploits and, like the rest of the family, thought that his political career had brought only suffering and shame. His influence over his youngest daughter appears to have been strengthened rather than undermined by the circumstances surrounding his arrest and deportation. Indeed, her unbounded youthful admiration for his heroism was, in later years, to colour her political views and shape her allegiance to the 'plain people' of Ireland.

Without doubt, William Smith O'Brien had many positive attributes. Described as 'a very sincere and courageous man',[8] he was full of passion and enthusiasm, and tried always to understand the realities of peasant existence, even learning Irish so that he would be better able to communicate with his tenants. Charlotte Grace, like her father, refused to be fettered by her social status and, in turn, openly castigated the evils inherent in the political system. The likeness between the two was acknowledged on more than one occasion by her nephew, Stephen Gwynn. 'I think one trait came down from this aristocrat with the big rent-roll,' he remarked, 'none of his family were likely to stop at anything merely because it was extreme and unusual. His second daughter, Charlotte, had perhaps most of his temper.'[9]

The 'set' to which the O'Brien family belonged during Charlotte Grace's formative years almost certainly played its part in moulding her views. It was dominated by the Spring Rice family, the largest landowners in County Limerick, and also included the De Vere family of Curraghchase.[10]

It is highly probable that the involvement of the Spring Rices and the De Veres in the emigration issue was, subsequently, to influence Charlotte Grace's decision to work with emigrant women.[11] At any rate, in Thomas Spring Rice, or 'Uncle Monteagle' as he was known to the O'Briens of Cahirmoyle, she found at times a useful ally, despite the fact that they held widely different views on many matters and that she, like her father, was staunchly nationalist. Family ties meant a great deal to her, so it was comforting that her close friends and family respected her views, even though they were opposed to her political convictions.

In 1888, a little book of sonnets, written by O'Brien, was published under the title *Cahirmoyle or The Old Home*.[12] It was dedicated to 'all those who love simple and true things'. In these poems, she recalled with great fondness her early years. The O'Briens owned five thousand acres of rich County Limerick land. Yet despite her superior social standing, Cahirmoyle's tenants were at all times regarded by Charlotte Grace as her friends and neighbours. In the sonnets she spoke of them as 'the simple folk I loved', and delighted in the fact that they frequently enjoyed Cahirmoyle hospitality, especially when it hosted the annual ball and its rooms reverberated to the sound of fiddles and stomping feet. In O'Brien's youth, despite the fact that times were hard, estates like Cahirmoyle could keep the worst excesses of the Famine at bay. As a result the wretched existence outside the walls impinged only in a very minor way on the lifestyle of its owners, and the younger members of the O'Brien family were shielded from much of the hardship of those years.

In childhood, the bonds of affection which existed between the children were exceptionally strong and Charlotte Grace, in particular, seems to have given love with an almost excessive passion, especially to her younger brother, Charles. In fact, she tended to view the Cahirmoyle children as a perfect, intact unit, believing that their cohesion imbued them with a certain invincibility and provided a bulwark against the loss of innocence.

It appears that O'Brien was a poor scholar who became more than a little impatient at times with academic endeavour. Unlike her brothers, she received no formal education and, as was the case with other young girls of her class, was groomed instead to become an accomplished wife and mother. Yet there is no evidence to suggest that she resented the boys' special status. At Cahirmoyle, she had a tutor and, when she was older, Miss D'Arcy, 'a lady of good Irish family',[13] came to work as her governess. Indeed, as a young child, it seems her frustration during lessons often spilled over into genuine distress when only her pets could provide comfort and consolation.

The Cahirmoyle sonnets are essentially happy reminiscences. If they have a flaw it is that they barely acknowledge the terrible upheaval of the years following Smith O'Brien's conviction for his part in the Young Ireland rebellion and the distress which this must have inflicted on his wife and young family. Indeed, it was only as a result of

Lady Charlotte O'Brien's foresight that the family managed to survive at all during this period and retain possession of their home and lands.[14] Yet it is clear that Charlotte Grace never blamed her father in any way for the suffering they had to endure. In fact, his actions were totally vindicated by her on the grounds that his motives were entirely altruistic and rooted in genuine patriotism. In the sonnets she expressed only sympathy for the demeaning nature of his experiences after his arrest and compassion for the man who was 'exiled from home with every branded thief'. In her eyes, Smith O'Brien was blameless. 'He was noble, he was not perfect', she wrote on one occasion, 'those very qualities that raised his public life were a difficulty in his private.'[15]

O'Brien's mother was, on the other hand, the person to whom Charlotte Grace owed her security as a child and her day to day happiness. She is fondly recalled sitting in a 'warm corner' of the old garden at Cahirmoyle, watching over her children at play. Unwavering and strong, she was capable of great affection and lavished her children with love. Even though she never shared her husband's political convictions which were, apparently not only 'reprobated by all his kin' but 'by all the society to which he and she belonged',[16] she displayed unwavering loyalty to him, both throughout the long ordeal of his trial and afterwards, when he was forced to live in exile. For her children, she represented strength of character and a sense of permanence in an otherwise uncertain environment. Daily, despite being pregnant, she visited William Smith in Kilmainham Gaol, travelling by hack car and remained as close as possible to him until his deportation, almost a year after his arrest. Lucy's great determination was, in fact, nowhere more apparent than in her resolve to share, with her seven young children, her husband's life in Tasmania. However, William's insistence that she remain in Ireland meant that she had to face a very uncertain future alone. There is no doubt that Lucy's death in 1861, just seven years after her husband had been granted a full pardon, and while her family was still not fully recovered from the rift his deportation had caused, was a tremendous loss to all her children. Her youngest daughter, Charlotte Grace, was still in her teens and felt her passing keenly. Effectively it brought her childhood to an end.

From this time onwards, the somewhat tentative relationship which had existed between Smith O'Brien and his children after his release deteriorated rapidly, with matters coming to a head when Edward, his eldest son, came of age and inherited the Cahirmoyle estate.[17] Bitter recriminations followed with the result that the elder O'Brien went to live in Killiney for a time with his two daughters, Charlotte Grace and her older sister Lucy.

This was the start of a period in O'Brien's life which was characterised by service to other members of her family. Lucy's marriage in 1862 meant that, thereafter, Smith O'Brien relied exclusively on her companionship. In a letter to her he wrote: 'You must be prepared to take a position in the world as the consoler of your father'.[18] At the time she was, once again, living at Cahirmoyle, more or less as a housekeeper for her brothers. However, on Edward's marriage to Mary Spring Rice in 1863, she moved out of the old house in County Limerick to devote herself entirely to the care of her father, who had now adopted a somewhat itinerant lifestyle. These years were not easy ones for Charlotte Grace. Smith O'Brien chose to live mainly in hotels and was constantly on the move. As his health declined, his manner became difficult also, and even though she was young and inexperienced, she had to cope alone with his mood swings. There is no doubt that the strain on her must have been very great, yet, his death in 1864 left a huge void in her life.

She had been a devoted daughter whose role as 'carer' was entirely in keeping with the expectations which society had of unmarried women. Now, her options were limited solely to living with Edward and Mary Spring Rice, the new mistress of Cahirmoyle. She was, understandably, consumed with anxiety and, to some degree, jealousy. Mary's presence in the house where she had spent her childhood meant adjusting to loss and change. However, her fears proved groundless, since she found a true friend and staunch ally in Mary, someone who shared many of her views and was sensitive to her needs. In fact, such a strong bond developed between the two women that O'Brien became almost a second mother to Mary's three young children. Yet, although she loved her nieces and nephew dearly, in a poem called 'Mary - Hyeres, 1866',[19] one senses her genuine sadness at not having become a mother herself.

Tragically, the happiness which they enjoyed was to be short-lived. Mary developed TB and died on the Riviera in 1868, just two years after the birth of her youngest daughter, Mary. Her only son, Dermod, was born in 1865. It was bitterly ironic that O'Brien's strong maternal instincts were to be satisfied in such tragic circumstances, as Mary Spring Rice had entrusted her with the upbringing of her 'well-beloved'[20] children. Although she was only twenty-three, O'Brien took her responsibilities very seriously indeed and was assiduous in her care of her three charges, lavishing as much love on them as if they had been her own.

After his wife's death, Edward became morose and withdrawn and had difficulty adjusting to Charlotte Grace as mistress of his home. It appears that her wide frame and 'rough' manner was in sharp contrast to the delicate bearing of Mary Spring Rice. This, coupled with the fact that she was quite awkward in her movements and apparently could not enter a room without knocking something over,[21] meant that there was a constant palpable tension between the two. His decision to rebuild Cahirmoyle may have been prompted by a desire to obliterate the painful memories which the house held for him, or may simply have been in accordance with the fashion of the time. At any rate, during the reconstruction, which lasted for four years, the entire family lived at Corgrig in Foynes, a small house which, it seems, suited Charlotte Grace.

At this point in her life she had started to write, and this outlet was to prove very important to her when communication with others became strained as a result of her growing deafness. The great passion in her life, however, continued to be the rearing of Mary Spring Rice's children. It was heartbreaking for her, therefore, when the two girls, Nell and Mary, left for boarding school in England in 1879 as their brother, Dermod, had done earlier. Once more, O'Brien was plagued by uncertainty and the fear of being left loveless and alone, especially since the children's departure came just a short while after the death of her favourite brother, Charles, in 1877. In fact, her dread of a solitary old age had been expressed as far back as 1870 and became a recurring theme in her work.[22] Her deafness, too, made it difficult for her not to succumb periodically to bouts of depression, and when her hearing finally deserted her in 1879 she was, understandably, utterly dismayed:

About my neck

The children cast their arms, no voices break

Upon my ear; no sounds of laughter come -

Child's laughter wrought of love, and life and bliss;

Heedless I leave the rest, had I but this![23]

Not even the success of her first and only novel, *Light and Shade*, which dealt with the Fenian Rising of 1867 and was written from personal contact with ex-Fenians, could lift her spirits and, in spite of many accolades, she remained morose and depressed.[24] Edward's decision to remarry and move his family to London where his future wife, Julia Marshall, had her home, further compounded this unhappiness, filling her with anxiety and the awful fear that she would lose contact with the three children who had once been so dependent on her.[25]

Luckily for O'Brien, she had built her own home in County Limerick in 1870. This was, possibly, an early attempt by her to establish her independence and assume some control over her future. It appears that 'a vision of a cottage at Foynes' was something that had obsessed her from the time she received her inheritance, at the age of twenty-one, and began to handle her own money.[26] Her garden at Ardanoir was most important to her and, in its own way, made a strong statement about her personality. In fact, in its development she refused to conform to the fashion of the time and to what she described as 'the pernicious facility of a "paper" garden'.[27] She displayed a similar reluctance to conform to fashion in dress, preferring that her 'broad square figure' which, according to Gwynn, 'had something of a peasant woman's dignity in its carriage', be loosely garbed in clothes which she made herself.[28] It was her view that nature should also defy the intervention of the designer's pencil at all costs and that rural gardens, especially, should blend with their surroundings by retaining a certain raw quality. O'Brien planted her garden herself on a bed of pencil slate, which she had literally hewn out with a pickaxe. The result was that over many months she developed at Ardanoir a sort of private paradise, where she liked to bask in the winter sunshine 'though the frost was caked white under the shadow of the hill'.[29] She hoped it would flourish and outlive her. Yet, even if it did not, her choice of plants - sweet briars, planted close to a fine rose, and daffodils - guaranteed a certain immortality and delighted her sense of fun. In 'The making of our home' she wrote:

> I will puzzle the botanist of another generation and when my bones are dust and my good spade rust, when my house is pulled down and my garden asphalt and bricks, my extra special wild briars and my daffodils will still linger on the hill side and scent the bloomy air for generations that know me not. [30]

It was to this simple haven, rented out to naval officers during her time spent at Cahirmoyle and at Corgrig, that she now went when Edward closed up her childhood home. It was a time of great turmoil for her, but also a time of challenge. In many respects the year 1880 was to be the turning point in her life.

Before 1880 O'Brien had been preoccupied with the demands of home and family, and her concerns had been mainly domestic ones. She had also clearly defined her political views in a number of poems written prior to this date.[31] In 'The workers for Ireland' she strongly identified with her country's nationalist heroes and martyrs, and affirmed her belief in the need to maintain the fight for freedom. Likewise, 'I dwell among my own people' reiterated her affinity to the Irish, whom she referred to as 'my people, my own countrymen, my friends'. Even the early sonnets addressed to Gladstone, while displaying faith in the Liberal administration, demonstrated that the needs of her country and its people always took precedence over ties of class or vested interest. The publication of an article entitled 'The Irish poor man',[32] towards the end of 1880, broadened the scope of her influence considerably, while demonstrating that some of her early idealism had now been shed and replaced by a more mature and incisive social and political analysis.

It was of course the period of the Land League, and O'Brien clearly sided with the tenantry in their fight for control of the land.[33] In 'The Irish poor man', she was passionate in her condemnation of those who advocated emigration as 'a panacea for all ills' and argued that, instead, it should be 'the natural throwing off from the body politic of the needless particles, not the draining away of the life-blood of a nation'.[34]

Generally speaking, she made no effort to hide her contempt for rack-renting landlords whose actions she likened to 'a capricious extraction of the pound of flesh'. Essentially, she believed in her country's ability to recover from the effects of the past and to provide each Irish woman and man with hope for the future. 'Ireland is suffering now from stagnation, not from over-population,' she wrote, 'bring back her successful exiles, and commerce will return, and knowledge of practical arts will arise; the life-blood of the nation will flow again.'[35] In many respects, then, her ideals and aspirations were directly opposed to those of her friends and family since, in what amounted to a class war, she 'took the side of her nation against the interest and the judgement of those nearest to her'.[36]

The *Munster News*, not surprisingly, gave significant coverage at the time to a letter written by O'Brien which openly challenged Aubrey De Vere's public rejection of the Land League and its tactics, especially that of repudiation of contract. The letter was particularly newsworthy since De Vere was a personal friend and kinsman of O'Brien. In it, she stressed that the common good should be the concern of all classes.[37] This splitting of her allegiance, however, placed a great strain on her, and left her feeling confused and angry. At one point she remarked:

> I get rather wild about politics, it is so hard to get things straight in one's head - the landlords with their outcry of robbery, put against the doings of landlordism - the people with their failure of right put against the just treatment they have received from some.[38]

At any rate, the stance she took in defence of non-parliamentary agitation must, surely, have affected for a time the relationship she had with her brothers and especially with Donough, reputed to be 'a strong Unionist and authoritarian'.[39] In spite of this, however, her support for the Irish cause never faltered; nor did she flinch from publicly denouncing the Liberal government under Gladstone, when she felt it acted ineptly. The 'Coercion Act', which came into effect early in 1881, particularly incensed her since, under its terms, Mr Forster, the Chief Secretary, 'had filled the Irish jails with people arrested on suspicion'.[40] Even though she was connected by ties of blood and friendship with the landlord class, she was convinced that self-government was the only possible solution to Ireland's problems. In 'Eighty Years' she wrote: 'I don't believe the Castle and its authorities dependent on English faction, could ever be other than rightly unpopular. No, I should step out of this train which has wrecked us - I should clear the lines, and fetch up a new engine'.[41]

At this time, the Ladies' Land League, organised by Fanny and Anna Parnell to continue the work of the Land League,[42] would have seemed the most likely outlet for her talent and enthusiasm, yet, within months of its formation in January 1881, O'Brien had already decided on the course her life was to take for the foreseeable future. While Michael Davitt and Parnell were to remain heroes of a kind, she was determined to devote all her energy to combating the dangers faced by vulnerable, emigrant Irish women.

A routine visit to her sister-in-law in Queenstown marked the start of the campaign for which she is best remembered, a campaign which was inextricably linked to the large-scale emigration of young, single Irish women in the second half of the nineteenth century.[43] It was on behalf of these women that O'Brien confronted the great shipping lines of the day and worked tirelessly to establish a network of support for them both in Ireland and in the archdiocese of New York.

Early in 1881, before her fateful visit to Queenstown, she had already begun to champion the cause of the vulnerable and the defenceless, and was determined to increase public awareness of the degradation to which young women were being subjected by bogus employment agencies, which, it seems, duped many of them into becoming prostitutes. Her tactics were simple. She believed in making public what Victorian society would have preferred to keep hidden. Throughout her campaign, therefore, she relied heavily on press coverage, an approach which proved to be quite successful. The *Munster News* was just one of many newspapers which sympathised with her views. At one point, its editor even agreed with a request from her not to carry any advertisements from London employment agencies, since she believed many of them were false.[44]

However, in the summer of 1881, she was absolutely appalled by what she found below decks on a tour of the

Germanic, a liner owned by the White Star Line which was docked at Queenstown prior to its departure for America, and she turned her attention instead to campaigning for improved conditions on board emigrant ships. Immediately, she sent her impressions of her visit to the *Pall Mall Gazette*, where her letter was published under the title 'Horrors of an emigrant ship'.[45] The effect was like 'a bursting bomb on the public'.[46] While she likened the single men's quarters to those on a slave ship, her description of the women's accommodation was so graphic that it shocked the Victorian public almost into disbelief. Many readers of the *Gazette* could identify with the shipboard accommodation which was available to first- and second-class passengers, but few could imagine what she described in steerage, where two enormous hammocks were suspended about three feet from the floor, each carrying one hundred people. Men, it seems, could sleep in these hammocks with women who were, or claimed to be, their wives. As a result, women in general had no privacy and single women were especially vulnerable to sexual harassment and assault.[47] O'Brien also accused the shipping company of grossly overloading the vessel on the occasion of her visit. Instead of carrying 1000 licensed passengers, she estimated that, in all, there was nearly double that number on board.

Once her letter was published, the matter was immediately raised in parliament and an official enquiry was promised. In the House of Commons, Chamberlain, who was then President of the Board of Trade, did everything he could to discredit O'Brien as a 'hair brained', silly woman, over-reacting to the situation. He even tried to dupe her into believing that she had been mistaken in her observations by inviting her to re-examine the vessel in the presence of a Board of Trade Inspector when it docked again in Queenstown. What he failed to point out was that arrangements on emigrant ships were altered from one voyage to the next and that, on the return journey from New York to Queenstown, the steerage accommodation was frequently transformed almost beyond recognition.

O'Brien became aware of the deceit, as did Parnell, who spoke in her favour, citing the fact that a Grand Jury in New York had already on a number of occasions indicted British steamship companies for overcrowding. T P O'Connor MP also sprang to her defence. He had, he said, reliable information to substantiate O'Brien's claims from an exconstituent of his in Boston.[48] However, not all Irish nationalists were as concerned. Many of them, instead, were more preoccupied with the struggle for independence. From Kilmainham Gaol, John Dillon, with whom O'Brien had been friendly in childhood, replied to her request for support by admitting that his knowledge of the problem was 'slight' and that, although abuses had been brought to his attention, he had neglected to act on the matter, due to the pressure of other business.[49]

Predictably, when the official report of the enquiry was presented by the Board of Trade to both houses of parliament in July 1881, it categorically denied O'Brien's allegations and even attempted to justify the conditions in steerage, on the grounds that fares were kept to a minimum and emigrants, as a class, were used to little better. Chamberlain remarked at the time:

> There are evils which can and ought to be removed, but an attempt to enforce, by process of law, too high a standard of comfort, or even of cleanliness, would be contrary to the feelings and the interests of the emigrants themselves.[50]

Although concern *was* expressed at the practice of carrying live cattle on emigrant ships, the enquiry was satisfied that the shipping companies operated within the law and recommended that things be left to legitimate competition. Indeed, W E Forster, the Chief Secretary, had expressed the same opinion when he wrote privately to O'Brien. 'Care must be taken', he said, 'not to impose unnecessary regulations. Regulations will probably mean increases of passage money and the emigrants would greatly complain at being obliged to pay more than is necessary.'[51]

O'Brien was devastated at the treatment she received in the House of Commons. Yet, in terms of the battle she was about to wage with the shipping companies, her letter to the *Pall Mall Gazette* had been an unqualified success. Not only had it raised public awareness of the emigrant's plight and instigated debate in the columns of the daily newspapers, but as a result, her cause now began to be championed in Parliament by a number of Irish MPs, the most prominent of whom was Count Arthur Moore from Tipperary.

Despite this support, O'Brien felt that even more needed to be done and so she changed the focus of her campaign somewhat by appealing directly to the Catholic church for assistance. The vast majority of emigrants were Catholics, and in letters published by the *Freeman's Journal* throughout the summer of 1881, she constantly reminded the church of its obligation to its parishioners, and of the power of the ecclesiastical network which it had at its disposal. She felt that the provision of chaplains, for example, both at the ports and on board ship, would go a long way towards minimising abuse. She made this point very clear, 'The Catholic church,' she said,

> had an obligation to look after the emigrant at Queenstown and have chaplains especially devoted to this work in communication with every priest in Ireland and every priest in America so that every woman should go direct from the hands of her own priest to the chaplain at Queenstown, from his hands to the chaplain at Castle Garden, from his hands to her parish priest, whether in New York or San Francisco. I know too well now, how many women and men too are lost for the want of such an organisation.[52]

Before long, letters supporting her views began to appear in the press, and the apathy of the church was condemned by many readers.[53] These letters, while helpful, were also a source of great frustration and annoyance, since they were mostly anonymous.[54] Undaunted, on 18 June she again appealed to the Catholic church for assistance through the pages of the *Freeman's Journal*, this time citing the words of a recent female emigrant who furnished her local priest with an eye-witness account of the shame and 'night-time confusion' on board ship. She also made an impassioned plea to both priests and parents to try to discourage young women from emigrating for at least a few months, until some reform of the system could be introduced.

For those who insisted on travelling, her advice was based on information contained in hundreds of letters from emigrant women. 'There is nothing I say', she remarked, 'but what I have line and verse for, in many, certainly genuine letters.' She cautioned women against travelling alone and advised those who wished to travel in a party to have their names entered on a single ticket, since otherwise they could be forced to separate at Queenstown and wait for up to a week for another ship. She also gave the women practical advice about food and clothing. The main target of this letter, however, was again the Catholic church. 'I beseech of the chiefs of the Church to stand forward and help now,' she said, 'it is their work, their responsibility, without them we could do nothing, with their aid an immediate improvement is possible.'[55]

Despite the church's continued silence, the scope of the debate was gradually extended in the newspapers and demands were soon made for an examination also of conditions at the ports, where emigrants often had to be housed and fed for many days. While it was obvious that depots, as well as official boarding houses, were needed, it seems no one wanted to accept responsibility for their provision. The shipping lines, in particular, were not convinced that the venture would be profitable, which meant that lodging houses were run solely by residents of the ports, more or less on an *ad hoc* basis. In Queenstown, the practices engaged in by the lodging-house keepers were dubious, to say the least. No licensing system was in operation, which meant that there was no register of premises or official inspections. Overcrowding was common. In one house, twenty-six people were crammed into a room measuring no more than seventeen feet by ten feet. Various ploys were also used to cheat the unsuspecting emigrants out of their meagre funds. It was quite a normal practice, for example, for fiddlers to be employed late at night to lure the emigrant downstairs to listen to music and, in his absence, for his bed to be rented to the next caller. This was particularly true during the months of April, May and June, when the steamers filled quickly and often refused passage to as many as 500 people.[56]

O'Brien abhorred this type of exploitation and was so concerned by the overcrowding and the increasing incidence of typhus in the town that she called, once more, on the church to intervene. Not only did she make personal contact with Bishop Croke and Cardinal Manning, but she also wrote to the Archbishop of Canterbury at this time, acquainting all three with the facts as she saw them. Afterwards she was optimistic that they would help her, but, as time passed, their indifference to her cause became apparent. Having promised in July, for example, not to allow the matter to rest, by December the Archbishop of Canterbury had a change of heart and wrote: 'I should have been very glad had I been able to help you on it, but the calls upon me are so numerous.' The response from Bishop Croke and Cardinal Manning was much the same.[57]

In the end, O'Brien came to realise that nothing would be done unless she took the matter in hand herself. Therefore, in November 1881, she left her small home in Foynes and moved to Queenstown, where she became a licensed lodging-house keeper. On her arrival in County Cork, she immediately called on the authorities to implement the conditions of the Public Health (Ireland) Act of 1878 which had, up to then, been ignored by the town commissioners. Their reluctance to enforce the law was not difficult to understand, since eight of the commissioners were themselves owners of lodging-houses in Queenstown.[58]

To alleviate the immediate suffering of female emigrants, she opened the O'Brien Emigrants' Home, offering as low a rate as was possible - just two shillings per adult - for bed, breakfast and an evening meal. It seems that, shortly after opening, the house was 'largely patronised' and, although intended originally only for women and children, O'Brien soon found herself admitting 'whole families to share the hospitality of her rooms and to take their meals there, sending the men out to select lodgings to sleep'.[59] To maximise space within the Home, where she had a licence to accommodate 105 lodgers, she herself lived and slept in a corner on the ground floor where there was room, behind a screen, for a table and a bed.[60] Outside on Admiralty Pier, she also provided refreshments for emigrants, at affordable prices, from a large wooden structure on wheels which was known locally as 'The Coffee Stall'.[61]

The residents of Queenstown, who felt O'Brien was threatening their livelihood, very shortly turned against her and made her life difficult. She was jostled by the townspeople as she went about her business, and jeered publicly whenever she went to the station to meet the emigrants coming off the trains. She was also ostracised by the local traders, who refused to supply her with essential items, so that food and clothing had to be delivered from Cork city, which was about fifteen miles away.[62]

In spite of this she persevered and eventually her resilience paid off. Once the shipping companies realised that she was highly respected by the emigrants and could influence their choice of line when they went to purchase their tickets, they thought it more expedient to concede to her demands than to antagonise her further. The emigrant trade was a highly lucrative one and few shipping lines could afford any negative publicity. O'Brien had anticipated this reaction. 'I knew I could force almost any reform I wanted,' she said, 'if I put myself directly in relationship with the emigrants.'[63] As a result, by the autumn of 1882, all the major shipping lines, with the exception of the Cunard, had made arrangements to separate single women from every other class. Stewardesses were also employed on the ships to cater specifically to the needs of female passengers, who could number as many as 500 at any given time. In addition, sanitary arrangements were greatly improved, and, where possible, women were no longer forced to leave their steerage at night in order to use the lavatories. Washbowls, soap and towels were now also provided.[64]

While O'Brien was always at pains to acknowledge the assistance and support she received from Irish MPs, there is no doubt that the success of her campaign was due, in large part, to the fact that she herself became a thorn in the side of all the large shipping companies. Not only did she relentlessly expose their shortcomings in the press and visit the ships on a regular basis, but she also became the emigrant's voice, making sure that their eye-witness accounts of the voyage were published.

It was a great disappointment to her, though, that the Catholic church chose to ignore her work. In many respects, that sense of hurt was compounded by the fact that the Irish clergy supported Vere Foster and to a lesser extent, James Hack Tuke, both proponents of assisted emigration schemes. In 1882, Hack Tuke helped 9,500 people to leave Ireland in family emigration schemes, while Vere Foster used his personal fortune to send over 22,000 women to America between 1880 and 1889. Although O'Brien regarded Vere Foster as an 'excellent man', she thought his scheme was a very dangerous experiment, since it lacked the support network which single women, 'innocent as babes', needed. She remarked at the time:

> The girls go their own way. No enquiry is made as to what becomes of them. They simply receive, on application, a bribe of two or three pounds to leave Ireland. In my opinion,

it is one of the grossest cases of misdirected charity the world has ever seen. What does it matter that it is supported by good men?[65]

In the autumn of 1882, because O'Brien realised that a vacuum still existed for many female emigrants once they arrived in Castle Garden, New York, she decided to go to America herself to see if anything could be done to improve matters. What she experienced there reaffirmed her views on the emigrant question and prompted her to speak out strongly in condemnation of government schemes which encouraged Irish men and women to leave the land. She remarked that 'one class only may benefit by clearing the land, that is the landlords ... the labourers are a sore in the landlord's side, a living shame and blot on his property.'[66]

Before she left Queenstown, she was forced to close down her refuge for emigrants, since she could not afford to employ a matron to run it in her absence.[67] Its closure was a severe blow to many women,[68] yet no effort was made by the Catholic clergy in Ireland either to step into the breach and supervise staffing arrangements on a temporary basis, or to establish an alternative shelter under their own control. In many respects, this sort of indifference was a reflection of the subordinate position of women in Irish society, and betrayed both a gender and a class bias.

On her arrival in New York, where she was brought free of charge by the White Star Line, O'Brien, characteristically, refused to stay in a hotel and opted instead to board with an Irish labouring family in a tenement building. She was appalled by the living conditions of the poor and especially by the extremely high infant mortality rate in Irish communities. After a fact-finding mission to Castle Garden, the immigration depot for the port of New York which was later replaced by Ellis Island, she concluded that the immigrants' problems were due, in large part, to inadequate services at the port. Even though Castle Garden housed an official labour bureau, most immigrants were unaware of its existence while, ironically, outside Castle Garden, bogus employment agencies were doing a roaring trade, though mostly as 'feeders' for vice rings. One of the main problems with Castle Garden was that official notices were often incomprehensible to illiterate and semi-literate women and men, and, indeed, to immigrants whose only language, in some cases, was Irish. No accommodation was provided at the port either, other than a large, dirty waiting room where prices for food and drink, railway tickets and baggage handling were all exorbitant. All of these factors combined to hasten the emigrant's departure from Castle Garden and into the arms of unscrupulous lodging-house keepers who were waiting to 'claim' them. O'Brien felt that, in addition to an immigrants' home, an efficiently run employment agency was necessary, as were female officials and inspectors.[69]

Her campaign in America was directed at the American government, Irish societies and the Catholic church. Happily, unlike her experience with the Irish Church, a meeting with Bishop Ireland in St Paul, Minnesota, was to prove very worthwhile. In fact, he became a useful ally who, time and again, assured her of his good wishes and continued support.[70] After their meeting, he made many representations on her behalf to Cardinal McCloskey, who eventually sanctioned the appointment of Father John Joseph Riordan as chaplain to Castle Garden. This was a major breakthrough in that, for the first time since her campaign began, the Catholic church acknowledged that it had a moral obligation to the Irish immigrant. On 1 January 1884, Fr Riordan established the mission of Our Lady of the Rosary, first at 7 Broadway and later at 7 State Street, New York. Between 1884 and 1890 this mission harboured 25,000 young women.[71] Bishop Ireland remained in touch with O'Brien after she returned to Queenstown, and continued to work on her behalf.[72]

In fact, it was largely through his friendship with William J Onahan that the Irish Catholic Colonization Association of the United States agreed to assume initial responsibility for the entire financial burden of the work at Castle Garden.[73]

Although ably assisted by Bishop Ireland, O'Brien's success in having a mission established in New York was due in no small part to the support which she herself generated for her cause. While she was in America, she travelled a total of 4,000 miles and lectured extensively, even though she was completely deaf and had never before spoken in public. Not only did she utilise the extensive network of ex-Fenians which existed in all large American cities, she was also befriended by individual, more moderate politicians such as A M Sullivan who assured her, even before her departure from Queenstown, that he would organise her lodgings in New York, and considered it 'a pleasure and a privilege' to meet her on her arrival.[74] John Boyle O'Reilly, a prominent exiled Fenian, gave her support through his newspaper the *Boston Pilot.*

The only impediment to her work in America arose from a policy of assisted emigration, outlined in the Arrears of Rent (Ireland) Act of 1882. Under this scheme, the British government paid Irish families £5 each if they agreed to emigrate. Nationalists on both sides of the Atlantic were incensed at the idea. Unfortunately the controversy which ensued for a time deflected attention from humanitarian issues, issues that O'Brien had only just succeeded in bringing before the public. In addition, because of her own work with the emigrants, she too became embroiled in the debate and was even accused, at one stage, of being an agent of the British government. In response, she left the public in no doubt where her allegiance lay, calling the subsidised emigration of young children and old people 'social murders'. However, she was adamant that the assisted emigrants needed her intervention, arguing that, on her return to Queenstown in 1882, she had come into contact with many of them who were, as she said herself, 'clad apparently from the pawn shops, unable to speak English, and as unfit to struggle in America as savages'.[75] She argued that she could not stand idly by while these people suffered, or adopt a position similar to the one taken by John Boyle O'Reilly, who advocated leaving the emigrants to die on the wharves in order to highlight the inhumanity and folly of British policy in Ireland. From Boston, he had written to her that 'nothing will be done by Irish men here to relieve the English government of its difficulties in getting rid of the people'.[76]

When O'Brien returned to Queenstown, she re-opened her Emigrants' Home but, through lack of funds, it was forced to close again after only another year. Sadly, although she intended to do so, she never made a return trip to America and never saw the mission on State Street, whose foundation owed so much to her own determination and energy. From 1883 she suffered ill health and was never really well again, especially after a bad carriage accident. 'The day's work was all I could manage,' she later recalled.[77] Bishop Ireland kept in contact with her and tried his best to revitalise her flagging spirits. In January 1884 he wrote to her from St Paul and encouraged her to 'keep a sharp eye on the Atlantic steamers and continue to expose abuses and demand corrective remedies'.[78]

While O'Brien was heartened by news of the mission's thorough work in New York, as time passed she became more and more disillusioned with the situation in Ireland. She had never really expected that her home in Queenstown would be forced to close down and had always felt that either the Catholic church or the State would take over its day-to-day operations. With characteristic optimism, she had written to her niece Mary, in 1882: 'I expect that another year or two will see the house on a public basis and I out of it altogether.'[79] It must have been a severe blow to have these hopes dashed and to return to her home in Foynes knowing that both Church and State had failed to respond to her call.

When O'Brien returned to Ardanoir she was in poor spirits. In fact, throughout 1883 she suffered from bouts of severe depression. Her sudden mood swings were, apparently, also related to a love affair which developed during her emigration work, but which ended unhappily.[80] It appears that she was 'deeply shaken'[81] by the affair and took many months to recover from its effects. It was not any wonder, therefore, that after what she referred to as 'the long past year, the sad past year'[82] she focused more and more on developing inner reserves of strength, and kept herself occupied as much as possible with various projects. One of her minor endeavours included the cultivation and sale of daffodils. Her brothers, Lucius and Donough, shared her interest in gardening and in botany, and she became quite close to both of them, frequently visiting the clergyman Lucius in the rectory at Adare and the old Deanery in Limerick, and the architect Donough in his little house above the Lax Weir, near Parteen.

Donough's house was a special haven. Both he and Charlotte Grace were, in many respects, kindred spirits, and they worked together to contribute plant records from the locality to Robert Lloyd Praeger, the distinguished botanist. After her return to Ardanoir, she also enjoyed the company of Matilda Knowles, a prominent lichenologist. O'Brien's preoccupation with natural history was not, however, a sign of a falling-off in her interest in political affairs, and her anger at the ineptitude of the London government was frequently expressed in verse. Gladstone's professed ignorance of the economic crisis in Ireland during 1879-1880, for example, prompted an angry response from her.[83] A number of years were to pass before Gladstone won back her trust and respect with the introduction of the Government of Ireland Bill in 1886 which, she felt, was at last a sign of his commitment to Home Rule.

Her literary endeavours were not confined solely to the realms of poetry, although she achieved considerable success in this genre and her work, which had a huge popular appeal, was published by the *Irish Monthly* on a regular basis from 1887 onwards.[84] She also wrote a number of prose essays at this time, with topics ranging from a simple appreciation of nature's wonders to a philosophical reflection on the position of women and the restrictions imposed on them by nineteenth-century society. Sometimes her work contained a curious blend of both approaches, as in 'An essay on birds', where the relations between her domesticated wild birds are used allegorically to illustrate her growing conviction that marriage was not always the best option for women.[85] 'The feminine animal' explored a similar theme. It, too, was concerned with the negative aspects of Victorian ideology, which extolled marriage and leisure for women of the middle and upper classes. In this essay, O'Brien strongly condemned the idleness which, she believed, women themselves cultivated. 'How can they do it?' she asked,

> ... idling, amusing themselves, with their senses perfect and their youth and their education and strength, and all the work of the world crying to them. It is enough to make the blood flame to think of it, and to see what women are making of this society they create - for it is their creation, this artificial society.[86]

Her vision of the future was one in which women spurned self-indulgence and inactivity and desired, instead, work outside the home where men, in turn, could 'meet and respect women in professional life'.

However, she believed that real equality between the sexes was possible only when women became mothers, since motherhood represented 'the force, the strength and the life man holds in his own individuality'. By contrast, 'The pains of solitude', written in 1892, is quite a grim essay. It explores the combined effect of deafness and physical isolation, opening with a quotation from Georges Sand - a woman for whom O'Brien had the utmost respect, and who believed that human nature could be utterly destroyed when subjected to absolute solitude. O'Brien, from experience, knew this to be true, and described how, in her own case, deafness coupled with loneliness had the power to separate her from the rest of humanity and threaten her sanity. 'Place a mind which has the necessity of labour in its being in absolute and prolonged solitude,' she wrote, 'and it will grind itself to pieces for default of other grist.'[87]

Thankfully, none of her other work expresses quite the same degree of sheer despair, and from 1898 onwards, a note of optimism is present in her writing, even when the subject matter deals with her own infirmity. In 'Pastoral Memories', for example, imagination negates the effect of deafness by giving 'hearing to the brain even when the ear is useless'.[88]

O'Brien converted from the Church of Ireland to Catholicism sometime around 1890. In so doing, she was not alone among her contemporaries.[89] It appears that her change of religion was generally well tolerated by her immediate family, who were aware of her great need to identify fully with 'her people', a term which was always used to denote her relationship with the peasant class. By all accounts, she practised her new faith with great fervour and devotion, although she never sacrificed her individuality, and continued to support Parnell even after his fall from grace and his condemnation by the Catholic hierarchy.

In fact, Parnell's death seemed to mark O'Brien's withdrawal from political debate and the beginning of her involvement with Douglas Hyde and the work of the Gaelic League, established in 1893. She found it easy to identify with Hyde and his followers who were concerned, primarily, with preserving the Irish language and Irish culture and traditions and with fostering a national identity and a distinct Irish character. On many occasions she had advocated rescuing what she termed the 'fragments' of 'Irish instinctive culture',[90] which had survived into the 1890s, and by so doing to blend traditional values with contemporary British and European ones. Hers was a broad vision which eschewed the extremism of some of her contemporaries and their preoccupation with past glories. In 1899 she wrote: 'Are we to return to our harps and ignore the orchestral music of the world? ... I myself would have nothing to do with '98 centenaries, or '48 for the matter of that ... the risings themselves were hopeless.'[91]

It appealed greatly to her that, although its neutrality was threatened on many occasions during her lifetime, from the outset the Gaelic League was non-political and non-denominational. By 1889, Hyde was already acquainted with O'Brien. In his diary he recalled a meeting with 'Miss O'Brien' in the Gwynn home in Dublin in March of that year. By August 1891, the friendship had developed to the point where he was invited to stay at Ardanoir, an invitation he accepted, breaking the journey in Limerick where he spent one night at the George Hotel. He obviously valued Charlotte Grace's friendship and her company, since he made every effort to communicate with her using sign-language.[92]

For her part, O'Brien had great respect for Hyde and wrote to him frequently with progress reports on her efforts to learn Irish - not an easy task for someone who was completely deaf. This physical handicap, coupled with her general ill health, meant that her participation in the activities of the League was always somewhat limited. Indeed, as a heart condition worsened, it is doubtful that she would even have been able to attend meetings had it not been for the devotion and care of her friend and companion, Peggy Briscoe, who, like her, belonged to the Foynes Branch.

In the 1890s she rented a house, Woodville, in Clonskeagh, County Dublin, which became a popular meeting place for writers and artists, among them the painter Walter Osborne. Here, she held *soirées* to introduce her nieces and nephews to Dublin society. She certainly enjoyed life in the capital, so much so that she eventually built her own house in Foxrock, calling it, not surprisingly, Fáilte (Welcome). However, when her sister Lucy and her family moved away from Dublin shortly afterwards, Fáilte lost a good deal of its charm and was sold to one of its long-standing tenants. In spite of this, however, O'Brien's trips to Dublin continued on a regular basis and when her nephew, Dermod O'Brien, then a struggling artist, set up home at 42 Mountjoy Square in 1901, she was such a frequent visitor that he conceded to her request to become a paying guest.[93] O'Brien wrote comparatively little during this period. Aside from contributions to *Irish Gardening* her writing was confined mostly to correspondence of a private nature.

In July 1905, although her health was poor, she shared the same platform with the nationalist priest, Father Casey, at an open air rally before 5,000 people in Abbeyfeale, County

Limerick. Her speech, expressing confidence in Ireland's future and advocating support for indigenous industries, was cheered to the echo by the crowd. On that occasion, as on many more, she was accompanied by Peggy Briscoe. It appears that O'Brien was especially pleased with her performance that day and with the reception she received from 'her own people'. Briscoe later recalled that on her return to her hotel room in Abbeyfeale, O'Brien proudly remarked, 'Well, Peggy, don't you think the old woman has done enough for today?'[94] These words were to prove strangely prophetic, since the *aeridheacht* in Abbeyfeale was her last appearance in public.

O'Brien died, apparently of heart failure, on 3 June 1909. Although she had been in poor health for quite some time, her death, when it came, was sudden and traumatic. Her sister-in-law Alice Spring Rice was one of the first to alert Dermod O'Brien to the fact that his aunt's condition had deteriorated, and to tell him of her stubborn refusal to see a doctor. She was, in fact extremely worried that O'Brien was taking thyroid tablets 'on her own initiative'. By contrast her niece Nellie, who was also unwell at this time, was not unduly concerned about O'Brien, as she felt it was just another 'bad turn' from which her aunt would recover. However, those members of the O'Brien family living close at hand were dismayed that she was ill. It was obvious that Peggy Briscoe was under great strain also, and was distraught at O'Brien's growing dependence on the 'thyroid' tablets. It appears that caring for O'Brien during these last days had developed into a battle of wits, with the entire family conspiring to keep medication out of her reach. Briefly she rallied, yet, within a short time, her condition had become quite serious again. On Saturday, 3 June, a telegram arrived at Cahirmoyle which requested Dermod to come to Ardanoir with a doctor. He did so, but within an hour of being examined by Dr Fogarty, and while Dermod was in Foynes sending news of her condition to her family, O'Brien died in Peggy's arms.[95]

The funeral took place on the Sunday. Father Richard O'Kennedy, an old friend, officiated at the Mass in the crowded local church and afterwards at Knockpatrick cemetery, her final resting place, situated just a short distance from Foynes and once a renowned place of pilgrimage. As far back as 1890 she had specifically asked to be buried within its windswept confines, since its desolation and dramatic character greatly appealed to her.[96]

While her death was felt keenly by many people, her immediate family was shocked by the news. Nellie, the main beneficiary of her will, was utterly devastated and was not fit enough even to travel to County Limerick for the funeral. Official expressions of sympathy, from the offices of the Gaelic League in Foynes and from the Foynes Workingmen's Club, were received.[97]

Irish Gardening carried both an editorial and a special tribute from Professor W F P Stockley, who recalled seeing:

> Miss O'Brien herself a horrible emigrant figure, lugging a huge hideous carpet bag into a Dublin tram, spurning alarmed attentions. She was just off for the Cove of Cork in the days when she would prove in her own person whether more tickets were given to the emigrants than there were places in ships. [98]

Interestingly, this reference of Stockley's is the only one which depicts her operating 'incognito', as it were, in order to gather evidence against the shipping lines. The *Irish Book Lover* also carried news of her death in its September issue where it too praised her philanthropic work as well as her literary ability. In May 1910, the *Irish Monthly*, in an article written by M C Keogh, paid a special tribute to O'Brien, when it acknowledged the rich complexity of her personality and her many varied interests. Of the woman behind the public image, the woman who loved her home and her garden, her 'children' and her writing and life in the open air, Keogh had this to say:

> [She was] good to the heart's core; pious, loyal, unselfish and sincere. A foe to conventionality, careless in dress, awkward in movement, unmethodical, eccentric - and thoroughly loveable [sic].[99]

Charlotte Grace O'Brien touched the lives of countless emigrant women, all of them for the better. There is no doubt that the time she spent in Queenstown will be most readily recalled whenever her name is remembered in the future.

Yet the influence she wielded within her immediate family was also considerable. Nellie O'Brien, for example, owed much to the upbringing she received from her aunt who inculcated in her, during her early years, a great love of Ireland and of the Irish people. Eventually, this found an outlet in Nellie's membership of the Gaelic League and, later on, in militant nationalism. Today, she is, perhaps, best remembered as the founder of the Irish College at Carrigaholt.

Stephen Gwynn also acknowledged the part played by his aunt in moulding his character and his political convictions. On one occasion, he even expressed doubt that his mother, Lucy, 'ever formed a political opinion', and credited his aunt instead with exerting a strong influence in this regard.[100]

Like all who mourned her passing, Keogh felt the world would be 'all the poorer'[101] in her absence. This is true, and yet the fact that she lies today more or less forgotten is a tragedy. Part of the inscription on her grave at Knockpatrick reads, *Is é an tiarna mo sholas agus mo shlínadh.*[102] There is a sad irony in the fact that this simple epitaph is written in the vernacular. For O'Brien, the language which she tried so hard to master represented the very essence of Irish culture and induced in her a sense of belonging and of a common heritage. Together with her conversion to Catholicism, her use of Irish reflected a lifelong preoccupation with recovering her Gaelic identity in order to satisfy some deep-rooted psychical need. In many respects, this was her greatest tribute to Ireland and to its people.

NOTES

1 See Luddy, Maria. 1995. *Woman and Philanthropy in Nineteenth-Century Ireland*. Cambridge.

2 These women did not belong exclusively to the Ascendancy class. While Alexander M. Sullivan provides an account of the literary contribution of three society women, 'Eva', 'Mary', and 'Speranza', to Irish national poetry during the Young Ireland era, he also recounts how, when high-ranking Fenian, James Stephens, was on the run, he was, 'for a long period .... secreted in the house of a Mrs Butler of Summer Hill, a woman of humble means'. See Sullivan, A M 1978. *New Ireland*. London, pp74-8, 269-70.

3 Gwynn, Stephen. 1909. *Charlotte Grace O'Brien: Selections from her writings and correspondence with a memoir*. Dublin, p.54.

4 In the established tradition of the ladies of the leisured upper classes, she spent much of her time tending the victims of famine-induced fevers. Because her husband spent long periods in London on parliamentary business, Lady O'Brien became an adept manager of their vast estate and acquired skills which were to stand her in good stead when she opened the first of her schools, for one hundred children, in Newmarket-on-Fergus in 1819.

5 Davis, Richard. 1989. *William Smith O'Brien*. Dublin, p.5.

6 *Ibid.*, p.8.

7 *Ibid.*, p.23.

8 O'Brien, Ivor. 1986. *O'Brien of Thomond: The O'Briens in Irish History 1500-1865*. Sussex, p.161.

9 Gwynn Stephen. 1926. *Experiences of a Literary Man*. London, p.14.

10 Fitzpatrick, David. 1988. 'Thomas Spring Rice and the peopling of Australia'. In *The Old Limerick Journal* 23, (Spring), p.42.

11 In many respects, O'Brien's voyages as a steerage passenger from Queenstown to Liverpool, and her tactical campaign, which relied heavily on press coverage and publicity in the House of Commons, re-echoed the exploits of her kinsman, Stephen De Vere. His report to the House of Commons in 1847, on the steerage accommodation provided for emigrant women, caused a sensation in political circles. As a result of his efforts, a Passenger Act was eventually passed in 1859 which introduced some improvements to the steerage section of ocean-going liners. See Hamilton, Frank. 1977. *The Changing Face of Limerick*. Limerick, p.19.

12 O'Brien, Charlotte Grace. 1888. *Cahirmoyle or The Old Home*. Limerick.

13 Gwynn, *Charlotte Grace O'Brien*, p.32.

14 It appears that, prior to the uprising, on his mother's insistence, Smith O'Brien conveyed Cahirmoyle and all his estates to trustees, to be held for his wife, Lucy, during her life and on her death for Edward his eldest son. This deed saved Cahirmoyle from confiscation and ensured that Lucy was financially secure after Smith O'Brien was deported to Tasmania as a felon. For further information see Cussen, Robert. 1964. 'Smith O'Brien and

Cahirmoyle'. In *The Monthly Observer* 1, 5 (July/August), pp1-2.

15 Gwynn, *Charlotte Grace O'Brien*, p.29.

16 *Ibid.*, p.10.

17 When Lucy died, legal proceedings were instigated on behalf of Smith O'Brien in an attempt to have him re-instated as rightful owner of Cahirmoyle. Eventually, the matter was settled out of court when Edward agreed to pay his father an allowance of £2,000 per annum for life. However, for his remaining years, Smith O'Brien refused to live at Cahirmoyle. See Cussen, 'Smith O'Brien', pp1-2.

18 Gwynn, *Charlotte Grace O'Brien*, p.32.

19 O'Brien, Charlotte Grace. 1886. *Lyrics*. London, p.2.

20 *Ibid.*, p.3.

21 Gwynn, *Charlotte Grace O'Brien*, p.37.

22 *Ibid.*, p.61.

23 O'Brien, Charlotte Grace. 1880. *A Tale of Venice: A Drama and Lyrics*. Dublin, p.123.

24 The opinions of both the Irish and English press were highly complimentary and encouraging.

25 Gwynn, *Charlotte Grace O'Brien*, pp42-3.

26 *Ibid.*, p.219.

27 *Ibid.*, p.223.

28 *Ibid.*, p.37.

29 *Ibid.*, p.228.

30 *Ibid.*, p.231.

31 For some examples of her early work see O'Brien, *A Tale of Venice*.

32 O'Brien, Charlotte Grace. 1880. 'The Irish poor man'. In *The Nineteenth Century* 8, 46, pp876-87.

33 Keogh, M C 1910. 'Charlotte Grace O'Brien'. In *The Irish Monthly* 38, p.242.

34 O'Brien, 'Irish poor man', pp876-87

35 *Ibid*

36 Gwynn, *Charlotte Grace O'Brien*, p.50.

37 *The Munster News and Limerick and Clare Advocate*, 26 January 1881.

38 Gwynn, *Charlotte Grace O'Brien*, p.50.

39 Gwynn, *Experiences*, p.14.

40 *Ibid.*, p.32.

41 O'Brien, Charlotte Grace. 1881. 'Eighty years'. In *The Nineteenth Century* 9, 49, p.413.

42 See article on Anna Parnell in this volume for information on the Ladies' Land League.

43 See Nolan, Janet. 1989. *Ourselves Alone: Women's Emigration from Ireland, 1885-1920*. Lexington. Diner Hasia, 1983. *Erin's Daughters in America: Irish Immigrant Women in the Nineteenth Century*, London; Fitzpatrick, David. 1984. *Irish Emigration, 1801-1921*, Dublin.

44 *The Munster News*, 15 January 1881.

45 *The Pall Mall Gazette*, 6 May 1881.

46 Joyce, Mannix. 1974 'Charlotte Grace O'Brien'. In *The Capuchin*

Annual. p.334.

47 At one point in the letter O'Brien wrote, 'Do not look on these abodes of misery now in the daylight and open for inspection - they are empty, swept and garnished; think that in the darkness of the night, the ship pitching in mid-ocean, a glimmering light or two makes visible to you this brutal and impure dream; this is the truth, the living horror ... '

48 *Freeman's Journal*, 31 May 1881.

49 O'Brien letters, University College, Cork.

50 *Reports with regard to the Accommodation and Treatment of Emigrants on board Atlantic steam ships*, HC 1881 [c-2995], lxxxii.

51 O'Brien letters, University College, Cork.

52 *Freeman's Journal*, 3 June 1881.

53 *Freeman's Journal*, 7, 9, 15 June 1881.

54 *Freeman's Journal*, 21 June 1881.

55 *Freeman's Journal*, 18 June 1881.

56 *Reports on the state of the Lodging-houses in Queenstown*, HC 1882 (237), 1xiv

57 O'Brien letters, University College, Cork.

58 *Reports on the state of the Lodging-houses in Queenstown.*

59 Cited in 'Cobh, The Queenstown Story', Permanent Exhibition, Cobh Heritage Centre, Cobh, County Cork.

60 O'Kennedy, Richard. 1910. 'With the emigrant'. In the *Irish Monthly* 38, 450, p.661.

61 Murphy, J T 1932. 'The coffee stall at Cobh: a symbol of progress'. Unpublished typescript.

62 O'Kennedy, 'With the emigrant', p.663.

63 Gwynn, *Charlotte Grace O'Brien*, pp64-5.

64 Ironically, it was the White Star Line, owners of the *Germanic*, which was most highly praised by O'Brien for the quality of its revised steerage accommodation. See Gwynn, *Charlotte Grace O'Brien*, pp65-9.

65 O'Brien, Charlotte Grace. 1884 'The emigrant in New York'. In *The Nineteenth Century* 16, 92 (October), pp546-7.

66 O'Brien, Charlotte Grace. 1881. 'The emigration and wasteland clauses'. In *The Fortnightly Review* , pp763-4.

67 Her only income was derived from rents on Ardanoir and possibly from tenants on part of the Cahirmoyle estate, which may have comprised her inheritance.

68 In 'The emigrant in New York', O'Brien noted that, in a single year in Queenstown, she probably looked after as many as 3,000 female emigrants.

69 For further information see O'Brien, 'The emigrant in New York'.

70 O'Brien letters, University College, Cork.

71 Nolan, John. 1891. 'Mission of Our Lady of the Rosary'. In *Irish Ecclesiastical Record* (September), pp776-85.

72 O'Brien letters, University College, Cork.

73 Henthorne, Mary E 1932. *The Irish Catholic Colonization Association of the United States*. Illinois. pp93-4

74 O'Brien letters, University College, Cork. O'Brien, while

accepting this offer, wished her arrival in New York to be as 'low-key' as possible.

75 O'Brien, 'The emigrant in New York', pp532-4.

76 O'Brien letters, University College, Cork.

77 Robinson, Lennox. 1948. *Palette and Plough*. Dublin, p.21.

78 O'Brien letters, University College, Cork.

79 Gwynn, *Charlotte Grace O'Brien*, p.88.

80 Unfortunately, little is known about the relationship, due mainly to the fact that family members and friends were determined to conceal the name of the person with whom she became involved. Where it does appear in her correspondence, it has been carefully erased. However, it seems that O'Brien never regretted falling in love no matter how painful the experience might have been. See Gwynn, *Charlotte Grace O'Brien*, p.36.

81 *Ibid.*, p.93.

82 O'Brien, *Lyrics*, p.43.

83 *Ibid.*, p.17.

84 *Lyrics*, published in 1886, contained many poems with political themes.

85 Gwynn, *Charlotte Grace O'Brien*, p.177.

86 *Ibid.*, pp183-7.

87 *Ibid.*, pp188-91.

88 *Ibid.*, pp197-9.

89 Aubrey de Vere of Curraghchase, whose only sister, Elinor, married Robert O'Brien of Dromoland, had become a Catholic as far back as 1851. Later, Dora Knox, a cousin of the O'Briens, also converted to Catholicism as did Stephen Gwynn's wife, May.

90 O'Brien, Charlotte Grace. 1899. 'Is the Irish nation dying?' In *The New Ireland Review* 11, 2 (April), p.66.

91 *Ibid.*

92 Daly, Dominic. 1974. *The Young Douglas Hyde*. Dublin, pp98-146.

93 Robinson, *Palette and Plough*, p.82.

94 Gwynn, *Charlotte Grace O'Brien*, p.125.

95 Dermod O'Brien papers, MS 4293, Trinity College, Dublin.

96 At the time she remarked: 'My! how weird it looked. The grandest place in this world to my individuality.' See Gwynn, *Charlotte Grace O'Brien*, p.129.

97 Dermod O'Brien papers MS 4293, Trinity College, Dublin.

98 *Irish Gardening*, July 1909

99 Keogh, 'Charlotte Grace O'Brien', p.244.

100 Gwynn, *Experiences*, pp15-33.

101 Keogh, 'Charlotte Grace O'Brien', p.245.

102 The translation reads: 'The Lord is my light and my salvation'.

Anna Parnell

(1852-1911)

Jane Côté and Dana Hearne

The best part of independence, the foundation of every other kind [is] the independence of the mind. [1]

In this chapter we propose first to recount the significant features of Anna Parnell's family history and then to analyse

263

that history - her upbringing and education, and the social and political context of her world. We will examine her own political activism in the Land War years; the significance of her memoir *The Tale of a Great Sham*, and the impact of her legacy for the women, both nationalist and feminist, of the early twentieth century.

Anna Parnell was born on the family estate, Avondale, County Wicklow on 13 May 1852, the fifth daughter of an Anglo-Irish Protestant landowner, John Henry Parnell and his American wife Delia Tudor Stewart Parnell. One of eleven children, six daughters and five sons[2], she was six years younger than her brother Charles Stewart, and four years younger than her sister Fanny, her closest friend and ally. Her Anglo-Irish great-grandfather Sir John Parnell (1744-1801), a member of the Privy Council and Chancellor of the Exchequer in Grattan's Parliament, had been dismissed from office for his opposition to the Act of Union of 1800. Although his son (Anna's grandfather) William Parnell (1780-1821) accepted the *fait accompli* of the Union, he wrote several polemical novels and pamphlets in which he pleaded for Catholic emancipation. As Member of Parliament for Wicklow (1817-20) he supported humanitarian reform in Ireland and unsuccessfully proposed a bill to protect children employed in Irish cotton factories. William Parnell found his experience in Parliament deeply disillusioning because so often justice and morality were sacrificed to expediency.

Anna's father, John Henry Parnell, preferred to devote his time to his estate, his large family, and to hunting and cricket. After the early death of his parents he had been much influenced by his evangelical aunt, Theodosia, Lady Powerscourt, who later became a member of the Plymouth Brethren. Although John Parnell remained a member of the Church of Ireland, he retained throughout his lifetime much of the strict, rather puritanical character of an evangelical Christian. A conservative in social and political views, he raised his children with the bluest of Tory principles. In later life Anna, who associated the Church of Ireland with oppressive British rule,[3] came to believe that established religion contributed to perpetuating injustice, and abandoned formal worship.

On her American mother's side Anna Parnell was descended from the Tudors of Boston and the Stewarts of

Philadelphia, families which included men of letters, holders of high office in peace and war, visionary and successful business entrepreneurs, and confident, highly literate women. Her great-grandfather William Tudor Senior had been Judge Advocate-General of the Continental army under General Washington, and later served several terms in the Massachusetts legislature. Anna's grandfather, Commodore Charles Stewart, became a hero of the War of 1812 for his naval victory over two British men-of-war, and later campaigned unsuccessfully for the Democratic Party's presidential nomination. In 1815 her great-uncle William Tudor Junior founded the influential *North American Review* (in which Fanny Parnell, under the name of her brother Charles, published an article on 'The Irish land question' in 1880). Tributes to the wit, learning and independent ways of Anna's grandmother, Delia Tudor Stewart, whom she knew well as a child, and of her great-grandmother Delia Jarvis Tudor, are found in several memoirs of the period.[4]

The Tudors combined American patriotism with admiration for English customs, laws and literature. As members of the élite they favoured moderate social change, achieved by gradual and constitutional means.[5] Commodore Stewart and his son Charles (for whom Anna's brother Charles Stewart was named), were lifelong members of the Democratic Party, and thus were on the conservative side of American politics. There was nothing, therefore, in Anna Parnell's family history to infuse her with a revolutionary spirit. Her mixed heritage did, however, give her the outsider's capacity to view the received opinions of her caste - the Anglo-Irish gentry - with a sceptical eye.

The sudden death of John Parnell in 1859 at the young age of 48, when Anna was seven years old, profoundly disrupted the lives of the whole family. Avondale, inherited by the thirteen-year-old Charles, was heavily indebted and had to be let to tenants until Charles's majority. The family was obliged to move, first to Dalkey, then to Kingstown (now Dún Laoghaire) and finally to Dublin, where they maintained a home until 1870. This departure was the beginning of the peripatetic existence which marked Anna Parnell's adult life.

Under the tutelage of their easygoing American mother, Anna and her sisters Fanny and Theodosia enjoyed a liberty of movement which would have been unthinkable had their more conventional father lived. The self-reliant individualism of the adult Anna owed much to the intellectual and physical freedom she enjoyed as a girl. Like most girls of her class, the sisters were educated by a series of governesses of varying ability and knowledge. Fortunately, Anna and Fanny had a taste for reading and study which they were permitted to indulge freely, thereby acquiring a considerable knowledge of Irish, English, American and French history and literature, political science and philosophy.

Their interest in Irish nationalist politics was precocious. In 1864 the sixteen-year-old Fanny began to publish, in the Fenian newspaper the *Irish People*, a series of poems which praised the Irish patriots who were prepared to 'prove the mettle of your swords by noble deeds'.

Anna moved to Paris with her mother and sisters in the late 1860s, but returned soon afterwards to Dublin to begin studies at the Royal Dublin Academy of Art. In the spring of 1875 she settled in London to continue her studies at the Heatherley School of Art, the only institution which then allowed women to paint from the nude model. She was talented enough to have a number of paintings accepted for showing in one of the leading London galleries.[6] However, with the arrival in London in April 1875 of her brother Charles to take up his duties as the new Member of Parliament for Meath, she became more and more absorbed in events at Westminster.

During the session of 1877 a small group of advanced Home Rulers, headed by Charles Parnell, frustrated by their inability to get a fair hearing in Parliament for Bills important to Ireland, began to retaliate by systematically obstructing the passage of English and Scottish Bills. Anna followed the action from the Ladies' Gallery of the House of Commons and published a witty three-part article 'How they do in the House of Commons: notes from the ladies' cage' in the *Celtic Monthly* (May-July 1880). In this first attempt at political reporting she recounted the events of that tumultuous session of 1877. She demonstrated an analytical turn of mind, an appreciation of the intricacies of parliamentary rules and procedure, and an understanding of the nature of representative parliamentary government. She argued that although majority decision prevails, the minority must refuse to acquiesce in the defeat of its own just claims to fair legislation (as the so-called Home Rule Party had been doing) and continue its struggle to make its claims heard by the tyrannical majority, no matter how unpopular this might make it. Anna Parnell's political beliefs concerning the 'tyranny of the majority' are clearly rooted in the writings of Tocqueville, John Stuart Mill and, above all, in the abolitionist writings of the American Transcendentalists, Thoreau and Lowell.

At the conclusion of the parliamentary session of 1877, she travelled to the United States of America to join her mother and sisters Fanny and Theodosia, who were living at Ironsides, the estate near Bordentown, New Jersey which Delia Parnell had inherited from her father Commodore Stewart. Looking back some twenty-five years later, Anna noted one particularly important result of the Obstructionists' tactics; they had brought the young and unknown MP Charles Stewart Parnell to prominence as the leader of a party of Irishmen whose activities were permeated by a flavour of success. Thus the foundation of the Land League was facilitated in October 1879.[7]

The circumstances of Anna Parnell's upbringing permitted a liberty of movement, both physical and intellectual, rare for a girl of her class and time. Living at a time when it was assumed that all women's primary goal was marriage and motherhood, and when this was one of the few options open to them which held out the promise of financial security, Anna opted for the independent life and became the subject of her own story. From the moment her brother Charles entered parliament in 1875, her life became focused on the possibility of political change. Her interest in her brother's political progress was intense. It is her involvement in the politics of the Land War and the nature of that involvement that is Anna Parnell's major claim to fame. Because she left a memoir of her experience in the Land League movement which made her own political position clear, we are able to analyse the engagement itself and the consequences for a woman who dared to step out of her culturally assigned place in such a conspicuously public way.

The agricultural depression of the late 1870s had led to evictions and near famine conditions in Ireland, particularly in the west. In response to this crisis, a group of tenant farmers in Mayo banded together in an organised opposition to evictions. Within months this local organisation had evolved into the Irish National Land League which was founded in Dublin on 21 October 1879. Charles Stewart Parnell, the acknowledged leader of the advanced Home

Rule Party at Westminster[8], was elected president. Thus, for the first time, the two major preoccupations of the Irish people, Home Rule and land reform, were symbolically united in one man. Michael Davitt[9] was chosen as the new League's secretary but he was in fact its animating spirit and principal organiser.

The aim of the Land League, summed up in the slogan 'The land of Ireland for the people of Ireland' was to make the Irish tenant farmers the owners of the land they tilled by inducing a reluctant government in England to supply them with interest free loans, thus enabling them to buy their holdings from their mainly Anglo-Irish landlords. Although the Land League membership included members of all political stripes including Fenians dedicated to the physical overthrow of English rule in Ireland, the Land League leadership was committed to pursuing its aims by strictly peaceful and constitutional means. This involved mass meetings, marches and public demonstrations organised by the League in Ireland while the Irish parlimentary party at Westminster pushed for the legislative changes needed to bring about both land reform and Home Rule.

While the ultimate aim of the Land League was to convert the Irish tenant farmers into the owners of their holdings, the aim in that autumn of 1879 was to gain immediate rent reductions. After three years of bad harvests and falling prices for agricultural produce, many tenant farmers, deeply in debt to the shopkeepers and to the banks, were unable to pay their rent and faced eviction. Consequently, the Land League's new president sailed to the United States of America and Canada to raise funds and support for the League among the millions of Irish migrants now settled in North America. The substantial amounts of money needed to carry on the land agitation could come only from 'the Irish nation beyond the seas'.

By the time Parnell arrived in New York in early January 1880, the knowledge that the poorest farmers of the south and southwest were facing starvation led him to immediately open the Irish Land League Famine Relief Fund. He then set off with John Dillon across the USA and Canada to raise the funds needed for famine relief and land agitation.[10]

Anna and Fanny, who had been following events in Ireland with intense interest, were in full agreement with their brother's policies. Like Charles, they were not, in principle, against insurrection, but were opposed to fighting England from 'the air'. They saw the Fenians' forays into 'battles' they had no hope of winning as counterproductive. Parliamentary action, allied to a concerted and determined opposition to unjust rents and evictions by the Irish farmers themselves, was an exciting new departure in which they were anxious to take part.

They left immediately for New York where they began to put in twelve-hour days in the offices of the Irish Land League Famine Relief Fund. Excellent administrators themselves, they were frequently frustrated by the failure of Land League headquarters in Dublin to acknowledge quickly and correctly the generous contributions of Irish-American individuals and societies. Their sharply-worded letters criticising Dublin's administrative shortcomings could not have endeared the outspoken sisters to the Land League executive.

On 11 March 1880, just before sailing home from New York to fight the general election of that year, Charles Parnell founded the Irish National Land League of the United States. Two months later - in May 1880 - Davitt arrived in New York to put the new organisation on a firm footing.

Fanny had returned to Bordentown while Anna remained in New York. Here she divided her time between the offices of the Land League Famine Relief Fund, which was winding up as the danger of famine receded, and the new headquarters of the United States Land League set up by Michael Davitt on Washington Square. Working closely with her at this time, Davitt came to appreciate Anna Parnell's practical administrative abilities, her dedication to the cause of land reform and Home Rule, and her understanding of the intricacies of parliamentary tactics and procedure, all of which she carefully spelled out to him in a letter in June 1880.[11]

By October 1880 Davitt had done all he could to put the American Land League on a firm footing, but the results were negligible and little money was being raised for the Land League in Ireland. Consequently, Fanny Parnell decided to found a women's league which, through energetic fundraising, would help the land agitation in Ireland and, in the process, inspire the American men's league to greater efforts. Within three weeks they had organised a public meeting, attended by over 3,000 people, which realised the large sum at the time of $1,000.

Fanny thought that Anna (who had returned to Ireland in the late summer of 1880) might found a similar organisation in Ireland, but Anna refused. She feared that Irish women would not come forward to participate.[12]

Davitt returned to Ireland in November 1880 aware that his continued activities as organiser and speaker on behalf of the Land League would cause the British authorities to return him to prison.[13] It was also evident that the government would soon suspend *habeas corpus* in Ireland to enable them to imprison without trial the leaders of the land agitation and bring the whole movement to a close before its most basic demands had been met. Recalling the success of Fanny Parnell's Ladies' Land League, Davitt decided to found a similar organisation in Ireland which would keep the land agitation alive during the men's anticipated imprisonment by distributing grants to evicted tenants and their families. At its head he envisaged Anna Parnell, with her administrative abilities and political acumen.

To his surprise the plan was opposed by Charles Stewart Parnell, John Dillon and Thomas Brennan, but since they had nothing better to suggest, they reluctantly concurred.

Anna accepted the challenge Davitt held out to her, perhaps believing that Irish women would be more likely to join an association sponsored by Michael Davitt, who had become, by then, as popular in Irish nationalist circles as her brother Charles. And although Davitt saw the proposed Ladies' Land League as a purely charitable and therefore suitably feminine organisation which would support evicted tenants, relieve cases of distress and keep up a semblance of organisation during the attempted repression which he saw was coming, Anna Parnell viewed it as distinctly political.[14] Accordingly, on 31 January 1881 the Ladies' Irish National Land League was formed at a public meeting held in Dublin. The titular president of the new organisation was Anna Deane, a successful businesswoman from the west of Ireland, but its effective leader from the beginning was Anna Parnell, one of four honorary secretaries. The executive of the Land League, now reluctantly reconciled to the presence of women in their organisation, sent a circular to all branch members to encourage their wives and daughters to join the Ladies' Land League.[15]

Three days later, on 3 February 1881, Davitt was returned to prison in England where he was deprived of all political news until his release in May, 1882. Thus he knew nothing about the activities of the organisation which had been founded at his urging, but which he nonetheless described twenty years later in distressingly inaccurate terms.

During the first few months of its existence, the Ladies' Land League took over much of the administration at Land League headquarters on Upper Sackville (now O'Connell) Street, Dublin, including processing applications for relief and distributing money to qualified tenants and their families. Aware of the need for careful accounting to avoid charges of mismanagement of money, Anna Parnell kept a record of all funds received and expended which she was able to present to Michael Davitt on his release from prison in May 1882.[16] Unfortunately, this did not prevent the myth of financial irresponsibility and extravagance on the part of the Ladies' Land League from taking hold.

As part of her Ladies' Land League activity Anna Parnell travelled extensively in Ireland and in those parts of England and Scotland where large Irish communities resided. Speaking at large open air meetings, she explained the aims of land agitation and encouraged the founding of Ladies' Land League branches. Before the end of the first year there were over 400 Ladies' Land League branches in Ireland, some consisting of only a few members, others of close to one hundred.

The leaders and executive of the Ladies' Land League came from the small Irish middle classes and included many young women such as Katherine Tynan[17], Jennie O'Toole (later Wyse Power)[18] and Hannah Lynch[19] who would later make their mark in Irish political and literary life. In country branches most of the members were farmers' wives and daughters and sometimes farmers in their own right, many of whom had been involved in land agitation from the very beginning. They were on average very young. On one occasion in late 1881, the fifteen year old Teresa Cantwell accompanied Jennie O'Toole, then eighteen, to a small country town where on their own they found housing for ten evicted farmers and their families.[20] After October 1881 when the government began to seize issues of the Land League newspaper *United Ireland* the young women had the plates printed in secret and smuggled out the newspapers in bundles under their voluminous skirts under the very eyes of the watching detectives. They then mailed them from their own home addresses for distribution throughout the country.[21]

271

In April 1881 *habeas corpus* was suspended in Ireland and large numbers of Land League members throughout the country were arrested 'on suspicion'. The Ladies' Land League immediately began supplying food to the prisoners and relief to their families, thus alleviating hardship and encouraging the tenant farmers to continue the agitation for rent reductions. As the agitation against the payment of 'unjust' rents continued unabated, the government arrested Charles Stewart Parnell in October 1881 and imprisoned him in Kilmainham Gaol where he was joined a few days later by most of the leaders of the Land League. In retaliation they issued a manifesto from prison exhorting the Irish farmers to pay no rent until the Land League leaders had been released.

The signatories of the Manifesto[22] did not really expect that those Irish tenant farmers able to pay their rent would refuse to do so and thus find themselves evicted from their homes and farms, without a roof over their heads or food on their tables. They also knew that the church hierarchy would not back such a move. Furthermore a new Land Act had come into force in August 1881 and, although far from meeting the demands of the Land League in making the farmers the owners of their holdings, it contained much to please them.[23] The No-Rent Manifesto was simply intended to mollify the more militant Irish-Americans who had been clamouring for such a strike for several months and were beginning to wonder why they should send money to Ireland while the landlords continued secure in their possessions.

The first consequence of the No-Rent Manifesto was the decision by the Chief Secretary, William Forster, to proclaim the Land League an illegal organisation. To his surprise the Land League obediently folded up and ceased to exist. And to the equal surprise of the leaders in Kilmainham, the Ladies' Land League, which had not been named in the proclamation and was now on its own, took the No-Rent Manifesto at face value and attempted to enforce it as best they could. They did this principally by the practical expedient of building over 200 pre-fabricated wooden huts. Anna Parnell reasoned that in a country very short of house room, it was illogical to expect tenant farmers to submit to eviction unless they could be assured of finding housing. She therefore ordered the huts from suppliers in Ireland and Scotland. They could then be quickly transported from Dublin with carpenters to erect them wherever a group of tenants was evicted for obeying the No-Rent Manifesto.[24]

Anna Parnell's decision to continue to build Land League huts in the spring of 1882 brought her on to a collision course with her brother. By this time Charles was determined to pursue his goal of Irish Home Rule through constitutional, parliamentary means alone. He was anxious, therefore, to save the remaining Land League funds in order to finance his parliamentary tactics once he and the Land League leaders were released from prison and life had returned to normal. Anna took the view that since many of the Irish-Americans who had contributed generously to the Land League agitation did so on the express understanding that their money would not be used for parliamentary purposes (which were anathema to American Fenians), she was justified in defying her brother and spending it for Land League purposes.[25]

Throughout the late winter of 1881 and early spring of 1882 there was a steady increase in the number of evictions, reaching a total of 14,600 in four years, more than in the thirty previous years.[26] Evictions in unprecedented numbers had always called secret societies into existence in Ireland. Now, with the imprisonment of close to 1,000 Land Leaguers, including some of the most responsible and influential men of the townlands, the way was open to young hotheads and physical force advocates. The peaceful weapon of boycotting or social ostracism was enforced by violent intimidation, night-time raids, burning of hay ricks, mutilation of animals and the like. Clearly the Ladies' Land League could do nothing to control these unruly elements in rural society. The number of young women who could travel about the country on Ladies' Land League business was small and they were constantly harassed by the police who attempted to prevent them from attending evictions or supervising the building of Land League huts. Indeed, thirteen members of the Ladies' Land League were imprisoned for terms ranging from a few days to a month; not, however, under the Coercion Act but under an ancient statute of Edward III originally designed to keep prostitutes off the streets.[27]

Gladstone, anxious to see an end to the continuing crisis in Ireland, struck an informal bargain with Charles Stewart Parnell, known as the Kilmainham Treaty, in April 1882. Parnell and the other Land League leaders were to be released from prison and Gladstone would push through an

Arrears Bill enabling the small impoverished farmers of the west and southwest to take advantage of the Land Act of 1881. Parnell undertook to cool down the agitation, not a difficult task once the Arrears Bill was passed, since this would end the cycle of evictions and resulting agrarian crime. Outraged by the release of Parnell and the other Land Leaguers, the Chief Secretary William Forster resigned.[28]

Soon after Parnell's release from prison the Ladies' Land League, disheartened by the failure of the No-Rent Manifesto and disillusioned by Parnell's acceptance of the Arrears Act as the final settlement of the land agitation, signalled their wish to disband. It took several months and some skilful manoeuvring before they extricated themselves from what had become a wearisome and unwelcome task. In the process, Anna Parnell became permanently estranged from her brother who, she believed, had behaved towards her and the Ladies' Land League in an unprincipled manner.[29]

The activities of the Ladies' Land League attracted considerable criticism and hostility from the outset. Conservative Catholic opinion in the voice of Archbishop McCabe[30] of Dublin viewed the Ladies' Land League as an attempt at 'degrading the women of Ireland' by men who had 'drawn the country into its present deplorable condition'.[31] Here McCabe revealed in one stroke his opposition to the Land League movement as well as his opposition to women stepping outside the confines of the home on what he saw as the 'pretext' of charity. Mary, the mother of God, was evoked as the model of chastity, holiness and silent care to which Irish women were called on to aspire. The Archbishop ended his pastoral letter with the warning: 'Do not tolerate in your sodalities the woman who so far disavows her birthright of modesty as to parade herself before the public gaze.'[32] For McCabe, women who assumed a visible and vocal public profile were on a par with prostitutes.[33] His language was so interpreted, and the Irish MP A M Sullivan[34] accused him of wronging the 'pure and devoted Catholic ladies ... who have given their humble aid to relieving the wives and children of evicted or imprisoned Irish peasants'.[35] Yet Sullivan and McCabe did not differ in their view of a woman's proper place in society - secluded in the home or, when out of the home, engaged in seemly and modest behaviour that would not draw down on them the lewd gaze of men, or contaminate them with the viciousness of the market-place or indeed, the political platform.[36]

But the women of the Ladies' Land League were not behaving in a ladylike way, and were decidedly political. We may note that this ideology of true womanhood and true femininity could not be applied to the vast majority of Irish women who worked alongside men digging potatoes, stacking turf, going to market, working as shop assistants, or in factories.[37] Nor did it apply to many of the middle-class women who actually joined the Ladies' Land League.[38]

Archbishop Croke[39] of Cashel also came to the defence of the Ladies. He supported Sullivan's vindication of the character of the 'ladies' of the Ladies' Land League and challenged the 'monstrous imputations' which McCabe cast on their activities.[40] He then departed from the prevailing ideological position regarding women's place in society and revealed that his criticism of McCabe was rooted in his nationalism, as he attacked McCabe for 'the peculiar political theories which he is known to hold in opposition to the cherished convictions of the ... overwhelming majority of the Irish priests and people'.[41] The Ladies' Land League were, for Croke, devoted nationalists fighting for land reform and the end of landlordism and British rule. Their political position justified their activities. Archbishop McCabe, in Croke's view, was not entitled to speak for the hierarchy on political matters, particularly since he looked at the land movement through 'spectacles provided by a Castle tradesman in Dublin'.[42] The ideology of femininity was employed by McCabe on behalf of a patriotism which envisaged separate spheres for women and men where women would continue 'to be the glory of their sex and the noble angels of stainless modesty', and repudiated by Croke on behalf of a patriotism which could envisage the equal participation of women and men in the political arena without fear of threat to that glory and modesty.[43] Clearly then, if threat was perceived, it was the threat of the breakdown of a patriarchal tradition of power and control, one which politician John Dillon at a later date warned would lead to the destruction of civilisation.[44]

This sense of threat was being voiced at a time when the question of women's enfranchisement, and other measures for a fuller life for women outside the domestic arena, had come on to the political agenda in Britain and Ireland. The position of the Catholic church on the issue of a woman's proper place was by no means a uniform one, and if the priest[45] or the bishop was a militant nationalist then women were encouraged to participate in the national struggle and applauded for doing so.

Throughout its eighteen months of existence, the Ladies' Land League was constantly on the front pages of the Irish, Irish-American, Irish-Canadian and English press. In its day it was seen as a movement of considerable significance and yet, like most of women's activities, it was submerged when the history of the period came to be written. Just as with the three-way exchange between McCabe, Sullivan and Croke, the media view of women's participation varied with the political position of the paper.

Anna Parnell's speeches were recorded verbatim in the provincial Irish press and reprinted in abbreviated form in national weeklies or dailies. To the more extreme opponents of the land agitation in England - for example the *London Standard* - the Ladies were 'pestilent disturber[s]' who should be 'lodged in Kilmainham'. The conservative pro-government Irish press - the *Irish Times* or the *Leinster Express* - gave substantial coverage to the important work the Ladies were performing for evicted tenants and imprisoned Land Leaguers. However, they demonstrated unease with both the land agitation and the presence of women in 'the noisy arena of public life' by ridiculing the Ladies themselves as 'patriots in petticoats' or even 'the screaming sisterhood'. In the pro-Land League press, the influential New York weekly, *Irish World*, the Land League's own organ, *United Ireland*, the Dublin *Nation* and *Freeman's Journal*, editorial comment was invariably laudatory and the Ladies themselves were modern 'Joans of Arc' courageously coming forward to take the place of the men in a national emergency.

The phrase 'national emergency' does of course imply that under normal circumstances they would not be expected to be in the public arena. Nowhere, even in the most hostile accounts, was there any suggestion that the Ladies' Land League had in any way encouraged or condoned violence.

The first lengthy, public 'post-mortem' on the Ladies' Land League appeared in an interview with Michael Davitt, published in the *New York World* of 9 and 16 July 1882. He declared that the Ladies' Land League had been thoroughly successful in fulfilling the two objects for which it had been formed: receiving and distributing 'all kinds of charity to support the evicted tenants and relieve all cases of distress, and keeping up a semblance of organisation during the period of repression'. Then, ignoring the existence of the Kilmainham Treaty which had precipitated Forster's resignation, he went on to add that the Ladies had saved the Land League and banished the Chief Secretary, William Forster, from Ireland. The British government, he asserted, had threatened to imprison the ladies of the League but the British people would not tolerate this and Forster had been forced to resign. Thus the Land League had won the fight and 'the finishing blow had been struck by the ladies of Ireland'.

This implausible conclusion may be seen as Davitt's attempt to disguise his own (amicable) break with Charles Stewart Parnell over the latter's decision to accept Gladstone's terms and end the land agitation at the very moment when, Davitt believed, it was close to achieving its goals. By attributing to the Ladies a spurious victory Davitt could omit all mention of the Kilmainham Treaty, the true cause of Forster's resignation and of Davitt's own rupture with Parnell and the Irish Party for over a decade.

Anna Parnell spurned this fictitious victory, for she was well aware that Forster had not been beaten - a fact that 'ought to have been quite plain to everybody'[46] - and that the land agitation had ended in failure. However, since there was nothing personally objectionable in Davitt's interview, she made no public comment on it.

During the remaining years of the decade Anna Parnell lived mainly in England with occasional visits to Ireland. She maintained contact with her friends from the Ladies' Land League days and for a period joined a group of painters in Marazion in Cornwall. In 1885 she travelled to London to speak at an open air meeting in support of Helen Taylor[47] who was campaigning to become the official candidate of the Radical Liberals in North Camberwell during the forthcoming parliamentary elections. Although Taylor, who was the first woman to attempt to stand for election to parliament, won her party's official nomination, the returning officer refused to accept the papers of a woman.

By the turn of the century Anna, now in her fifties, was nearly destitute. Successive financial crises of the previous decades had reduced her capital to a mere subsistence. Furthermore, her eldest brother John Howard Parnell had ceased to pay her the £100 annual income which had been left to her by her father. This income was tied to the estate inherited by John, who was prone to investing in losing speculative ventures.[48]

In 1904, over twenty years after the Ladies' Land League had been disbanded, Davitt published *The Fall of Feudalism in Ireland* which was instantly hailed as a classic of Irish political literature and the true story of the Land League agitation. In a chapter devoted to the Ladies' Land League he again attributed the defeat of Forster and the so-called success of the Land League to the action of the Ladies. This time, however, the success was no longer attributed to the chivalry of Englishmen whose unwillingness to see Irish ladies in prison had forced the Chief Secretary to resign. Now it was attributed to the action of the Ladies themselves who, Davitt claimed, had encouraged the Irish farmers to commit acts of violence and outrage, thus making Ireland ungovernable and forcing the British government to settle in favour of the Land League.

Anna Parnell was devastated by these 'vicious lies'.[49] Depressed and near suicidal at Davitt's betrayal, ill and almost destitute, she might well have died in the streets had not her old friends, Kate Molony and Jennie Wyse Power, come to her aid. They worked out a complicated scheme (designed to save Anna's pride and spirit of independence) whereby the Dublin publishers Sealey, Bryers & Walker would offer Anna £50 for some poems they 'understood' she wished to publish.[50] Unknown to Anna, the £50 paid to her as well as all the expenses of publication were supplied by John Dillon.

A few months later, her health and spirits recovered, Anna wrote to the publishers of *The Fall of Feudalism in Ireland* to protest Davitt's several 'wanton, malicious and impudent libels'[51] concerning her. Although reviews of his book in English newspapers - all carefully preserved in his papers - quoted extensively from his chapter on the Ladies' Land League in order to demonstrate his own and the Land League's 'tenderness to crime', Davitt professed not to understand why Anna was upset. After all, he claimed, he had only meant to be 'complimentary to her'.[52] Despairing at her failure to have Davitt rectify his gross distortion of the work of the Ladies' Land League, Anna Parnell wrote *The Tale of a Great Sham*, her own account of the Land League - the 'great sham' of the title.

Despite unflagging attempts she was never able to find a publisher for the 70,000-word manuscript. Thus Davitt's *Fall of Feudalism*, which portrayed 'Irish girls as being a pack of murderers, mutilators, hysterical idiots and fools', became the authority on which later authors relied to 'libel and ridicule' the Ladies.[53]

The first was F Hugh O'Donnell, whose *History of the Irish Parliamentary Party*, published in London in 1910, compares Anna Parnell to the Grande Mademoiselle and the Ladies' Land League to 'Captain Moonlight in Petticoats'. Others followed, invariably accepting Davitt's 1904 portrait of the Ladies' Land League (if it was mentioned at all) as a band of harridans sowing seeds of dissension and murder throughout the country.[54]

In 1908, when Anna was invited to campaign on behalf of the Sinn Féin candidate in North Leitrim, she accepted with alacrity. Although the Sinn Féin philosophy of self-reliance was certainly attractive to Anna, she was now too thoroughly disillusioned with all Irish politicians to believe in any of them. 'If he were a Unionist I should call on the electors to vote for him just the same,' she wrote.[55] What she did welcome was the chance to tell publicly her own story concerning the 'falsehoods, cowardice and imbecility' of the Land League leaders, thus enabling her 'to put a stop to the doings of that gang of scoundrels in and out of parliament who have been dominating Ireland since 1880'.[56]

Although she spoke at several meetings, all fully reported in the *Sligo Champion* and the *Leitrim Observer*, a pelting with eggs and tomatoes helped to convince her that 'the character of Irishmen is at present incompatible with any great change for the better in Ireland',[57] and from then on she concentrated her efforts on finding a publisher for *The Tale of a Great Sham*.

In 1910 Anna Parnell came into a small inheritance, probably from the settling of her mother's estate. This enabled her to live decently in the attractive resort town of Ilfracombe, North Devon, and to devote small sums to her efforts to find a publisher. She also obtained the help of the young Helena Molony[58] to whom Anna sent her manuscript in hopes that Molony would be more successful than she had been in seeing *The Tale of a Great Sham* into print.

On 20 September 1911, while enjoying her daily swim at the 'Tunnels' bath, Anna Parnell accidentally drowned. Her grave in the cemetery of the Church of England's Holy

Trinity in Ilfracombe overlooks the sea and is marked by a plain stone engraved with a simple inscription: 'In loving memory of Catherine Maria Anna Mercer Parnell, died September 20, 1911, aged 59. Oh death, where is thy sting?'

The Tale of a Great Sham fulfils two functions. It presents Anna Parnell's own political philosophy, and it writes herself and the Ladies' Land League back into history in a way that enables us to evaluate her on her own terms. The memoir is Parnell's own account of her experience and the experience of the Ladies' Land League during its existence from January 1881 to August 1882. She touches on questions of power, political perspective, nationalism and imperialism. It becomes clear that, although the women of the Ladies' Land League were invited by the male League to take part in the Land League movement at a critical juncture in its history, neither Michael Davitt who was pressing for this move, nor other leading members of the Land League executive who were hostile to it, had any idea that the women would do more than dispense relief funds and 'keep up a semblance of organisation'[59] in the event that the men were imprisoned.

Parnell's memoir shows that she had no thought other than to carry forward what she perceived to be the revolutionary aims of the male Land League. She did not align herself with the current ideology about womanly behaviour. That she was competent and knowledgeable about the issues of land and politics in Ireland was attested to by all who knew her. Irish people needed to be in control of their own destiny and, in Parnell's view, this could only be achieved through political independence. Her consciousness of the subordinate position of women is manifest in *The Tale* and in Côté's biography.[60] At the beginning she speaks about the importance of the franchise, particularly after the Secret Ballot Act of 1872 which freed electors from the control of their landlords.[61] Observing that government by consent would now have some real meaning, she added that she was speaking of the consent of 'the only portion of the people that counts, the adult males'.[62] She speaks bitterly, from personal experience, about the Irish custom among the landlord and upper classes 'of giving all, or nearly all, to the sons, and little or nothing to the daughters'.[63] When she speaks of the damage done to the women of the Ladies' Land League as a result of their connection with a political sham, she observes that 'the character of Irish men is at present incompatible with any great change for the better in Ireland'.

She continues:

> I say 'Irishmen' because, whatever the relative values
> of men and women may be, it is certain that the
> former cannot be done without, when it is a question
> of altering the status of a country. If the men of that
> country have made up their minds it shall not be
> done, then the women cannot bring it about.[64]

When she tried later, as we saw, to express publicly her
sense of betrayal at the hands of the men, she was pelted
with rotten fruit for her pains. She even exhorted men to stay
away so that the women would be free to conduct their own
organisation without interference and not be discouraged
from coming to meetings and joining the League. To the
women of Rathdowney she said: 'You cannot alter your
stature, the scripture says, but you can mould your course of
life any way you please.'[65] She urged women to fight against
the injustice of British rule and not to expect to be praised for
so doing.

'Perhaps,' she said to a public meeting in March 1881,
'when we are dead and gone and another generation grown
up ... they will point to us as having set a noble example to
all the women of Ireland.'[6]

The Tale is an important historical document and in the
words of the Irish historian, Roy Foster, it is indispensable to
the study of the Parnell years. Let us focus briefly then on
the three major themes that Anna Parnell treats in her *Tale*:
her political analysis of Land League politics; her concept of
nationalism; her portrayal of her own experience and that of
the Ladies' Land League working alongside men in the
struggle for Irish independence. *The Tale* constantly speaks of
the 'failure' of the Land League. Parnell's reasons for so
describing the Land League are twofold. One is related to the
strategy adopted by the League known as 'Rent at the Point
of a Bayonet', and the other is related to what she sees as the
worthlessness of Gladstone's land legislation.

The strategy known as 'Rent at the point of a Bayonet'
with its defiant, martial wording implies an unflinching
determination to face eviction at the point of the landlord's
bayonet rather than to pay an unjust rent. Certainly Anna

Parnell understood it to be just this when she agreed to head the Ladies' Land League. In fact what the policy amounted to was a noisy and prolonged refusal by tenants to pay what they considered to be an excessive rent until all legal delays were exhausted and they were on the point of being evicted. They then, at the urging of the Land League leadership, paid the rent while the Land League assumed responsibility for the legal costs incurred by the delay. Once the landlords realised that rents would be paid 'at the end' they had no incentive to lower the rent; they need only wait until the noisy agitation came to an end and the tenants paid off their full rents. To Anna Parnell the policy was not consistent with sanity and it was 'impossible to tell what induced the Land League to adopt such a plan'.[67]

When, therefore, the Land League leaders issued their No-Rent Manifesto from prison in October 1881, the Irish tenant farmers simply continued as before. That is they declared their support for the Manifesto but continued to pay their rent when on the point of eviction. As Anna ironically observed, 'It was just as easy to say they would pay no rent as to say they would pay only so much, when in both cases they meant to pay the whole'.[68] Thus the best efforts of the Ladies' Land League to enforce the Manifesto were defeated. But what if, Parnell speculated in her memoir, the Land League had from the beginning induced the farmers to put up a real opposition to the payment of unjust rents, thus allowing them to perceive the possibility of success before them. The chances of a general strike against rent such as that urged by the No-Rent Manifesto might have had a real chance of success and the Land League might not have ended in failure. Thus, for Anna Parnell, it was the 'Rent at the point of a bayonet' policy that for her constituted the failure of the Land League - the 'Great Sham' of the title.

The outcome of the Land League movement was the Land Act of 1881, in Anna Parnell's view 'the ridiculous mouse resulting from the upheaval of the whole island',[69] and the Kilmainham Treaty by which Charles Parnell ended the land agitation after securing an immediate settlement of the arrears question for some 130,000 small and poor tenants.[70] In return Charles Parnell and his colleagues could withdraw the No-Rent Manifesto, end outrage and intimidation and co-operate with the Liberal Party so the government could refrain from further coercive measures.[71]

In Ireland, the Kilmainham Treaty was generally seen as
a victory for Charles Parnell; in England, opponents of the
government saw it as a surrender to him; while Davitt and
the revolutionary wing of the Land League saw it as a
surrender to the government. Davitt's views in *The Fall of
Feudalism in Ireland* and Anna Parnell's in *The Tale of a Great
Sham* are closely akin. Both saw the Kilmainham accord as a
surrender of the League's basic demand, i.e. peasant
proprietorship, and as a premature disbandment of the
League's fighting forces.

Even Gladstone was amazed at how little was being
asked of him and how much was being offered in return. In
a private letter he wrote that the promise seemed 'if any
thing wider than we wanted and the sole condition was the
settlement of the arrears'.[72]

The major argument of Parnell's *Tale* is that the initial
promise of the Land League was not fulfilled, that whatever
apparent successes it did achieve were fictitious, and that
this need not have been the case. The final defeat lay in
abandoning the claim to independence as a right, and
instead forming an alliance with a 'wretched, hypocritical,
bloodthirsty miscreant ...' as she described Gladstone.[73]

The other dimension of *The Tale* needing discussion is the
apparent inability of the men on the Land League executive
to work on an equal footing with nationalist women. From
the first, Parnell tells us, there was marked hostility
displayed by the Land League executive towards the Ladies.
This was coupled with an absence of any indication as to
how the women were expected to proceed. The latter charted
their own course only to find that this was not acceptable
either. The relationship between the two Leagues became so
difficult that Anna Parnell suggested the dissolution of the
Ladies' Land League. This suggestion angered the men who
seemingly were determined to have their cake and eat it too;
they felt free to express their resentment at the presence of
women in their midst while relying on the highly competent
work they were performing in attending evictions, providing
relief to imprisoned Land Leaguers and their families, and so
on.

When Parnell emerged from Kilmainham in April 1882,
the Ladies, disillusioned by the failure of the No-Rent
Manifesto and Parnell's decision to end the land agitation,
signalled their wish to disband. Faced with the continued
resistance of the men the Ladies agreed to continue

processing applications for relief for a short time longer. In July the executive of the Ladies' Land League learned that the money they were paying out for Land League purposes was not being covered by drafts from the Land League's treasury in Paris[74] and their bank overdraft had reached £5,000. They then learned of the thoroughly underhand trap that had been laid for them. The Land League informed the Ladies that their overdraft would be honoured if they in turn gave a signed agreement to disband their organisation but continue to 'consider all applications for grants made to the Land League, and make recommendations on them for that body'.[75] In other words, the Ladies were to become subservient clerical assistants. Anna Parnell later recalled:

> Our long connection with them seemed to have brought very little understanding to them of our character if they supposed their action would have any effect on us beyond strengthening our determination not to have any more to do with them.[76]

The impasse caused by this reprehensible act was ended when the Ladies discovered that by altering one word in the agreement they rendered themselves responsible only for making recommendations on the cases of applications towards whom their own League had incurred responsibility. They immediately disbanded as an organisation although a few members stayed on in Land League offices for a few months to wind up their outstanding affairs.

Although the events surrounding the demise of the Ladies' Land League are clearly revealed in chapter XI of Parnell's *The Tale*, the myth that Charles Parnell 'snuffed out'[77] the Ladies' Land League because of its extravagance and extremism[78] continues and will continue as long as attempts to set the record straight go so quickly out of print and are not deemed worthy of reprinting.[79]

It was some time after the formation of the Ladies' Land League before the women came to realise how profoundly the two Leagues differed in their aims. When the outcome of the struggle materialised in the Kilmainham Treaty, it need not surprise us that Anna Parnell saw this as a defeat of the League's highest hopes, nor that it was unthinkable for her to continue her involvement with the Land League when its revolutionary vigour was finally extinguished.

In the conclusion of her memoir, Anna Parnell fluctuates between tentative optimism and outright pessimism, and finally takes the view that all hope of effective resistance to British domination would have to wait until the last residues of the parliamentary tradition were extinguished. The Irish character had been weakened, she thought, by centuries of dependence, and the Home Rule mentality - by now apparently fully internalised - had exacerbated that spirit of dependence. Aligning themselves with Gladstone at the expense of their erstwhile saviour Charles Parnell was the final blow inflicted by the Irish people on the Republican ideal of independence. The Irish Party, and the Irish people as long as they supported that party, would continue to regard their own fate as being bound up with the fate of the Liberal Government and by extension the Liberal (or liberalised) Empire.

Under these circumstances, argued Parnell, England's difficulty would be 'Ireland's opportunity to assist her'.[80] Parnell argues that the 'demand' for Home Rule must be abandoned and an end put to contemplation of partial solutions to the Irish question.[81] The moral fibre of the nation had been practically extinguished and was in urgent need of renewal. She speculates that, 'in spite of its poor prospects, armed rebellion seems likely to be the next thing either tried or played at, here'.[82]

Apart from the value of the memoir as a historical document it seems to us that its most important insight concerns power, and specifically the power of women to be effective in the presence of men who cannot conceive of their having a legitimate and equal place in the 'public sphere'. Although these women were drawn into the struggle at the specific request of the men, it was not possible, even for a man like Davitt, to imagine women participating in a way which departed from their historically defined roles as women. The Irish National League, the organisation which succeeded the Land League, defined itself as 'an open organisation in which the ladies will not take part'.[83] Clearly the men did not like 'unmanageable revolutionaries'.[84]

Anna Parnell's experience as a woman engaged in the struggle for national independence would be a constant reminder to the women of the following generation, particularly the feminist women, of their political vulnerability so long as they lacked the political status of men.[85] Within the nationalist community, women who put feminist issues first were often seen as traitors to the cause of Irish nationalism. Yet Anna Parnell's experience points to the dilemma faced by those women who put their energies into national independence struggles while their own status as subordinates to men and patriarchal power structures are still intact. At the time Parnell made a choice to fight for Ireland's right to self-determination, other battles were being waged specifically on behalf of women. Some of these are examined in other studies in this book, and they included campaigns for improved education for women, wider employment opportunities, better working conditions, improved property and marital rights, as well as rights to the municipal and parliamentary franchises. Parnell was familiar with and sympathetic to these campaigns even if she did not give them her first allegiance.[86]

Most of the women who took part in specifically feminist politics during the nineteenth century supported the Union. In the 1880s when Parnell was politically active, the Land War and the question of Home Rule overwhelmed all other concerns for nationalist women. It was not until the first decade of the twentieth century that women from the nationalist community became involved in the suffrage campaign in any large numbers, and that feminist issues came to occupy a more central position among the major movements of the period. The choice of where to give one's primary political allegiance was no easier in this later period than it had been earlier. Within the nationalist community women who opted to give their primary allegiance to feminism and to put women's demands for equal political, social and economic status first did so in a climate of considerable hostility. The hostility was based on a specific view of nationalism, a nationalism which branded feminism as anti-nationalist - 'a foreign import' - and saw it as a distraction from the main goal rather than an integral part of a wider concept of nationalism.

The memory of the women's experience of the Land League days lived on in the hearts and minds of politically active nationalist women in the new century whichever choice they made. In 1912 Jennie Wyse Power, veteran of the Ladies' Land League and now vice-president of Sinn Féin, defended the 'militant' tactics of the Irish Women's Franchise League in protest against the Irish Parliamentary Party's failure to insist on the inclusion of women's suffrage in the Home Rule Bill, saying: 'Irish people with memories of agitation should be slow to blame women who have been goaded into revolution by government tactics.' She concluded by asking, as 'one who has suffered', that 'all Irish men ... realise that this is a women's question'.[87]

Might Anna Parnell have been described as a feminist even though she was not active in feminist causes? The answer is undoubtedly yes, by virtue of the life she lived and the views she held. In her thought-provoking essay 'Defining feminism', Karen Offen suggests three criteria essential to the characterisation of a feminist. By Offen's definition a feminist 'recognises the validity of women's own interpretations of their lived experience and needs'; that person exhibits a 'consciousness of, discomfort at, or even anger at institutionalised injustice (or inequity) towards women as a group by men as a group in a given society...'; and advocates 'the elimination of that injustice by challenging, through efforts to alter prevailing ideas and/or social institutions and practices, the coercive power, force, or authority that upholds male prerogatives in that particular culture'.[88] Through her life, her speeches and her own written record, Anna Parnell fulfils all of these criteria.

In retrieving a life such as Anna Parnell's and examining it from a feminist perspective, we are able to give it back the power it has lost through the alternative renditions of 'the woman out of place', the 'shrill', the 'strident' woman, the woman who had finally to be 'suppressed' as the myth would have it - all terms which today, as feminist literary critic Carolyn Heilbrun has remarked, might be rendered by the term 'feminist'.[89] Anna Parnell expressed in her life and work the feminist recognition of a woman's right to power and control over her own life, as well as to act in the 'public' domain; the right to her own story and, to the greatest possible extent, the right to create that story. As Heilbrun observes,

> Although feminists early discovered that the private is the public, women's exercise of power and control, and the admission and expression of anger necessary to that exercise, has been until recently declared unacceptable.[90]

The true representation of power is not domination but rather 'the ability to take one's place in whatever discourse is essential to action and the right to have one's part matter'.[91] Anna Parnell had the first but was denied the second. By telling her own story and through the work of feminist retrieval, the value of her contribution to women and to Irish life can be re-instated, and her hope realised that the women of the Ladies' Land League would be pointed to as 'having set a noble example to all the women of Ireland'.[92]

NOTES

1 Anna Parnell in Côté, Jane. 1991. *Fanny and Anna Parnell: Ireland's Patriot Sisters*. Dublin, p.53.

2 William (1836-60); Delia (1837-188?); Hayes (1838-54); Emily (1841-1918); John Howard (1842-1923?); Sophia (1845-77); Charles Stewart (1846-91); Fanny Isabel (1848-1882); Henry Tudor (1850-1915); Catherine Maria Anna Mercer (1852-1911); Theodosia (1853-1920).

3 See the many poems on this theme contained in Anna Parnell. 1905. *Old Tales and New*. Dublin.

4 See, for example, de Segur, Compte. 1927. *Memoires. 3 Vols*. Paris. I, p.407. The count also remembered Delia Stewart for her 'witty writings'.

5 It is a serious misreading of history to assume, as C S Parnell's biographers seem to have done, that the colonial elite in the Thirteen Colonies was composed of radical political thinkers or given to strong anti-English sentiments. Only after every effort to conciliate the mother country had failed did the colonial leaders such as John Adams reluctantly accept the need to fight for the rights which they believed they as 'free-born English subjects in distant dominions' were entitled to.

6 At the 1874 Annual Exhibition of the Royal Society of British Artists at their Suffolk Street Gallery two paintings of Anna Parnell's, one oil and one watercolour, were shown. A third picture was exhibited at their Spring Exhibition of the following year. No further record of paintings by Anna Parnell is to be found in the lists of English or Irish gallery showings.

7 Parnell. Anna. 1986. Hearne, Dana (ed). *The Tale of a Great Sham*. Dublin, p.52.

8 It was not until 17 May 1880 that Charles Parnell was officially elected leader of the Irish Parliamentary Party.

9 A former Fenian who had served seven years of a fifteen-year prison sentence for Fenian activities.

10 These funds were to be kept separate since moderate Irish Americans would donate for famine relief but were reluctant to encourage land agitation which they feared would be taken over by advocates of physical force, i.e. the Fenians.

11 See A Parnell to M Davitt, undated but c. June 1880, Michael Davitt papers (9378/1087), Trinity College, Dublin.

12 See TeBrake, Janet K 1992. 'Irish peasant women in revolt: the Land League years'. In *Irish Historical Studies*, xxviii, 109 May; and Côté, *Fanny and Anna Parnell*, p.4.

13 Davitt had been released on a ticket of leave (parole) and could be returned to prison at the will of the authorities.

14 Dana Hearne, 'Introduction', in Parnell, *The Tale*, p.24

15 Some peasant women who were farmers in their own right were already members of their local Land League branches but were not eligible for membership of the branch executive.

16 Cashman, D B 1883. *The Life of Michael Davitt*. London, p.233.

17 Katherine Tynan (1861-1931), novelist, poet and nationalist.

18 Jennie Wyse Power (1858-1941), later a member of Inghinidhe na hEireann, Sinn Féin and Cumman na mBan, and a senator in the Irish Free State.

19 Hannah Lynch (1862-1904), journalist, translator, biographer and novelist.

20 Report of speech by Jennie (O'Toole) Wyse Power in *Sinn Féin Weekly*, 16 October 1909. Also, police report for 20 December 1881, entitled 'Lady Land Leaguers', National Archives, Dublin.

21 *Sinn Féin Weekly*, 16 October 1909.

22 Charles Stewart Parnell, John Dillon, Patrick Egan (who was in Paris), Michael Davitt (who was in Portland Prison in England and knew nothing about it), Thomas Brennan and Thomas Sexton.

23 The Land Act of 1881 provided for the 'Three F's': fixed tenure as long as the rent was paid; fair rents fixed by a three-man land court; and free sale of the tenant's improvements when he gave up his holding. Further provisions allowed for tenant purchase from landlords but the terms were too onerous to allow most tenants to take advantage of them.

24 Belatedly Anna Parnell discovered that most of the tenant farmers who occupied the huts had been evicted not because they had refused to pay rent, but because they had been unable to do so. Furthermore, many of them saved enough money out of the allowances given to them by the Ladies' Land League to pay their arrears and reclaim their holdings. Thus, money contributed by Irish-Americans to end landlordism in Ireland instead went to pay the landlord's rent.

25 In a letter of 16 February 1908 to the former secretary of the Ladies' Land League in Kiltyclogher, Parnell relates how, in 1882, she defied her brother's express orders not to build any more huts, and built 60 huts for evicted tenants. The letter is in the possession of Mrs Mary Slevin, Kiltyclogher.

26 Only tenants in possession of their holdings in August 1881 when the new Land Act came into operation and who were not in arrears with rent were eligible to have their rents judicially set in the Land Courts. Consequently, landlords tried to evict tenants who were in rent arrears, in order to replace them with new ones who would not be eligible to enter the Land Court.

27 Côté, *Fanny and Anna Parnell*, pp207-8.

28 Almost all the tenant farmers who were evicted had not refused to pay rent but were simply too impoverished to do so.

29 The disbandment of the Ladies' Land League is discussed in more detail later in this article.

30 Edward McCabe (1816-1885); created archbishop of Dublin in 1879, and cardinal in 1882.

31 Côté, *Fanny and Anna Parnell*, p.169.

32 *Ibid.*, pp169-170.

33 Drawing a parallel in this way between politically active women and prostitutes calls into mind the double standard which saw prostitutes as a 'necessary' evil while at the same time vilifying

them.

34 Alexander Martin Sullivan (1830-1884), journalist with the *Nation* and later its proprietor; Home Rule MP for Louth 1874-1880, and for Meath 1880-1881.

35 Côté, *Fanny and Anna Parnell*, p.170.

36 Note that an ideology of 'true femininity' which suggests that women need to protect themselves from the 'lewd' gaze of men entrenches a stereotypical view of men as basely sensual and brutal.

37 Côté, *Fanny and Anna Parnell*, p.171.

38 *Ibid.*, p.172.

39 Thomas William Croke (1824-1902); created Bishop of Auckland in New Zealand 1870, Archbishop of Cashel 1875.

40 Côté, *Fanny and Anna Parnell*, p.172.

41 *Ibid.*

42 *Ibid.*, p.174.

43 See *ibid.*, p.176 for some interesting details about the lives of vigorous action and public service of his two sisters.

44 Sheehy Skeffington, Hanna. n.d. 'Reminiscences of an Irish suffragette'. In Sheehy Skeffington, Andrée and Owens, Rosemary. 1975. *Votes for Women*. Dublin, p.18.

45 For the case of Fr Sheehy see Côté, *Fanny and Anna Parnell*, p.174.

46 Parnell, *The Tale*, p.128.

47 Helen Taylor, English suffragist, land reformer and social activist. President of the Irish Prisoners' Sustentation Fund, founded in Dublin in November 1882 to raise money for the support of imprisoned Land Leaguers. See, Côté, *Fanny and Anna Parnell*, pp186-8.

48 *Ibid.*, p.85.

49 See letter from Anna Parnell to the editor of *The Peasant and Irish Irelander*, 5 October 1907.

50 Published under the title *Old Tales and New*, it was printed in Dublin in 1905. The poems, mainly political, are bitterly anti-colonial. Very few copies were sold.

51 See the Michael Davitt papers, TCD, 9511/5599-5604 for the three-way correspondence between Davitt, his publisher, Harper's, and Anna Parnell.

52 For a discussion of Davitt's possible reasons for his treatment of the Ladies' Land League, see Côté, *Fanny and Anna Parnell*, pp37-45,238.

53 Anna Parnell to the editor, *The Peasant and Irish Irelander*, 5 October 1907.

54 For example, Lord Eversley. *Gladstone and Ireland*. London. and St John, Ervine. 1936. *Parnell*. London.

55 Anna Parnell to Mrs Lennon, 16 February 1908. Letter, possession of Mrs Slevin, Kiltyclogher.

56 *Ibid.*

57 Parnell, *The Tale*, p.173.

58 Helena Molony (1884-1967), nationalist, feminist, actress, trade unionist. Member of Inghinidhe na hEireann and editor of its monthly paper started in 1908, *Bean na hEireann*. She was

imprisoned for her part in the 1916 rising as a member of the
Citizen Army. She worked for most of her life with the Irish
Women Workers' Union.

59 The phrase used by Michael Davitt in *The Fall of Feudalism in
Ireland* (1904). For A Parnell's understanding of her mission, see *The
Tale*, p.88.

60 Note also Foster, R F 1976. *Charles Stewart Parnell; the Man and
His Family*, Sussex.

61 The Secret Ballot Act of 1872 freed tenants from the fear of
reprisals if they chose to cast their votes against the known wishes
of their landlords.

62 The election Anna Parnell referred to here is that of 1880. The
comment therefore about the franchise is not correct since it was
not till 1884 that an extension of the franchise occurred, increasing
the electorate from 200,000 to 700,000. Historian Edmund Curtis
remarks that the Franchise Act of 1884 had established 'almost
universal' suffrage in both countries - *A History of Ireland* (London,
1963), pp381-2. Parnell, albeit inexact in her dates, pointedly brings
to our attention that this 'almost universal' suffrage does not
include women.

63 *The Tale*, p.85.

64 *Ibid.*, pp29, 173.

65 *Ibid.*, p.167.

66 *Ibid.*, p.168. On the question of the suffrage see Côté, *Fanny and
Anna Parnell*, p.290, footnote 14, and pp227-9.

67 Parnell, *The Tale*, Chapter 8.

68 *Ibid.* p. 112.

69 *Ibid.* p.99.

70 *Ibid.*, ch 8.

71 Hearne, 'Introduction', p.11.

72 *Ibid*

73 *Ibid.*, p.12.

74 Where it had been removed for safety under the care of Patrick
Egan just before the Land League was proscribed.

75 Parnell, *The Tale* p.154.

76 *Ibid.* p.155

77 Moody, T W 1982. *Davitt and the Irish Revolution*. Oxford, p.534.

78 Hearne, 'Introduction', p.25. To describe Anna Parnell as an
'extremist' is misleading. To call her an agrarian radical, a
republican and an anti-imperialist would be more accurate. One
suspects that it is the last which provokes some historians to
categorise her as 'an extremist'. The anti-English rhetoric that
abounds in the manuscript is indeed one of its gravest defects, not
because of her anti-imperialist stand, but because the language in
which she expresses it diminishes the power of her political
argument. On 'extravagance' see chapter IV of *The Tale*, and
Cashman *Life of Davitt*, p.233, for details of the Ladies' Land League
expenditures. Whether these expenditures or any of the
expenditures which the Ladies' Land League laid out from October
1881 to May 1882 were extravagant depends largely on one's

political viewpoint. Their expenditures had a revolutionary purpose and were undertaken at a time when the revolutionary spirit of the Land League was on the wane and continued when that spirit was at its last gasp. To call such expenditures mere extravagance was little more than an excuse, and an extremely crude one at that, to obliterate a revolutionary group whose presence was now, under such changed circumstances, an embarrassment to the newly converted Land League leadership.

79 Two recent works - i.e. TeBrake's 'Irish peasant women' and Marie O'Neill's biography of Jennie Wyse Power, *From Parnell to De Valera*, Dublin, 1990, were clearly written without consultation with either Côté's biography or Hearne's edition of *The Tale*. The feminist press which published *The Tale* went out of business due to lack of capital. Dana Hearne suggested to Gill & MacMillan that the centenary year of Charles Stewart Parnell's death (1991) would be the perfect occasion to reprint *The Tale*, but was told that this would not be an economically viable plan since large sales could not be expected. If this is correct, despite the view of some highly reputable Irish historians that *The Tale* is indispensable to the study of the Land War years, we can only conclude that Irish historians in general and teachers of Irish history in general are not encouraging the inclusion of feminist scholarship in their approaches to the writing and teaching of history. The only explanation for such exclusion is ignorance of the meanings and importance of such scholarship.

80 Parnell, *The Tale*, p. 180.

81 See Bew, Paul, 1980. *Charles Stewart Parnell*, Dublin. Especially his concluding chapter for an interesting analysis of Parnell's legacy.

82 Parnell, *The Tale*, p.178.

83 Cited in Ward, Margaret. 1983. *Unmaneagable Revolutionaries: Women and Irish Nationalism*. Dingle, p.36.

84 The term is borrowed from Margaret Ward and is ascribed to De Valera who so termed the women who wished to take part in the revolution alongside the men.

85 For a discussion of the nationalist-feminist debate, see Ward, *Unmaneagable Revolutionaries*, pp69-73. Hearne, Dana. 1992. 'The Development of Irish Feminist Thought; a Critical Historical Analysis of the *Irish Citizen* 1912-1920'. Unpublished PhD thesis, York University.

86 Côté, *Fanny and Anna Parnell*, pp227-9.

87 Cullen Owens, Rosemary. 1984. *Smashing Times: a History of the Irish Women's Suffrage Movement 1876-1922*. Dublin. pp56-58.

88 Offen, Karen. 'Defining feminism; a comparative historical analysis'. In *Signs: Journal of Culture and Society*, 14, 1 p. 152.

89 Heilbrun, Carolyn. 1988. *Writing a Woman's Life* . New York, p.15.

90 *Ibid.*, p.17.

91 *Ibid.*, p.18.

92 Côté, *Fanny and Anna Parnell*, p.168.

Index

295

Also from Attic Press

In Their Own Voice
Women and Irish Nationalism
by Margaret Ward

For a full list of Attic Press titles,
please contact the publishers at

Attic Press
29 Upper Mount Street
Dublin 2, Ireland
Tel: (353 1) 661 6128   Fax: (353 1) 661 6176